Françoise Blin de Bourdon
Woman of Influence

THE STORY OF THE COFOUNDRESS OF THE SISTERS OF NOTRE DAME

Jo Ann M. Recker, S.N.D. de N.

PAULIST PRESS
New York/Mahwah, N.J.

Book design by Theresa M. Sparacio

Cover design by Cynthia Dunne

Library of Congress Cataloging-in-Publication Data

Recker, Jo Ann Marie.
Françoise Blin de Bourdon, woman of influence : the story of the cofoundress of the Sisters of Notre Dame / Jo Ann M. Recker.
p. cm.
Includes bibliographical references and index.
ISBN 0-8091-4017-9 (alk. paper)
1. Saint Joseph, Mother, 1756–1838. 2. Sisters of Notre Dame de Namur–Biography. 1. Title.

BX4485.3.Z8 R43 2001
271′.97–dc21
[B]

00-066568

Published by Paulist Press
997 Macarthur Boulevard
Mahwah, New Jersey 07430

www.paulistpress.com

Printed and bound in the
United States of America

CONTENTS

Dedicated to
Sister Margaret Lanahan,
and all
my friends
and sisters in community,
the Sisters of Notre Dame de Namur.

ACKNOWLEDGMENTS

The motherhouse of the Sisters of Notre Dame de Namur shared in the devastation experienced in Belgium during the twentieth century's two world wars. The bombings that took place destroyed much of the precious heritage of the congregation, including many original documents that pertained to the foundress, Saint Julie Billiart, and the cofoundress, Françoise Blin de Bourdon. Fortunately for future researchers and for those who love the congregation and its history, a collection of hand-copied notebooks or *cahiers,* which had by then reached various parts of the Notre Dame world, were spared and eventually found their way back to the archives of the motherhouse. These notebooks, containing copies of original documents and carefully written in elegant script, had been made by Sisters of Notre Dame at the end of the nineteenth century in preparation for the process of beatification of the foundresses.

Aristotle postulated that human happiness or fulfillment depended somehow upon friendship; accordingly, nothing worthwhile is accomplished without friends. For this reason, I gratefully acknowledge my foremothers, sisters, and friends in the community of Notre Dame who have, in one way or another, contributed to this endeavor. First, I acknowledge those nameless nineteenth-century copyists in the community of Notre Dame together with those who, in more recent times, have painstakingly worked toward other editions of the letters of Julie Billiart and the publication of a selection of the letters of Françoise Blin in English. These, as well as the other studies of Françoise and Julie, cited in the bibliography, have been of inestimable value to this present work.

Sister Lucy Tinsley of California began the work on the letters of Françoise Blin, or Mother St. Joseph, and she is responsible for their translation. Sister Lucy died in November of 1986. Meanwhile, in South Belgium, Sister Madeleine Croix reviewed the French text and supplied copious explanatory notes.

Sister Mary Frances McCarthy of Maryland continued Sister Lucy's work and prepared the letters for publication. She was assisted in the task of selecting and annotating the English version by Sisters Julie McDonough (Maryland) and Edith Ryan (Ohio).

More recently, Sister Suzanne-Madeleine Bloquaux of Marche, Belgium, has deftly and expeditiously word-processed all 1,256 extant letters of Françoise Blin so that access is now available on disk—an undeniable boon to anyone wishing to work with them. In addition, the assistance of the current general archivist of the congregation, Sister Colette Valschaerts (Belgium South), in making available all relevant archival materials, and that of Sister Marie-Francine Vanderperre (Belgium South), congregational librarian, Sister Jean Bunn, archivist of the British Province, Sister Anne Stevenson (Ipswich), the director of communications for the Sisters of Notre Dame, and Sister Marie-Rose Lepers (Belgium South), provincial secretary, has been invaluable. Always unfailingly gracious, these women give definition to the appellation "sister."

This study owes its inspiration to the Sister of Notre Dame who served as congregational general archivist for many years and who first introduced me to the documents pertaining to our heritage as they are preserved at Namur, Sister Marie-Chantal Schweitzer. It was her careful cataloging of many if not most of these materials, her unparalleled knowledge of Notre Dame history and, first and foremost, her contagiously deep love of the congregation that provided the impetus for this project. Our foundress, Julie Billiart, and cofoundress, Françoise Blin de Bourdon, become so much more immediately accessible as living persons because of such sisters as she. Surely, what was said of Sister Marie-Thérèse Van de Putte, the fourth mother general of the Sisters of Notre Dame de Namur, could be said of Sister Marie-Chantal: *"Elle estima la congrégation comme sa mère et l'aima comme son enfant. Elle s'y dévoua corps et âme."*[1]

Sister Roseanne Murphy of the California province completed in 1995 a much-needed and long-awaited update of the life of the foundress, Julie Billiart. Also published by Paulist Press, *Julie Billiart: Woman of Courage,* along with its author, were inspirations for and encouragement toward this present work. And, as he had been for Roseanne's book, Larry Boadt, C.S.P., was once again a believer from the beginning in this project. His own admiration for our foundresses is deeply appreciated.

All those Sisters of Notre Dame from five continents of the globe who participated in the Julie Renewal Program in Namur, Belgium, during the summer of 1997 gave their wholehearted and enthusiastic support to my initial study of our foundresses and their friendship-based spirituality. Their affirmation of this direction provided the framework for *Françoise Blin de Bourdon, Woman of Influence.* To each of them, I give my thanks.

The Second Vatican Council (October 11, 1962–December 8, 1965) encouraged all religious communities to be renewed and refreshed by drinking deeply from their sources, the special charism of their founders and foundresses. The congregation of the Sisters of Notre Dame de Namur has accordingly been reenergized by international summer programs in Namur, the Julie Renewal Sessions, by publications such as those written by Sister Mary Linscott, general moderator from 1969 to 1978, as well as by those stimulated by successive general governments and, especially, the current general moderator, Sister Ellen Gielty. Sister Ellen has specifically emphasized the importance of the cofoundress, Françoise Blin, as friend and collaborator of Julie Billiart. One such recently completed undertaking nurtured by Ellen is the publication of a selection of letters in French, *Je suis tout à vous: Lettres choisies de Mère St. Joseph.*

My sincere gratitude as well to a friend, Ms. Joan Buckley, whose patient reading and intelligent critique of the manuscript provided me with confidence and reassurance.

Certainly, without the daily support of all my sisters in the Congregation of the Sisters of Notre Dame de Namur, especially those in the Ohio Province and those in my "home away from home" at Namur, none of this would have been conceivable. There is no doubt that the Namur community is the living heart of the "mother" house. To each sister there and here, I am most lovingly grateful.

PREFACE

Influence n. 1. A power indirectly or intangibly affecting a person or a course of events.

1. a. Power to sway or affect based on prestige, wealth, ability, or position.
2. b. One exercising such power. c. An effect or change produced by such power.

   Lat. influens, pr. part. of *influere,* to flow in: *in* = in + *fluere*- to flow[1]

The story of Françoise Blin de Bourdon is the story of a woman's possibilities for influencing the course of history. In this case, it is the story of an aristocratic daughter of ancien régime or pre-revolutionary France. Surely, it could be said, those who possess the wealth of a society possess the power and the means to influence. But there are, as history teaches us, very different ways of wielding power, of affecting—for good or for ill—the course of events and the lives of others. One not readily acknowledged yet a significant and lasting way, is the way of friendship.

The essential aspects of the love of friendship, as characterized historically by classical writers, the doctors of the Church, as well as by more contemporary theologians, are threefold: friendship is benevolent in that the friends not only wish each other well but seek actively the other's good, wanting what is best for another precisely because the other is loved; the friendship is mutual or reciprocal, the friends recognize and share each other's love; the friendship, being solidly established in the good or purpose which is the center of the friendship, is transformative. The friend comes to see the other as another self and, through the love that bonds them, each becomes like the other, not only in interests and ideals, but also in goodness and character.

Inherent in this notion of transformation that is friendship is the ability to flow out of and into—out of the narrow confines of self-absorption and into the world of the other. The openness to the other carries with it the possibility of self-emptying as the friends are shaped and identified by the good that forms their relationship. Therein lies the potential for influence in its most positive sense.

Françoise Blin had a tremendous capacity for friendship. How easy it could have been for her to have chosen to remain enclosed in a world of privilege and self-directed wealth. She was raised on a vast and sumptuous country estate in Picardy, France, educated in the century's best schools for girls of the aristocracy and introduced to the court at Versailles where she was able to entertain quite promising offers of marriage. What made her choose to do otherwise?

An easy and perhaps obvious answer is that suffering has a way of forcing individuals to look beyond the glitter and glamor of a privileged existence to life's deeper meaning. And Françoise Blin did live in an era and a nation of both unprecedented splendor and unparalleled tragedy—eighteenth-century France, the site of the court of Louis XVI and the battleground of the world's most epoch-defining revolution. She and her family could have elected, as did so many of their class, to flee their country, taking with them as much of their wealth as their coffers could hold, to be counted among the many aristocratic émigrés. This was not her or her family's choice.

Another perhaps obvious answer is that one's religion functions as a stabilizing force, anchoring the individual in life's higher aims amidst the tumultuous and shifting seas of competing values. Yet, the tenets of the French Catholic Church during the period known as the Enlightenment were never more challenged than they were by the skeptically rationalistic arguments promulgated by the philosophic "lights" of the century: Voltaire, Diderot, Rousseau. Then, the Church during the Revolution was torn asunder internally by a schism between the juring (those who were considered, rightly or wrongly, to have compromised their faith by swearing allegiance to the republican credo) and nonjuring (consequently hunted, persecuted, executed) members of the Catholic clergy. What was one to believe in times of such upheaval? Whom was one to follow? Françoise's own father, the viscount Blin de Bourdon, had long worshiped at the altar of Voltarian skepticism.

The answer offered by this study of Mademoiselle de Gézaincourt, Françoise Blin's title of privilege, is that her real power of influence lay in her choice of and capacity for the transformative power of friendship. From the first seeds of love sown, primarily, by her grandmother who raised her, to a childhood friend to whom she was faithful throughout her life, Jeanne de Croquoison de Franssu, to her closest friend and spiritual mother, Julie Billiart, with whom she founded the Sisters of Notre Dame de Namur, to her dear religious sister and confidante, Victoire Anastasia Leleu or Soeur Anastasie, Françoise exhibited throughout her life a unique ability for self-transcendence and a true caring for the good of the other.

The ancient world, those philosophers such as Aristotle and Cicero, saw friendship as grounded in mutual goodness; the Christian tradition has seen this goodness as a manifestation of the presence of a God known to be all good. Saint Augustine (354–430 C.E.) viewed friendship as the very relationship in which Christian love or *agape,* the universal love open to everyone, is learned. Friendships centered in Christ, contrary to being impediments to *agape,* are those schools of discipleship in which friends learn to love all whom God loves, even their enemies.[2] God-given gifts, friends are brought together by God for the very purpose of helping one another seek and return to God. The twelfth-century Cistercian abbot, Aelred of Rievaulx (1110–67 C.E.), asserted that "God is friendship," and made the Trinity, that divine community of friendship, friendship's cause as well as its exemplar. In God, person *is* community inasmuch as Father, Son and Spirit are identified through the benevolent and reciprocal relationship each has with the other. Aelred's originality lay in his assigning limits to friendship: without a mutual love of Christ, he affirmed, no friendship is a true one.[3] Thus, Christ is a partner in every Christian friendship and Jesus enables friendship to grow into agapic love, into a friendship that is self-sacrificing, enduring, loyal and committed. Saint Thomas Aquinas (1225–74 C.E.) radicalized the notion of friendship by speaking of it not only as a relationship one shares with other human beings, but also the relationship one is called to have with God. For this doctor of the Church, to be Christian means to live in friendship with God.[4] In the seventeenth century, Saint Francis de Sales (1567–1622 C.E.) proclaimed his belief that friendship with God is something the human heart is made for: "You have created my heart for Yourself oh Lord, and never will it have rest if it does not have it in You."[5] He saw this eternal love originating with loves in this life but only consummated in the next life. While the ancients thought that human happiness depended upon friendship, the doctors of Christianity taught that human persons best image God when they make of life a community of friendship love in which good will and affection are given and received. Friendship is the true remnant of that universally mutual love that existed before the Fall and before the love of universal charity, *caritas* or *agape,* was made necessary. *In via,* there is no consolation greater than the mutual understanding of true friendship.

An image of the divine that came to hold much meaning for the devout of eighteenth-century France was that of the Sacred Heart of Jesus, and a feast was instituted by Pope Clement XIII in 1765. Françoise was introduced to this devotion during her formative years as a young student, and she would cherish and nurture her deepening friendship with God as reflected in the redemptive, self-emptying love of the Sacred Heart, throughout her life.

Here was truly a woman of influence, a woman who, in being willing to flow out of self and into transforming union with others, was able to seek the highest good of the other. Her influence resonates to the present day through all the lives affected by her: Françoise Blin de Bourdon, Mother St. Joseph, Sister of Notre Dame.

Jo Ann M. Recker, S.N.D. de N.
Xavier University
Cincinnati, Ohio

Chapter I

TO THE MANOR BORN 1756–1794

Two estates in Picardy, France, were united on December 16, 1748, when the forty-two-year-old Pierre-Louis Blin de Bourdon, viscount of Domart en Ponthieu, married the seventeen-year-old Marie-Louise-Claudine de Fouquesolles, daughter of the baron of Fouquesolles, viscount of Doullens. The country manor of Gézaincourt, with its ponds, flowerbeds and tree-lined avenues, had been part of the Fouquesolles family legacy since the seventeenth century. Its slopes, gently inclining toward the Authie riverbed, were alternately dotted with fertile fields, pastures of grazing cattle, bright and plentiful poppies and cornflowers. Cottages of the surrounding village sheltered a population of some six hundred residents of this department of the Somme, residents whose lives depended in one way or another on the existence of the château and the agricultural exploitation of its valley.

The Blin family, one of the oldest in Picardy, traced its heritage to the thirteenth-century ancestor and benefactor of the church of Beauvais, Jean de Blin, lord of Rainvilliers. Sterling in reputation, the noble family name had given rise to an adage, *"Bon comme un Blin."*

Five years after their union, the couple had given birth to three children in quick succession: Louis-Marie-César, Marie-Louise-Aimée, and then on March 8, 1756, the year of the outbreak of the Seven Years War,[1] their third and last child, Marie-Louise-Françoise, was born. Her baptismal day, March 9, the feast of Saint Frances of Rome (Francesca da Roma), and consequently her patroness, was one of customary local rejoicing with the entire populace celebrating the holiday. The new baby's maternal grandmother, the baroness de Fouquesolles, and a maternal uncle, François Debuine Du Hamel, were asked to be godparents.

The country and the Church into which the youngest Blin de Bourdon was born were each in a state of ominous restiveness. Louis XV had come to the throne in 1743 and proved to be more interested in eating, hunting, traveling from palace to palace and amusing himself with extravagant and spendthrift mistresses—notably Madame de Pompadour—than in ruling. By the end of his reign, he would succeed in seriously diminishing the power and prestige of the Bourbon monarchy. Attempts had been made by several of the king's ministers to redress the inequities in France's taxation system, for which the commoners bore the heaviest burden. These efforts led to an ongoing tug of war between the monarchy and both the Paris Parlement and the Church hierarchy, the members of which were from the privileged and largely exempted social classes.

Throne and altar were in close alliance. Though hardly edifying in his daily life, the king was outwardly pious, assisted at all required Church services and did not hesitate to communicate his loathing for the philosophers of the Enlightenment who railed against religious beliefs. Though the Catholic clergy formed the first Order of the State, the monarchy was long accustomed to ultimate authority in ecclesiastical matters. By virtue of the Concordat of 1516, the crown named the bishops and the abbots of the great monasteries, received requested subsidies from the Church and, by the Gallican tradition embodied in the organic articles of 1682, was able to exclude the pope from intervening between the king and his clergy. Papal decrees, along with laws promulgated by Church councils, could not be published in France without prior royal approval; churchmen could not be judged by any authority outside of the French kingdom.[2]

Bishoprics, with few exceptions, were reserved for members of the noble families. Not a few clerical dignitaries came to their state in life not from a sense of vocation but quite simply because they were the younger sons of aristocratic families or were prevented by some disability from following a career in the army. It was also possible that future clerics had relatives already placed in the ecclesiastical hierarchy whom they could succeed. Some were atheists and shared in the frivolity and secularism of the fashionable society of the time. They remained primarily great lords, enjoying the pleasures of Paris and the wealthy, luxurious existence of courtiers.

At the same time the secular clergy, the local parish priests and their assistants, were more respected and influential than they had ever been. The reforms of the seventeenth-century French School of Spirituality and the institution of the diocesan seminary system had provided the Gallican Church with priests whom the lay society could respect.[3] For the most part enlightened in outlook and exemplary in conduct, they were leaders of local life, and the ties between priest and people were often close and affectionate. The parish priest "kept the parish register, and one had no legal existence or valid marriage, nor indeed was one legally dead, until he had scribbled the archaic formula in his duplicate notebooks."[4] Primary education was under his purview as well as the rudimentary social services. In stark contrast to the wealth of the regular clergy, bishops and abbots, these humbler brethren of the secular clergy were frequently very poorly paid, receiving a *congrue* or small annual pension. This gross inequity between the aristocratic minority installed in the Church's highest posts and the plebeian clerical masses who had no hope of advancement would have its repercussions before the century's close.

Briefly, such was the civil and ecclesiastical state of affairs when Françoise's mother had returned to her family home at Gézaincourt for the birth of her third child and for the ensuing period of restorative confinement. Only twenty-five years of age and with two other children, ages two and three, Madame Blin was subsequently persuaded to leave the newborn at the manor house in the care of her maternal grandparents.

Little Françoise thrived in the loving environment provided by the baron and baroness in their vast and beautiful country home and gardens. Her grandmother, with the assistance of a governess, Mademoiselle Ursule, introduced the young child to her earliest educational experiences, both religious and secular.

Sensitive and headstrong, the child both delighted and exasperated her guardians.

One day, having been forbidden to go to a particular terrace on the grounds of the château, she defied the order not once but six times, each time asserting by screaming at the top of her lungs, "I'm going there because I want to!" and after each episode of flagrant disobedience her grandmother consistently and patiently applied the threatened punishment. On another such occasion, Françoise was taking rainy-day pleasure in jumping on drawing-room furniture. Told in vain by her governess, Ursule, to desist, she was "exiled" by her grandmother to the staircase landing that had previously served this purpose. "But, Grandmother," she menaced, knowing her grandmother's abhorrence of loud noise, "if you send me there, I'll scream as loud as I can!" Her grandmother did not acquiesce, and every few steps Françoise carried through with her threat. Neither governess nor grandmother paid any attention. Finally, the stubborn child called out, "Grandmother, don't you hear me? I will scream even louder!" Madame de Fouquesolles simply and firmly responded, "Climb to the top." Françoise obeyed but repeated at each step, "I won't stay and I'll scream!" Having reached the landing, she cried and screamed to such an extent that at last the governess was sent to retrieve the recalcitrant child. Released, triumphant and not a bit contrite, Françoise gloated to the weary baroness, "You see, Grandmother? I told you so. You see how I screamed!" Whereupon, Madame de Fouquesolles saw that the real wisdom of the situation lay not in directly confronting such a tenacious will but in appealing to the child's incipient piety. She spoke to her granddaughter about the child Jesus at Nazareth and of his obedience in all things to his parents. So well did she succeed in describing the sentiments of those who truly wish to show love for Jesus that Françoise burst into tears and hugging her grandmother affirmed, "Don't be sad anymore, Grandmother. I will try to please little Jesus." She then exacted a punishment upon herself, went of her own volition to the detested landing and remained there in silence for about one-half hour in reparation.[5]

A desire to show love for God quickly began to guide the young child's life. At age five, while playing in the flower gardens, Françoise was stung by a wasp and began to cry. In an effort to console her, Ursule exhorted her charge to use the pain in expiation for her sins. "Grandmother says I haven't sinned yet," she stated while wiping away her tears. "But for love of the child Jesus I won't cry anymore." And she kept her word.[6]

While still very young, Françoise had the opportunity to become acquainted with the Carmelite community of Amiens. During one visit the nuns were entertaining the little girl by letting her enter into the turn, or revolving opening, which permitted access to and from the cloister. Having been left inside a bit too long to be to her liking, she scolded, "Can the good God be happy when you torment little children! For your penance, since Grandmother always gives a punishment when I've been bad, you will keep me here for three days! I'll have a great time and I'll torment you, too!"[7]

Though she would later refer to herself as being difficult and even at times an "enfant terrible," she was nonetheless drawn more and more to the chapel of the manor house. She would pull her governess by her apron to accompany her, interrupting her games to spend a few minutes in adoration before the Blessed Sacrament. As she grew, she was permitted to attend Mass in the chapel on Sundays and on some weekdays and, kneeling between the baron and baroness, was an edifying site for the villagers in attendance. So earnest was her respect for the ceremony that the little girl knelt statue-still, hands joined and head bowed.

Candor and wit were hallmarks of her personality. Raised primarily among adults during the early years of her young life, it is not too surprising that she demonstrated such verbal precociousness that visitors to the château were known to remark with admiration about her cleverness and intelligence. Not wishing to have her granddaughter's head turned by being so much the center of attention and the recipient of too many compliments, Madame de Fouquesolles made the difficult decision to send Françoise to boarding school during the summers, the height of the social season in the French countryside.

Beginning with the summer of 1762, six-year-old Françoise boarded with the Benedictines at St. Michel in Doullens. The reputation of the school, the regularity of the monastic life, for which the abbess was appointed by the king himself, and its prosperity was such that the daughters of all the best families of the region were sent there. Modeled on the educational system established at Saint-Cyr by Madame de Maintenon, a strict discipline was maintained in an effort to shape the young girl's developing judgment, to affirm her will in the pursuit of good.[8] Françoise reflected much later in life that "the education provided there was solid. One could say that our saintly teachers foresaw the terrors of the Revolution and that their mission was, above all, to form women destined for great things. We experienced few of life's pleasures and holidays were rare. On the other hand, the regularity and seriousness of the atmosphere encouraged the reflection and piety that I saw in favor there."[9]

Such an atmosphere was apparently conducive to Françoise's own spiritual development. At the time of her first confession and with her typical candor, she asked Ursule what one could confess during subsequent confessions. It was inconceivable to her, obviously, that someone could offend a second time a God so generous in dispensing his forgiveness.[10] At age eight, it is probable that Françoise was confirmed at St. Michel during the pastoral visit of Bishop de la Motte[11] to that institution. Then, in 1767, when she was eleven years old, she made her first communion, an event that was to leave an indelible impression. In later years, as superior general of the Sisters of Notre Dame, she insisted that the preparation of children for their first reception of this treasured sacrament would have the highest priority, and she would let the sisters and their young charges know of her special prayers and sacrifices for them prior to this date. She was never able to refer to the impending reception of their first communion without emotion.

The year 1767 was significant for another reason. In October the bishop, Monseigneur de la Motte, responded to the desire Queen Marie Leckzinska had made known to an assembly of the clergy two years earlier in Paris, and he had a Mass and office composed in honor of the newly created feast of the Sacred Heart of Jesus.[12] According to the bishop's decree, the feast was to be observed in the diocese of Amiens on the Sunday following the octave of Corpus Christi. The abbess of St. Michel consequently had an altar in the monastery chapel dedicated to the Sacred Heart, and a confraternity was established there. The occasion was marked by a solemn ceremony at the abbey. Françoise later observed that it was there that she learned to honor the Sacred Heart of Jesus, the victim of human ingratitude.[13]

Not able to endure even the entire summer season without seeing their beloved granddaughter, both the baron and baroness de Fouquesolles either visited her at St. Michel or sent for her to spend some days back at Gézaincourt. Then, and during the remainder of the year at the manor house, Françoise willingly accompanied her grandmother on her rounds to those whose lives depended on the château distributing food, offering medical ministrations and whatever other assistance could be provided.

In 1768, Françoise was sent for two to three years to the Ursulines in Amiens to complete her education.[14] While remaining faithful to her first educators in Doullens and taking any opportunity to return to visit them, she distinguished herself as a scholar in Amiens, as she had with the Benedictines. While there, she made the acquaintance of another daughter of the aristocracy, Jeanne de Croquison de la Cour de Fiefs. Jeanne, the third of four children—two boys and two girls—was five years older than Françoise. Her father held the honor of being a member of the bodyguard of the king and was president-treasurer of France for the city of Amiens, where he resided in his town house in the Faubourg-Noyon. These two school friends shared, among the typical schoolgirl interests, an attraction for the Carmelites. However, in 1772, acquiescing to a right of parental authority, Jeanne married Adrien-Jacques Wignier de Franssu when she was twenty-one and he forty-three, a widower still in mourning for his first wife, who had passed away less than a year earlier after only a few months of marriage.

Ursuline educators aimed at giving their pupils a deep and entirely personal experience. Profane subjects (such as French, Latin, Greek, history, geography, philosophy, modern languages, fine art, grammar, rhetoric, science and agriculture) were taught by schoolmistresses who were to function as spiritual mothers in order to train students to live a Christian life. Educated in intellect, heart and will, each pupil's particular gifts, her personal aptitude, the dominant trait around which her personality should be built, were discerned. Educating the wives and mothers of the future, the Ursulines helped the young woman make her own personal synthesis, to look for a personal sense in her life, to realize the plan of God in her regard.[15] In like manner, having finished her studies and nineteen years of age, Françoise wrote on the frontispiece of her personally composed *Rule of Life,* "To find my happiness in attentiveness to the happiness of others."[16] Taking leave of her beloved grandparents and the manor house at Gézaincourt, the young woman returned to her paternal home and daughterly responsibilities at Bourdon.

This spacious manor house, built by Françoise's parents the year of their marriage and located to the north of Amiens on the road to Abbeville, was situated between the marshy banks of the Somme and the fertile valley so often the subject of discord between France and Holland. Many of the 370 inhabitants of the village of Bourdon, during this second half of the eighteenth century, were peasant laborers engaged in cultivating the fields or in cutting peat, the source of a rather prosperous industry. It was to this home that the young aristocrat returned and where she was warmly received by the siblings she only knew through family visits either at Gézaincourt or at Bourdon: Louis-Marie-César, now twenty-two, a career military man in the regiment of Artois and in the company of the eldest sons of some of France's most noble families, and her sister Marie-Louise-Aimée.

Attractive as well as intelligent, Mademoiselle de Gézaincourt, as she was known, made her mark among members of that society which strove above all to please and which excelled in the art of *"savoir-vivre."* As Talleyrand said, "He who has not lived in the years around 1780 has not known the pleasure of life," provided, of course, that one belonged to the upper classes and had no prejudices in favor of morality.[17] Within the more or less exclusive families of the nobility there was a gap that reflected the great differences in wealth between them. The right to be presented at court was confined to a small number, and the Blin de Bourdons numbered among these elite few.

Gatherings with friends were spent enjoying music, engaging in games and conversing. Later testimonials would affirm that Françoise's company was always greatly desired, whether she was asked to sing or so that those present could simply enjoy the vivacity and spontaneity of her wit. Nonetheless, these months of more sustained and intimate sharing with her brother whenever the young officer returned from military camp or the barracks revealed to the two of them a mutual affinity for the simpler joys of life, for works of charity, for the wish to achieve something worthwhile.

In June of 1775, King Louis XVI was crowned at Reims, and soon the young king, but twenty years of age, and his bride, Marie-Antoinette, nineteen, began to entertain lavishly in Paris and in the provinces, notably at Versailles. Françoise, having been presented at court, attended these festivities and became acquainted with the pious sister of the king, Madame Elisabeth, to whom she would later refer as "the most touching victim of the Revolution."[18]

Like his grandfather, Louis XV,[19] Louis XVI loved hunting, though to a fault. In his diary, the notation *"rien,"* or "nothing" indicated that he had not indulged in his passion for the sport that day. Described as "almost pathetically well-meaning and full of good intentions," he was at the same time, "thoroughly weak, vacillating and of very mediocre intelligence"[20] He possessed an enormous appetite for the pleasures of the table, while his queen, eventually to be nicknamed Madame Deficit, indulged in her favorite amusements–gambling, music, dancing and amateur theatricals.

In another June, six years later, Louis-César Blin de Bourdon married Elisabeth Pingré de Fieffes, also from an ancient family of Picardy, and the year 1781 did not close before Françoise's sister, Marie-Louise-Aimée, married, in December, the equerry Monsieur Gaspard Félix. Both new couples established themselves in Amiens, where the young viscount purchased a town home on the rue des Augustins.

Having been for so many years the only child in the company of her grandparents, Françoise found herself at the age of twenty-five alone with her parents. Her father, now in his seventy-fourth year, had long been imbued with the philosophy of the renowned Voltaire, and he had, in similar skeptical fashion, absented himself for many years from the family's religious activities. The embodiment of the eighteenth-century Enlightenment, Voltaire was particularly antagonistic to Christianity, challenging excesses of sacerdotalism and superstition, scorning miracles, mysteries, and myths in his youth and mockingly cynical toward doctrines such as the Trinity and the Incarnation, indeed all supernatural creeds, in his later years.

Doubtlessly deeply saddened by the long-standing cynicism of her father, Françoise, always influenced more by the faith of her mother's family, felt keenly the results of an accident that befell her mother in the summer of 1783. While returning from a visit to Amiens, the axle of her carriage broke and subsequent to a serious fall, Madame Blin suffered acutely for the following ten months. Her youngest daughter remained devotedly by her bedside. In February, 1784, they learned of the death of Madame Blin's father, the baron de Fouquesolles; shortly thereafter Madame Blin herself passed away on April 2 at the age of fifty-three. The combination of Françoise's confinement to care for her mother as well as the loss of two who were very dear led to many hours of quiet and intense reflection. Revealingly, among her notation of memorable dates is one for 1783 in which she refers to a *"demi-conversion,"* a half-conversion, the complete meaning of which would become more apparent after another entry made three years later. After several weeks spent consoling her bereaved father, Françoise responded to her grandmother's request to stay with her once again at Gézaincourt. Madame de Fouquesolles sorely needed the consolation which only the granddaughter she still affectionately called *"la petite"* could offer. This arrangement was made more feasible by the return to Bourdon of Françoise's sister and brother-in-law, Monsieur and Madame Félix.

Thus it was that at age twenty-eight, the *"demoiselle de Gézaincourt"* rejoined her beloved *"bonne Maman."* Nine years had passed in the interim during which Françoise had become well acquainted with all the grandeur that eighteenth-century Europe had to offer. "The lords of pedigree or wealth kept Versailles and Paris dancing with dinners, receptions, and balls. In the upper classes the arts included eating and conversation. The French cuisine was the envy of Europe. French wit had now reached a refinement where it had worn all topics thin, and boredom clouded brilliance."[21] Perhaps it was a firsthand experience of such boredom in the midst of courtly extravagance that had kept alive in the young aristocrat a desire for something more, for she continued to nurture her life of prayer and to find her happiness in attentiveness to the happiness of others.[22] It was in this spirit that she took up her duties as chatelaine of the vast domain at Gézaincourt. Along with the general administrative and economic governance, she tended to the various needs of the populace. Accompanied by her former governess, Mademoiselle Ursule, she even served as a ministering nurse, becoming well known for her herbal cures. Like her patroness, Saint Frances of Rome, who credited her healing miracles to a simple homemade ointment, Françoise's successful remedies began to attract notice not only in her own village but in neighboring ones as well. An avid gardener, she valued both the beautiful and the practical, cultivating flowers to please the eye and sooth the soul, and medicinal plants to tend the body. As a consequence, she was affectionately entitled the "Angel of the Château."

In 1786, another entry among her personal list of memorable dates is the notation, *"conversion entière,"* a full or complete conversion with the resolve to remove from her life all that could separate her from her end or goal.[23] Indeed, it seemed to be the understanding of her family that she was considering embracing the religious life and that it was only her devotion to her grandmother that caused the postponement of her entrance into a Carmelite monastery.[24]

Absorbed as she was with the daily demands of her new post and while thus able to avoid the social rounds so much a part of her milieu, she nonetheless made time for receiving visits from close friends such as her childhood schoolmate, Jeanne de Croquison, now Madame de Franssu, and for the annual summer stays of family members from Bourdon and Amiens. Her love for these summer gatherings of those closest to her would remain throughout her life.

The seemingly idyllic existence at Gézaincourt was relatively short-lived, for a Revolution had been brewing. Though there had been a rise in prosperity in France during the eighteenth century, most of the new affluence had been confined to the middle class or bourgeoisie. The majority of the nobility, or Second Estate, lived in their manors, as did those of Bourdon and Gézaincourt, and provided agricultural management. They served their country in the military, the courts, schools and hospitals and engaged in charitable works assisted by the clergy, or First Estate. Meanwhile, peasant proprietors were developing more of their own institutions for local administration. At the same time, they were expected to pay on average 10 percent of their produce or income to the local seigneur and another 8 or 10 percent for ecclesiastical tithes. As well, there were additional taxes to be paid to the state, market and sales taxes, and fees to the parish priest for baptisms, marriages and burials. Criticism had been levied by the Third Estate, or commoners, against the nobility for leaving vast areas of their estates uncultivated and for creating financial chaos through their decisions while many of those in urban areas were starving. A number of the Second Estate joined the philosophes, such as Voltaire, Diderot and Montesquieu in condemning the outdated prerogatives of their caste. They advocated reforms such as the equalization of taxes, the curbing of governmental extravagances and the organization of charities. Nonetheless, the generally held notion was that the nobility had outlived its usefulness and had ceased to earn its keep. The contrast in lifestyle between the extravagance of the court and the rich lords and the impoverished and hungry populace became too much to bear.[25] In many locales, the peasants banded together, armed themselves and attacked the local châteaux, burning the homes and debtor-listing manorial rolls of inflexible and unyielding nobles.[26]

A series of individual calamities occurred simultaneously in the months immediately preceding the cataclysmic event. An economic depression, which began in 1778, was made worse in 1788, when the harvest was appalling. In 1787, an edict had removed all form of control from the corn trade. Consequently, when the harvest failed, granaries were found to be empty and prices rose dramatically, reaching their height in July of 1789. Peasants, having little or no produce to sell, could derive little benefit from high prices.

During the same period, a lack of foresight on the part of the government aggravated the employment situation. For example, the sudden opening of French frontiers to English industry (whose superiority in using mechanical systems was overwhelming) seriously distressed the knitted goods industry. In 1785, there had been 5,672 looms working in Amiens and Abbeville, whereas in 1789, 3,668 of these were silent, and this threw an estimated thirty-six thousand people out of work. Cloth production fell by half in a period of two years. The situation was similar everywhere and in all industries.[27]

After the taking of the Bastille in July of 1789 and Louis XVI's unsuccessful attempt to flee the country with his immediate family and their subsequent imprisonment, the populace became increasingly hostile. Gézaincourt had been spared primarily because of the traditionally amicable relations between manor house and villagers. Amiens, where Françoise's brother resided, was also relatively calm due to the presence of the rather level-headed governor of the province, André Dumont.[28] However, the more radical Jacobins now in control in Paris began to cast a covetous eye on the property of the citizen Blin-Bourdon and, early in 1793, the octogenarian's name was listed with those of the detested émigrés. Accused of treachery, all those suspected of desertion saw their possessions sold at public auctions and their names posted on lists of the condemned. The younger viscount Blin made an appeal to the republican authorities on behalf of his elderly father, in effect proving that he had never absented himself from France, indeed had not even left his estate in Bourdon for the past 12 years. He pleaded, as well, that the family properties and goods not be confiscated, and he documented the penurious existence to which the Bourdon estate and its dependents had already been reduced by virtue of the fact that for more than a year the old man had received nothing of the produce of his holdings. By way of response, in December of 1793, both viscounts, father and son, were imprisoned in Amiens.[29] Françoise's brother-in-law, Monsieur Félix, was accused of conspiring with his sister-in-law, Madame de Herte, who had forwarded money to her husband, an émigré. Then, on the following ides of March, Françoise's sister and twelve-year-old nephew joined Louis-Félix in incarceration at the convent of Providence currently serving as a revolutionary prison.

At the time of his arrest, Françoise's father had been visiting at Gézaincourt and both Françoise and her grandmother were spared by hiding in the loft of a village house. Once calm had been restored, they returned to the château and were amazed by the fact that their home and its contents had been left undisturbed. Harboring the Blessed Sacrament from the chapel in one of the rooms of the manor house at the behest of the parish priest, Françoise and her grandmother devoted their time to prayer and to the consolation of the tenantry, who continued to assure them of their gratitude and fidelity. Then, on a February evening in 1794, a revolutionary mob descended upon the village and proceeded to the château. While Françoise was in the midst of her evening prayer in the presence of the Blessed Sacrament hidden within her home, she was alerted by the clanking of arms and the stamping hoofs of rearing horses. Planning to forestall resistance by arriving without a warning, the revolutionaries had intended to take away both Françoise and her grandmother. However, a general alarm aroused the villagers, who themselves surrounded the manor house brandishing pitchforks and guns. Françoise, disarmingly poised, introduced herself to the leader of the mob and inquired as to the motive for their arrival at her home at 11:00 in the evening. Stunned by her calm and dignified demeanor, the frenzied band was reduced to stammering the official order of arrest issued by the governing committee in Amiens. In response, the villagers registered their protest by shouting that they would not let anyone touch "their mothers" as long as a single drop of blood coursed in their veins.[30] A two-hour debate ensued in the midst of an indescribable brouhaha and was concluded only when Françoise effectively negotiated an exchange; she would dismiss her defenders and go without resistance if her grandmother were able to remain unharmed at the château. The deal was concluded and Françoise went unaccompanied except for the bellicose brigands who refused her request to bid a last farewell to her beloved grandmother. Consoled by the thought that she had been able to spare the life of the one who had nurtured her own for so many years, in the early morning hours,

Mademoiselle de Gézaincourt was put in a cart drawn by four workhorses. "I felt then all the revulsion that one quite naturally feels when faced with the assurance of a violent death. But these moments of anguish were of short duration; I offered to God the sacrifice of my life and begged him for courage and resignation. Prayer restored peace to my soul."[31]

At about 8:00 in the morning, the cortege reached the gates of Amiens and Françoise was led to her place of confinement, *La Providence,* formerly home of the Daughters of Madame de Miramion, or the Miramionnes, a teaching congregation that had also had an establishment in Ferté-sous-Jouarre. It was while incarcerated there, along with about six hundred to seven hundred others in a space designed for about one-half that number, that Françoise learned of the imprisonment of her father, brother, sister-in-law and nephew. After a mere few weeks and by a message brought clandestinely by a former servant, she was struck with the heartbreaking news that her grandmother had died on March 28. Though those around Madame de Fouquesolles had tried to keep from the eighty-eight-year-old woman news of Françoise's arrest, the aged chatelaine's intuition led her to surmise her granddaughter's fate. The anguish she suffered was too much for her feeble frame to bear. Overwhelmed by sorrow, she no longer had either the desire or the ability to eat, refusing anything that was offered by stating, "I'll wait for *'la petite.'*"[32]

An English woman who had been suspected of espionage and was consequently imprisoned in *La Providence* described conditions as they existed at the time of Françoise's confinement. She wrote that, in spite of the miseries to which they were exposed, they played the *violin,* dressed up, composed poetry and visited one another as if oblivious of their circumstances. Three or four beds were stacked one upon another so that room could be made for gaming tables. From Françoise's perspective, such frivolous behavior in those close quarters made any real recollection very difficult. Despite these circumstances, she pursued her rule of life by trying to find her own happiness in attentiveness to the happiness of those around her. Food was as scarce on the inside of the prison as it was on the outside, and prisoners were left to their own devices for maintaining subsistence. Some of the incarcerated, like Françoise, had access to what family, former servants or friends were able to supply them. However, the poor who formed the majority in the prison had no such resources, and Françoise fasted in order to share what she was able to obtain with the less fortunate, the forgotten and neglected.

Needing to augment the number of prisons in order to house the multiplying numbers of the detained, republican authorities requisitioned additional schools and convents for the purpose. The inmates of *La Providence* were offered a transfer to the former Carmelite convent in Amiens and Françoise alone of all those detained at *La Providence* gladly accepted the opportunity to return to this place of happy memory from her childhood. Escorted across town by two well-armed guards, Françoise was optimistic. "I was trembling from head to foot but, at the bottom of my heart, I held on to a glimmer of hope: so many times during these weeks of real anguish, I had had proof that God really never abandons his own."[33]

Further reason for hope, if she had been aware of it at the time, was the fact that in the interim the villagers of Gézaincourt, bereft of their beloved chatelaine, the Baroness de Fouquesolles, were determined not to lose as well their *"bonne demoiselle"* or the "good lady" of the manor house. To this effect, they joined together to draw up a formal document attesting to the exemplary public-mindedness of the citizenness Blin. This document was filed with the district administration and bore the signatures of everyone in Gézaincourt.[34] The salutary influence of Françoise Blin de Bourdon was already beginning to bear its fruit.

Chapter II

FOR CARMEL BOUND
1794–1803

The Carmelite nuns were still in residence in the convent at the time of Françoise's internment, providing a comfort to the young woman who had been refused her request to be united with the others of her family held there. Though confined to a different section, nonetheless, Françoise could sometimes hear the religious at prayer and at recreation. One day their usual tranquility was quite obviously disturbed by cries of surprise and fright followed by sounds of running feet, overturned chairs and lastly by an outburst of good-natured laughter. A mouse had made an unexpected appearance in the cloister and provoked a reaction that even the most troubled era of the Revolution had not engendered. "An unseen witness to the light-hearted gaiety, I said to myself, 'What happiness it is to belong to God! One's heart remains joyful even on the eve of mounting the scaffold!'"[1]

In June of 1794, the moderate provincial governor, André Dumont, was recalled to Paris and replaced by Joseph Lebon,[2] reputed to have kept his busy scaffold permanently erected in the city of Arras. A monstrous fanatic, he was said to have dined regularly with his executioner while displaying a miniature guillotine rather than fresh flowers as the centerpiece of his table. Another indication of his sadistic tendencies was his daily publication of the list of the condemned, a list circulated in the gazettes of the day. It was in this manner that Françoise learned of her impending execution as well as that of her father and brother. "Although in the habit of contemplating my own death," she was later to avow, "its announcement and the thought that I would only again see those dear to me on the scaffold caused me a pang of anguish and I felt already a kind of agony. It did not last long by the loving mercy of our Divine Savior. This crisis of nature was followed by a profound calm and I redoubled my prayers with the assurance that the Almighty would be our strength at the last moment."[3]

The Carmelites of Compiègne were executed on July 17, 1794, just ten days before the fall of the force behind the Reign of Terror, Robespierre.[4] The proposed executions at Amiens were stayed, and the Carmelites of that city were spared. On the evening of August 3, Françoise's young nephew, Alexander, ran to his aunt to announce that he and his grandfather had been freed and that she too was now free to leave her prison. Greatly relieved, but at the same time a bit reluctant to abandon her proximity to the cloister and to renounce the opportunity for some final reflective moments of thanksgiving, Françoise said to her nephew, "My child, I have already finished my night prayers. Tomorrow, I will return home to be reunited with my father and with you."[5] The next day, she happily rejoined her liberated family.

With the exception of the elderly viscount Blin, who was recalled to Bourdon to care for his estates, the other family members were delayed in Amiens to settle matters regarding the inheritance of the baroness de Fouquesolles. This delay meant that Françoise had to postpone her desired entrance into Carmel for a few months.

In the meantime, an old family friend from Paris, the countess Baudoin,[6] lost both father and husband to the Revolution and was currently seeking lodging in Amiens for an infirm friend. This friend, Julie Billiart, had herself been in hiding for several years. Daughter of a Third Estate family from the countryside of Picardy, Julie had had the occasion to make the acquaintance of several noble women in the Beauvais region while assisting them in their charitable works before the Revolution. Already referred to as the "Saint of Cuvilly," her home village, Julie was noted for the depth of her spiritual life and her ability to make accessible the mysteries of their faith to young and old, rich and poor alike.[7]

Paralyzed for twenty-two years by what today would probably be diagnosed as multiple sclerosis, and even in time losing facility in speech as the paralysis rendered articulation painful and incoherent, she had harbored nonjuring priests.[8] "*La dévote,*" as some sarcastically called her, became a target of revolutionary fervor. Hidden first at the château of Madame Pont l'Abbé [9] at Gournay-sur-Aronde, Julie afterwards spent about three years in several different locations in Compiègne. Now Madame Baudoin wished to have Julie in a place of more security and where she and her three daughters could find ready consolation in her presence. There was a small apartment in the town home of Françoise Blin's brother on the rue des Augustins in Amiens that was available, and so, in October of 1794, Madame Baudoin sent a carriage for Julie. The invalid was accompanied by her niece, Félicité, who had been devotedly caring for her aunt since they left Cuvilly together in 1790. Julie was now about forty-three years of age and Félicité, twenty.

Françoise, by her own admission, had "leisure in abundance" and was quite willing to respond to Madame Baudoin's invitation to meet Julie in the rented rooms of the hôtel Blin, though "when she found she could not understand the invalid's labored speech the visits seemed less attractive. But somehow as the days passed she found them to her taste and came more often."[10] During these early days of their relationship, Françoise would read to Julie during those hours when Julie was alone and Félicité was at market or delivering her lace orders.[11] She would also bring broth to the invalid and help her take it. Gradually, however, Julie's winning personality triumphed over her physical limitations, and what began as a work of mercy was transformed into one of the most beautiful examples of a spiritual friendship between two women in the recorded history of religious life.

Both women had an affinity for things spiritual and a deep inner life, and both had emerged from their respective sufferings more faith-filled and committed to growth in goodness. That reality which the Greeks and Romans, when discussing friendship, called resemblance or equality drew them together almost immediately. Saint Augustine had described how he would feel the need to approach, to know and to bind himself in friendship to a person whose love for Christ had been proved in some trial or persecution. He would, then, have a great respect for the other and love him for his virtue as much as for his love of God.[12] Such seemed to be the case for Julie and Françoise, whose love for Christ had been proved prior to this October date of 1794.

Significantly, at the time of these first encounters, it was Françoise who was ministering to Julie.[13] The manifestation of God in the other provides the "sweetness" of the attraction a person sometimes, though not always, enjoys in a friend from the beginning of a friendship. One of the foundations of the friendship, it should grow in time. According to Saint Francis de Sales, the love of friendship is not merely a feeling but a resolute effort following a decision, and if that movement of grace, that "rush of affections" which Cicero attributed to nature, does not accompany a resolute choice, friendship will not begin.[14] It is a tribute to Françoise's character that she overcame an understandable initial repugnance and persisted in what was at first an act of charity. It was decidedly a response to grace and the acceptance of a sacred gift, a sacrament.[15]

In Paris, the countess Baudoin had made the acquaintance of Father Thomas, a priest currently in hiding in Amiens.[16] She introduced him to Julie and Françoise and he soon became their confessor and counselor. The friends with whom he had been staying returned to their home in Brittany, and he was offered a room in the Blin town home, where he began to quietly celebrate daily Mass. Learning of Françoise's intention to enter the Carmelites and of her wish to grow in her prayer life, he asked Julie to serve as her spiritual director once he came to know more intimately the nature of the latter's own prayer and spiritual maturity.

Lise, the youngest daughter of the countess, along with some friends who accompanied her to Amiens, Jeanne and Aglaë de Méry and Françoise and Joséphine Doria, in time began to form a little community around the bedside of Julie. Under Father Thomas's guidance, they followed a rule of life, which included chanting in common the Office of the Blessed Virgin,[17] and addressed Julie by an accepted monastic title, *"Ma Mère."* They also engaged in good works, especially assisting the local churches in their work with the poor.

Business in Gézaincourt recalled Françoise there in July of 1795, after she renewed her consecration to the Sacred Heart, on July 2, in the presence of Father Thomas, Julie, and their young companions. Destined for the property and title of the estate since birth, no sooner was the transfer of these goods to her made official than Françoise renounced her holdings in Gézaincourt in favor of her brother and gave an equivalent value in goods to her sister. Seeing that a kind of religious indifference had settled in among the villagers after her abrupt seizure by Revolutionaries, Françoise immediately occupied herself with restoring an active faith life among them. Julie was well aware of her new friend's love for and inclination to experience God in the beauties of nature. Thus, her first letter to Françoise conveyed both her already well-developed personal affection and her delight that Françoise was able once again to take pleasure in the countryside of her childhood. Communication of affection, taking initial steps toward the eventual awareness of mutuality, is constitutive of an Augustinian understanding of friendship. "There is no greater invitation to love than to lovingly make the first advances," Augustine concluded.[18] Julie's letters of this early period are filled with such expressions.

> Oh, how often I thought of you during your journey! How much all the works of the Lord must have caused you to raise your mind to him! If I had any desire, it would be to see these objects so worthy of our respect and admiration. You will often be able to read in this great book of nature. What grandeur there is to be discovered in it! But only those souls can find it who have the happiness of seeing God everywhere![19]

One of Françoise's more welcome responsibilities during this stay in the country was the preparation of her nephew, Alexander, for his first communion. Acknowledging human respect because for a time she was the only one among the villagers to receive communion, Françoise received from Julie the counsel, " No, I am not in the least surprised that you have felt human respect reawakening because you are the only one to receive Holy Communion. You should be happy, my dear friend, that God is willing to use you in giving such a good example to others."[20] Obviously, Françoise was human enough to have provided Julie with a physical description of the priest who celebrated the Masses that she attended! For Julie wrote: "I have thanked the Lord for granting you the grace of having holy Mass by means of this good priest. So much the better if he is not attractive to the eye, provided you find him full of the spirit of God, as I hope you do, according to what you have been told about him."[21]

A law passed in 1795 made it possible for the faithful to reclaim their parish churches. This was one step toward the restoration of Catholic worship. Some religious activity was now tolerated by the decree of February 21, 1795, though "bells and other external signs of religion, including ecclesiastical dress, were prohibited; the Republic was not to recognize nor pay for any religion but, according to article VII of the Declaration of Rights, it guaranteed the free exercise of all."[22] That Church and State were separated was now a fact, but the freedom that the Church was given had been grudgingly conceded. The state would pay no salaries. Sunday still had to be a working day since the *décadi,* or tenth day, inaugurated during the period of aggressive de-Christianization of the two preceding years, continued to be the official holiday. The burden was placed on local authorities and police spies to be on the lookout for infringements regarding bells and other "exterior signs," to see that religious sentiment was contained within proper bounds.[23]

However, the speedy and complete implementation of this law varied according to the whims of the local administrators. The year 1795 also marks the establishment of the Directory, that government of the First Republic of France that in reaction to the Reign of Terror installed five executive Directors to administer the country. The years from 1795 to 1799 were characterized by rampant inflation, political conspiracies from Left and Right and a general moral decline, since the postrevolutionary morality based purely on civic spirit was ineffective in inspiring high-minded action.

Toward the end of 1795, Françoise was called to Bourdon to rejoin her father. Given his age and the state of his health, he wanted to have his youngest daughter with him for what he feared might be his imminent death. As she had in Gézaincourt,

Françoise found the local church at Bourdon drastically changed during the nine years of Revolution. In addition to the fact that the villagers, along with the head of the Blin family, seemed indifferent in matters of religion, the church structure too had been despoiled by the revolutionaries. Françoise set about doing what she could to prepare her father for eternity during his final months. She shared her concern for his spiritual state with her spiritual mother, and Julie sent her the following prudent advice: "Offer him many little marks of affection and filial love, even without talking about anything. Who knows the time when God will act, my dear friend? That is why we must not become tired of waiting for the most favorable time; the good God himself has waited for us so long."[24]

Gradually, due to Françoise's efforts, a sense of a religious spirit began to be reestablished at Bourdon, for Julie wrote in February of 1796: "My dear friend, I have received your letter with consolation, because it seems that our good God wants to make use of you to teach the little children to know and love him. I congratulate you and I advise you strongly to devote yourself entirely to this work."[25] Then, toward Easter, Françoise was rewarded to see that her father's health had greatly improved, and she decided to return to Amiens for the purpose of making a thirty-day retreat under the direction of Father Thomas. This retreat proved to be one blessed with the experience of contemplative prayer. Insights regarding an intimate relation between God and the individual were reflected in her journal notation for May 3: "My night prayer was not spent with Jesus Christ but with God in a manner devoid of form and seldom interrupted by distractions. It was experienced as a rather profound and gentle rest where, from time to time, a few words came easily and where my heart, each time, was stirred a bit more."[26] Begun on April 16, the retreat was interrupted after May 5 because her father suffered a relapse. Françoise returned immediately to Bourdon. But, once again, her father's health ameliorated to the point where her brother decided to invite his sister to Gézaincourt. There he had been proving to be a beloved and benign authority, continuing the family tradition of generosity and benevolence. He had given villagers access to the park on the estate and regularly distributed alms, occasionally depleting the stock of food and firewood that had been in reserve for the château itself. Françoise accepted his invitation and spent several autumn weeks in her childhood home in the company of her brother and sister-in-law, with whom she had grown very close.

That summer, Madame Baudoin died during a stay in Paris. She had left behind in Amiens her youngest daughter, Lise, the one most attached to Julie Billiart. Françoise followed with great interest all the news of the little community residing in the Blin town house as regularly communicated by Julie when, in December, her father took what proved to be a final turn for the worse. All seemed lost with respect to her quietly patient efforts to lead him back to the faith he had so long ago abandoned, but he, always so accepting of her continued devotion to Catholicism and ultimately so affected by her influence, did at last make his peace with God. Father and daughter daily recited prayers together, saying often the penitential Psalms along with the *Te Deum,* and it was in such a spiritual state that, on February 1, the elderly viscount Blin de Bourdon passed away. Julie's letter of consolation was quick in coming: "My dear child, so the good God has taken your father. May the Lord grant him peace and be merciful to him. I have asked him for this with all my heart. You must thank the good God for the dispositions in which your father died. You could not have wished for more consoling ones."[27]

Ever since the time of her "complete conversion" of 1786, Françoise Blin had remained unwavering in her resolve to give away all that she had and to follow Christ. For so long she had interpreted this self-donation to be synonymous with an entrance into a Carmelite monastery. Her family was understanding and supportive, though they reminded her of all the good she was able to do without being a Carmelite and already had done, good that was still in need of nurturing at Gézaincourt and Bourdon. They pointed out that she was beyond the age of adjusting easily to such a restraint on her liberty, to such an austere way of life. Knowing her as a previously headstrong child and seeing her resolve as well as her refusal of promising offers of marriage, however, they did not long persist in objecting. She wished to emulate Christ in his radical poverty, a desire that was reflected in some of Julie's letters:

> As for the evangelical counsel you mention of selling all and giving to the poor; the good God does not ask everybody to practice it with the same perfection. But he does ask us to share what we have, as you have done with me, my dear friend.[28] I must not forget to say a word about evangelical perfection. You write that the poor are the beloved members of Christ. I have realized that limiting you to giving alms was not what you needed to reach the object of your desires. May what I say satisfy you, my dear and loving friend, since you want to serve the poor through being poor yourself.[29]

After the death of her father, Françoise was free to pursue her life project and consecrate her life to God, with the help of God's grace. However, a doubt was obstructing her previous clarity regarding the form this would take. What she did not know and what Julie, wishing to respect her freedom, had not told her was that she, Françoise, had featured prominently in a mystical experience Julie had had while in hiding in Compiègne. It was there that she saw in prayer the interior vision of a group of religious women gathered about the foot of the cross. They were dressed in a fashion not yet known to an established community of nuns; individual faces, again previously unknown to Julie, were well delineated and foremost among them was that of Françoise Blin de Bourdon, whom Julie had yet to meet. Concurrent with the vision, Julie heard the words, "Behold the daughters whom I will give to you in an institute which will be marked by my cross." Trusting that God would in due time let her know when to reveal any of this to her new friend, as well as exactly what to reveal, Julie practiced as well as encouraged patience and confidence in Divine Providence. Since Françoise indicated that she was having doubts regarding Carmel, Julie felt freer to share some of her own intuitions as evidenced in these excerpts from two letters written after the death of the viscount Blin.

> Do not think, my daughter, that I shall not experience much consolation in seeing you again. Yes, my dear child, I feel that you are my eldest daughter. Though you said that I do

> not think of my children, I can assure you that I rejoice at the thought of seeing you again and of embracing you. But look, let me tell you with simplicity of heart what follows. As soon as I heard of your father's death, I saw you throwing yourself into my arms. This sight struck my heart with great feeling. It seemed to me that this was to be the moment when the good God would give you to me, and me to you, in such a strong tie that death alone would separate us.[30] As he has given us the same exclusive wish to seek to glorify him in all things, you must unite yourself with me, my dear child, as far as you can, so that we may fall in with the plans Providence has for us. I have no doubt that the good God has some special plan for you. We shall only go step by step, always consulting the holy will of God.[31]

In an effort to discern the will of God concerning the direction she should take, Françoise returned to Amiens in May with the intention of making a ten-day retreat under the direction of Father Thomas. Surely this time of doubt must have been difficult to a woman who was previously always so sure of her own mind. A journal entry reflected her struggle: " My imitation [32] told me: 'wait for the Lord, have courage, take renewed strength. Do not lose confidence or give way, but constantly risk soul and body for the glory of God. I will reward you fully and I will be with you in all your troubles.' After all that, I...renewed my resolutions. We will see what good will come of it." [33] Another entry indicated more clarity: "Today, you consulted the Lord who made you understand that you must not only consult but wait on his determination....I also see that any temporal goods I have in my hands are there to use for the other more precious members of the Body of Christ." [34] Indeed, at the end of this retreat, Françoise relinquished the rather sure route of a tried and true form of religious life, that of monasticism in the Carmelite tradition. In exchange, she embraced the unknown. She chose to align herself with her friend and spiritual mother, Julie Billiart, in a new form of religious community that had yet to take shape.

This decision was surely not an easy one, and interpersonal difficulties apparently arose in a series of miscommunications. Certain discrepancies perceived by Françoise in Julie's letters left her feeling uneasy and led to a certain degree of mistrust. To her credit, Françoise shared these perceptions with her friend, and Julie responded in like simplicity:

> You think, my dear child, that I do not pay enough attention in reading your letters? You would be very unjust to my heart in thinking that. You know how interested I am in all that concerns you....I do not doubt the devil makes every effort at this moment to disgust you with me....And no doubt, my daughter, you will see very great imperfections in me; yes, they exist. It is only according to my own experience that I can charitably sympathize with the imperfections, the problems and the miseries of others. I find all that in myself, my daughter, but with the grace of God my dispositions are not to foster them in myself but to get rid of them. Do not spare me, my dear child. Tell me all the faults you see in me and ask the good God that I may become a saint, whatever the price may be. There is still much work to be done, I warn you.[35]

Françoise Blin and Julie Billiart were to discover that misunderstandings are unavoidable in friendship. Being a relationship which Saint Francis de Sales described as a "gentle struggle," they would learn that the proof of the quality of the love of friendship is in choosing to stay with the struggle. It was just such a quality of love that Françoise would exhibit by putting aside her misgivings and making the decision to throw in her lot with Julie.

Gradually, in Amiens and the surrounding area, the little group of the rue des Augustins received high commendations for their care of the poor, their kindness toward the sick and the suffering, their unique ability to instruct the catechism and to prepare young and old for the reception of the sacraments. But the work that God promised would be marked with the sign of the cross of Jesus was never to be long without its sorrows.

Lise Baudoin, daughter of the countess and beloved spiritual daughter of Julie Billiart, decided to leave the little community and live with one of her sisters in Paris, a sister who was, unfortunately, to die not long thereafter. Lise was followed by Aglaë who also departed to be with her sister. Aglaë herself died only two years later. Jeanne de Méry and Françoise Doria pursued a virtuous life in the married state, and Joséphine Doria left Julie and Françoise Blin in order to enter the community of the

Visitation nuns. "So, after four or five years, only Mademoiselle Blin was left with our mother, for God gave Frances the grace to resist the affection of her brother and sister-in-law, who would have liked to have her with them, especially as she had an income and would be no burden to them; they were, besides, congenial and happy together. But this was not what God asked of her."[36]

After the fall of Robespierre in 1794, religious and political reaction to the Revolution had intensified. To a great extent, the Catholic Church, led by nonjuring clergy, regained its hold on the populace. That same populace began to voice its regrets for the *bonhomme* Louis XVI and monarchical philosophies were being discussed by returning émigrés. In a move destined to stem the tide toward monarchism, the firmly republican Directors staged a coup ousting those sympathetic to a conservative revival. The revised Directory gave the radicals almost absolute power and marked the beginning of a new period of terror. With the enactment of the law of September 5, 1797, all civil servants, and priests were considered to be numbered among them, were to take a new oath, one that replaced a swearing of allegiance to the Constitution with an oath of hatred for royalty. Those who refused to take it were hunted, deported and treated with barbarity. Having lived quietly as a priest in Amiens, Father Thomas was nonetheless well noted for his zeal and courage. Not surprisingly, his name figured on a list of those deemed undesirable, and on three occasions he narrowly slipped their grasp as radical republican inspectors ransacked the Blin town house in their search for him. On the last attempt, one member of the search party saw Father Thomas as he attempted to disappear up a ladder leading to a hayloft. In his haste to follow the priest, the man dropped his lantern and Father Thomas profited from the momentary darkness and confusion to flee. Reluctantly, he saw that the time had come to leave Amiens. Françoise and Julie determined to accompany him, accepting refuge in the Doria château at Bettencourt, a little village about twenty miles from Amiens. At approximately 9:00 P.M. on July 16, 1799, the three left under cover of darkness.

The ensuing years were anything but dark ones for them. Both Julie and Françoise became quite ill soon after their arrival in

Bettencourt (Françoise with smallpox). In time, however, Julie's health began to improve noticeably, and she was able to exchange her bed for an armchair and to speak with greater facility. "They spent four happy years at Bettencourt, all three devoting themselves to the people of the village, teaching religion, along with reading and writing. With God's grace, they did some good to the villagers of this little place." [37] Resuming the charitable and catechistic work they had undertaken in Amiens, they were able to effect so much good that many years later the local parish priest declared that if the Christian spirit had remained strong and vigorous in his parish, the fact must be attributed to the "holy women from the château."[38] In every friendship there is a second stage of hidden growth during which the friends communicate and participate in each other's qualities. Undoubtedly, the years between 1799 and 1803 at Bettencourt provided just such an opportunity.

Napoleon Bonaparte had returned victorious from his campaigns in 1799 and, capitalizing on the weakness of the Directory, soon had himself declared first consul in a new governmental configuration. A politically astute skeptic, he concluded that the social order was best maintained by means of a fear of the supernatural. Seeing the Catholic Church as a most effective instrument of control, in 1801 he negotiated a Concordat with Pope Pius VII (1800–1823). Thereafter, the French government would recognize and finance Catholicism as the religion of the majority of the French, though not the state religion. Full freedom of worship was affirmed but the Church was to withdraw its claims to all properties confiscated during the Revolution. The state would recompense the bishops with an annual salary, and parish priests would be paid a smaller salary. Bishops were to be nominated by the French government and swear fealty to the state but needed to receive final approval by the pope. By means of 121 Organic Articles added to the Concordat, the preeminence of the state over the Church in France was protected.

> No papal bull, brief, or legate, no decree of a general council or national synod, was to enter France without explicit permission from the government. Civil marriage was to be a legal prerequisite to a religious marriage. All students for the Catholic priesthood were to be taught Bossuet's "Gallican

> Articles" of 1682, which affirmed the legal independence of the French Catholic Church from *"ultramontane"* (over-the-mountains) rule.[39]

In the fall of 1801 then, the Fathers of the Faith opened a college, or secondary school, for boys in Amiens. Father Varin,[40] the superior of this group and a friend of Father Thomas, was at the time assisting Madame Sophie Barat[41] and some of her friends with the establishment of a similar institution for girls. Seeing in Julie Billiart a unique gift for the teaching of the catechism, Varin suggested to her the establishment of a congregation of religious women for the purpose of instructing the poorer classes. Françoise, being of noble birth and well educated, he thought to be more suited to Madame Barat's Congregation of the Ladies of Christian Instruction, whose purpose was to be the education of the upper classes. And wouldn't Françoise's fortune, he intimated, be put to excellent use were it at the disposal of Madame Barat's establishment? What potential for influence there would be in forming the nation's future leaders!

However, the time of Françoise's doubts were well past. She had made the decision to learn and practice virtue with Julie, in whose company she might be formed in the good that comprised the basis of their relationship. She put herself at Julie's disposal for the work that God wanted for them to do among the poor. With these dispositions and with very happy memories of the time spent in Bettencourt, Françoise returned to Amiens with Julie. Shortly afterwards Julie's niece, Félicité, returned to Bettencourt to marry Monsieur Thérasse, the schoolmaster at Saint-Ouen with whom she had fallen in love while in Bettencourt. Father Thomas's cousin, Constance Blondel, was willing to replace Julie's niece in caring for her, and Félicité, now thirty years of age, was bid a reluctant farewell by her aunt, who had felt that her niece had a vocation to the religious life. The time of persecution had also at long last ended and, in February of 1803, Father Thomas was recalled to the city. The Carmelites openly resumed their cloistered life, and the Poor Clares, dispersed by the Revolution, received official permission to reorganize themselves. The suite of rooms formerly occupied at the Blin hôtel were no longer available, so the two friends rented a small house on the rue du Puits à Brandil. With

Father Thomas still serving as chaplain, they zealously resumed their instruction of poor children, encouraged by the bishop of Amiens, Monseigneur Villaret, who had set about establishing catechism classes in his diocese.

Father Varin persisted in his effort to have Julie found a new congregation and enjoined upon her the duty of praying for subjects for this new institute. France was in dire need of educators in the aftermath of the Revolution. Scores of its sons and daughters lived in abysmal poverty due to the war, harvest failures, chronic shortages and widespread epidemics. Those who were not orphaned were woefully ignorant. State institutions were overburdened and supplied with insufficient funds, if any at all. Though the voice of reason questioned the viability of this course of action given Julie's still paralyzed state, the two friends did as Father Varin bid and asked the Carmelites of Amiens to pray with them. A roomier and more comfortable lodging in the city, a former orphanage (named the "Blue Children's Home" due to the orphans' blue uniforms) became available on the rue Neuve and, in August, the move was made. A third young woman from Reims who had been with the Ladies of Christian Instruction, Catherine Duchâtel, soon associated herself with Julie and Françoise in living a kind of community life and in instructing children of the poor in their faith. No sooner had they moved than Father Varin entrusted eight orphan girls to their care, only three of whom had a small pension.

Françoise Blin de Bourdon, the woman who had previously seen herself among the daughters of Saint Teresa, had embarked on a different course entirely. Acknowledging a woman only five years her senior as her spiritual mother, undertaking a form of religious life that was yet without definition for either of them and mothering eight orphans in a location not far from her brother's elegant town home in Amiens, Françoise put her life and her fortune at the disposal of God's poor.

Chapter III

EN ROUTE TO NAMUR 1804–1808

In her *Memoirs,* Françoise confined her own self-portrait with respect to subsequent events to the following:

> Here it may be useful to say a word or two about the first temporal benefactor of our Institute. Mademoiselle Frances Blin was born of parents who, like many people of means, lived in the spirit of the world. Since their daughter was brought up in this spirit, there is nothing to be gained by going into details about her early life. Suffice it to say that this worldly spirit governed her until she was thirty, and then God, to whom all things are possible, led her by another way. Unreservedly, of her own will, inspired solely by God, she used all she had for the good of the Institute, and God, whose will is the salvation of souls, used this means for her salvation, canceling her faults and failings. As I say, her response to God's will was useful for our work–this is mentioned so that everyone in the Institute, especially those aware of her spiritual needs, may keep her in their prayers in life and after death since she was, so to speak, God's instrument in our behalf. Mère Julie, in a spirit of humility and Christian prudence, which never relies on itself alone, consulted her as collaborator and friend–insofar as friendship is possible in the religious life–and the two were one in heart and mind.[1]

Humble and self-effacing in her own description of the role she would play in the creation and development of a new congregation of women religious, Françoise Blin would bring much more than financial resources to the enterprise. Not the least of these contributions would be her wonderful capacity for spiritual friendship.

On February 2, 1804, following their move to a larger house on the rue Neuve, the three women, Julie Billiart, Françoise Blin and Catherine Duchâtel, solemnly consecrated themselves to God during a Mass offered by Father Varin. In a simple ceremony, they made or renewed a vow of chastity and promised to devote themselves to the Christian education of girls and to the formation of teachers who would go wherever needed to meet the needs of the poor. They then renewed their act of consecration to the Sacred Heart and to the Immaculate Heart of Mary and, honoring the feast of the Purification, took the name of Sisters of Notre Dame. Father Varin presented them with a rule drafted in 1797 for the Sisters of Mary in Rome with the understanding that it be used on an experimental basis. Shortly after this ceremony, Catherine's health declined to a point where she asked to return to the Ladies of Christian Instruction. She died six months later.

Once again, Julie and Françoise were alone with their fledgling undertaking, though this time not for long. On February 20, two postulants presented themselves: Victoire Leleu, whose brother Louis was a Father of the Faith from Chépy, in Picardy, and her good friend, Justine Garson.[2] Both were in their twenties and had some education. Geneviève Gosselin, a native of Bettencourt, followed in March.

In April, Pope Pius VII declared a Jubilee Year inaugurating a series of missions throughout France in thanksgiving for the restoration of public worship in France. The Fathers of the Faith in Amiens enlisted the assistance of the Sisters of Notre Dame to instruct the women and girls for the mission that lasted from April 29 to May 24. One of the priests who distinguished himself by the zeal of his preaching was Father Enfantin, a young man of twenty-eight years and ordained for only four years.[3] Seeing Julie being brought to the cathedral in a sedan chair on Sundays and four or five times during the week, he thought about how much more effective she might be were she able to walk. Consequently, he approached Julie after the close of the mission with a request to make a novena to the Sacred Heart with him for an unnamed special intention. On Friday, June 1, the feast of the Sacred Heart and the fifth day of the novena, Father Enfantin saw Julie alone in the garden of her home. He commanded her, if she had any faith, to walk in the name of Jesus. She arose, took one step and then another. Father Enfantin ordered her not to tell anyone of her cure, with the exception of Father Thomas, until the close of the novena. Julie exercised remarkable restraint in obeying his order because even her best friend did not learn until four days later. Françoise's own joy upon being made aware of Julie's cure, whom she had only known to this point as a saintly invalid, is evident in her recounting of the event: "Finally, on Tuesday, when thanksgiving after Communion was over, we went down as usual to breakfast. We were in silence when two of the children who were near the door cried out: 'Mother is walking downstairs!' We were so amazed that we made no move to meet her. Our mother came in with a firm step while we fell on our knees to praise the Lord. Then we went to chapel and sang the *Te Deum* in thanksgiving. After her cure we did not have the joy of keeping her with us long...."[4] Indeed, Julie's cure marked the beginning of a series of separations, because the remainder of her life was punctuated by many trips undertaken in order to establish new foundations or to visit existing ones.

As soon as June 14, Julie left with Victoire Leleu for a mission in St-Valery-sur-Somme that lasted until July 18. This mission was followed immediately by another in Abbeville so that Julie's first absence lasted for almost two months. Françoise remained in Amiens and served as superior of the community, taught catechism to the children and trained the novices. Regarded by Julie as the eldest daughter of the Notre Dame family, she assumed any assigned responsibilities with docility and self-abnegation. Though "to the manor born," she wholeheartedly embraced her present condition. That there was occasion for much mortification and self-sacrifice is surely apparent from her spiritual journal of the period. On June 29, she wrote: "My prayer was covered in thick clouds but toward the end, I felt the presence of God through them. The day began in peace and ended in confusion because of all the busyness with letters and other temporal affairs that always have a way of disturbing me."[5]

Her path would be literally sown with opportunities for sacrifice, because she was called to engage in many activities that ran counter to her native temperament. Having been accustomed to the company of persons her own age and older, she now found herself among children and young persons. Material discomforts related to dress, food and housing added to the possibilities for self-abnegation. It is hardly surprising then that on July 4, her journal read: "A tissue of distractions in prayer and for several days the irritation of images of created things, especially those that were most pleasing to me such as the places where I spent my youth."[6] At war with her natural inclinations and desirous of doing only what would bring her into closer union with God, she wrote on July 7: "Rather cold in prayer but I know that I am close to God and that makes me happy. I so often feel in such a hurry to see myself rid of all that is an obstacle to my belonging completely to God."[7] Given her upbringing and education, Françoise was an ideal model for the younger religious. Refined, dignified and extremely generous, she did not deem any occupation to be beneath her, and she could be seen washing dishes, cooking and cleaning as well as teaching. She was usually the first to begin the more mundane tasks and the last to leave them. With her considerable experience managing affairs at Gézaincourt, she brought to her new task a wonderfully developed capacity for administration. She exuded calm and confidence whether she dealt with untrained recruits or with civic authorities. At last, as Françoise recorded in her *Memoirs,* "Our mother returned to Amiens a few days before the Assumption after being away for almost two months; she had left at the end of her retreat. You can imagine how glad we were to have her home. This was her first absence and we missed her very much."[8]

Though religious women were still regarded with too much suspicion to wear religious dress, the clothing of the young aspirants had been uniformly dyed violet. When the sisters went out they wore a fairly large black mantel of common woolen material with a white pleated cap tied under the chin; it was the customary costume of peasant women in Picardy. Françoise accompanied Julie to the market so attired, much to the embarrassment of her family, who attempted to dissuade her from appearing publicly in that fashion.

The interior struggle she endured was a very human one. She admitted in her journal that she found it difficult to admit her age, and she wondered about the source of this example of human respect. Other entries reflected her efforts to overcome showing distaste for foods that were served in community or for the babel of the children. "Nothing, nothing, nothing, a big emptiness, a little boredom, and I feel more like being still than speaking," she noted about her prayer on July 25.[9] That was followed the next day by, "I am unhappy with myself. Ten years have gone by and I am exactly the same." She prayed to Saint John of the Cross for the ability to lose herself in God and quite understandably acknowledged that the heat of the summer could chill her spirit of devotion. She admitted to days of "temptation and war" with self as well as to days when prayer seemed completely "empty," and expressed gratitude for those times when she felt palpably touched by grace and found it easy to cling to nothing but God.[10]

In contrast to this noblewoman who was attempting to live simply in her humble surroundings on the rue Neuve, a drama of another sort entirely was being enacted in the Notre Dame Cathedral, in Paris. On December 2, 1804, a Corsican soldier of obscure Italian nobility, Napoleon Bonaparte, had himself anointed by Pope Pius VII as the first emperor of the French. "The Emperor promised to 'observe the law, justice, and peace for the Church as for his people,' and 'to see that its Pontiffs enjoyed the respect and the honour due to them.'"[11] During the ceremony, the arrogant young general, determined to negate any possible future assertion that it was the pope who had invested him with the imperial dignity, took the blessed crown from the hands of the pontiff in order to place it on his own head. He then proceeded to crown as empress his wife, Josephine.

The subservient role that Pius VII was forced to play at the coronation was mirrored in the subservience of the Catholic Church to the French government. Changes needed to be made in the church leadership, and these changes required the blessing of the state. Noteworthy among them was the installation of Bishop Jean-François Demandolx, who arrived in Amiens on

December 17, and the transfer of Bishop de Vallaret to Casale in Piedmont.[12]

In the meanwhile, the provisional rule of the Sisters of Notre Dame was being wisely adapted by Julie and Françoise to suit the requirements of the new congregation.[13] The principal aspects that distinguished it from most previously established religious communities were elements for which women had been struggling with the institutional church for more than two hundred years: the congregation's houses would stretch beyond diocesan boundaries and would be united by a mother general, to whom every member should have access.[14] Julie and Françoise were also very much in accord that there would not be the traditional distinction between lay and choir sisters, between those who engaged in menial tasks and those who chiefly prayed.

Young French women continued to present themselves to the two foundresses. In 1805, Josephine Evrard, Angélique Bicheron, Elisabeth Michel, Catherine Daullée and Thérèse Boutrainghan and several others joined the community on the rue Neuve.[15] That July 2, the feast of the Presentation, Father Varin presented the community with a longer edition of the rule again by way of trial. It stated that the purpose of the congregation was the education of young girls, the poor especially. The rule received the enthusiastic endorsement of Bishop Demandolx, with his official episcopal seal.[16] Then, on October 15, the feast of Saint Teresa, Julie Billiart, Françoise Blin, Victoire Leleu and Justine Garson pronounced their vows in accordance with the new rule and took new names: Julie became Sister St. Ignace,[17] Françoise, Sister St. Joseph, Victoire Leleu, Sister Anastasie and Justine Garson, Sister St. John. The following day, Julie was elected mother general.

The care of orphans had been entrusted to the sisters.[18] One such was a child of twelve named Madeleine who had come to the rue Neuve, on August 19, 1805, in an advanced stage of consumption. Under Françoise's tutelage, Madeleine made remarkable strides in her study of the faith. Her simplicity, innocence and engaging disposition endeared her to everyone. She made her first communion and received the sacrament two more times. "The last time," Françoise wrote, "she was suffering so much during Mass that she could do nothing but weep and cry out....After that she grew weaker every day and at the end seemed to wish to die and was unafraid....This death brought us consolation and the confidence that we had a little protectress in heaven."[19]

Not all boarders were a source of consolation for the cofoundress. One, for example, was accepted through the influence of a prominent family in Amiens. Charming in appearance, precocious, and quick-witted, Firmine was quite able to create a bit of chaos with her boisterousness and petulance. It is no wonder that she featured a number of times in Françoise's spiritual notes! "I foresaw that Firmine would be a subject of sacrifice for me, but God is giving me the grace to know that true union with Him is achieved by the accomplishment of His will....Temptation with respect to Firmine. I had achieved a little recollection which needed, it seems, solitude and silence; it is gone!...What a miserable day! No great failings but almost always beside myself....Oh, Firmine, Firmine, you are somehow mixed up in it all."[20]

After two years of experience with orphaned boarders and poor day students, Julie and Françoise realized that a more sustained contact with these children would yield more fruit. With the advice of local authorities and the offer of a larger house by Bishop Demandolx, in August of 1806 the community moved and opened a school.

> [W]e left the house on the rue Neuve for a larger one in the Faubourg-Noyon.[21] This house was still not exactly what we wanted, and Mère Julie moved only out of obedience, for she was not satisfied with the house, and the rent was too high...Our new house belonged to the bishop, to whom it had been given to contribute to the support of his seminary. We paid one thousand francs rent and had to spend over four thousand more on necessary repairs. The bishop, in view of these improvements, gave us six hundred francs and leased the house to us for nine consecutive years. At that time he was kind to us.[22]

In less than a year, the number of sisters increased to thirty and there were eight boarders. "It is noteworthy that to begin this work God called only those with few worldly possessions. Mother Blin was the only exception, and certainly it was God's mercy which admitted her among his servants and accepted her offering."[23] Françoise's childhood friend, the now widowed Madame de Franssu, took up residence with them, wanting to live there as a guest while helping to further the work of the new community by assisting with household expenses. She brought with her a former religious who had been expelled from her convent during the height of the Revolution.

In lieu of an official circular or prospectus, since no printed piece concerning private schools was allowed without official approbation, a novice accompanied by a postulant fifteen years of age went out in the streets ringing a bell and announcing: "The Sisters of Notre Dame are opening a free school for little girls; go and tell your mothers!"[24] On the first day of classes, more than sixty children arrived at the school. The sisters added to their catechism classes instruction in reading, writing, arithmetic and sewing, and Françoise drew upon her considerable educational background with the Benedictines and Ursulines to begin the training of teachers. Noted for her clarity of expression and precision of thought, her calm, dignified manner, measured voice and gestures, she proved to be an ideal role model for the aspiring class mistresses. Novices attempting to internalize these same qualities were known to practice in the garden and, not unlike the Greek orator, Demosthenes, addressed the trees as they would rows of children in a classroom.[25]

The two priests who were considered by Julie and Françoise to be the "founders" of the institute, Father Varin and Father Thomas, were required to leave Amiens. Father Varin was needed in Paris and Father Thomas in Bordeaux. To replace him as ecclesiastical superior of the Sisters of Notre Dame, Father Varin appointed Father LeBlanc, superior of the Fathers of the Faith in Amiens.[26] As confessor for the Sisters of Notre Dame as well as for the Ladies of Christian Instruction, Varin named the young cleric, Louis-Étienne de Sambucy.[27] This latter appointment inaugurated a period of intense suffering for the foundresses of both women's congregations.[28]

Invited by Father LeBlanc to accompany him on a trip to Flanders, Julie was introduced to the Bishop Fallot de Beaumont of Ghent, who made known to her his desire to have convents in

Flanders. Subsequent to additional visits and the meeting of Flemish-speaking recruits, Julie established a house in St. Nicolas that December. Other houses in France were begun: Montdidier, on February 21, 1807, and Rubempré the following year. Meanwhile, Monseigneur Pisani de la Gaude, the Bishop of Namur, was asking for an establishment in his city.[29] Then, Bishop de Beaumont asked Julie to consider incorporating into her congregation another with the name Sisters of Notre Dame in Bordeaux. These sisters were a branch of an order founded in the seventeenth century by Jeanne de Lestonnac, and they shared the goal of the Sisters of Notre Dame in Amiens: to educate poor children. All of these proposals necessitated numerous trips by Julie, negotiating, making preparations, accompanying the sisters to their new home and staying until both convent and school were on sound footing.[30]

Julie's many trips greatly annoyed the young Father de Sambucy, who did not share the foundresses' vision for the congregation. Seeing Julie as ambitious and autocratic, he attempted to undermine her credibility with the bishop of Amiens. Though full of respect for the cofoundress, for her social rank as well as for her virtue, Sambucy could not help but observe the perfect harmony that linked Françoise with Julie. "Mère Julie's character was very different from Mother Blin's," Françoise acknowledged, "but they were so united that there was never any real disagreement between them. Mother Blin always deferred to the wishes of Mère Julie, so that everything was exactly the same whether the latter was there or not."[31]

Father de Sambucy believed that women religious should continue to be cloistered, leading a monastic type of life. His own sister had been an Ursuline nun before the Revolution and had later entered with Madame Sophie Barat's congregation. Intellectually gifted but headstrong, he viewed himself more as a founder than simply a confessor to both the Sisters of Notre Dame and the Ladies of Christian Instruction. He attempted to alienate both the bishop and the young sisters from Julie and then succeeded in having Bishop Demandolx name Françoise as the new superior of Namur, effectively removing both foundresses from the house at Amiens. "And as for Mother Blin he thought he was rid of her once and for all. I say rid because she was a real obstacle to his plans. As I have said, her mind and heart were one with Mère Julie's....He kept saying that while she was in the house he could do nothing constructive, and in a sense he was right, his estimate was correct."[32] Julie's original plan was that Françoise should stay in Amiens as superior. Her designation of those sisters who were to go to Namur had already been approved by the bishop. Thus the sisters were unprepared for his last-minute change of heart, and Françoise did not even have time to bid farewell to her family. Before they left the city, on June 30, 1807, Father de Sambucy saw to it that he had power of attorney over the rents and revenues that Françoise continued to receive for the good of the community. Madame de Franssu had also provided the congregation with monies, and one of Françoise's properties had been sold. With this capital, Julie intended to buy a larger house for the growing community. However, Sambucy persuaded her to loan it to Sophie Barat so that her group could purchase the "Maison de l'Oratoire,"[33] which to that point the Ladies of Christian Instruction had been merely renting because of insufficient funds. The day after Julie and Françoise left the house for the new foundation in Namur, the bishop named Sambucy ecclesiastical superior of the Sisters of Notre Dame, effectively replacing Father LeBlanc. Sambucy lost no time in convening the community and telling the sisters that he had been invested by the bishop with full authority over the Amiens house. He had the sisters change their names, substituting the more aristocratic title "Madame" for the simple "Sister," which was the custom initiated by the foundresses.[34] He then gave the young Thérèse Boutrainghan the title Mère Victoire and the role of superior and proceeded to intercept any mail from the sisters addressed to the foundresses.[35]

The sisters arrived in Namur by the Brussels gate on the evening of July 7, 1807, and already by July 23, Father LeBlanc reached Namur and told Julie and Françoise that they now had no more influence in the convent at Amiens than he. The two foundresses began to realize the real threat to their continued existence there. But the time had come for Julie to leave for Bordeaux, and she hoped that on her return she might be able to stop in Amiens to see what she could do to rectify matters. "On July 25, therefore, Julie set out for Bordeaux, where the new community was all the more anxious to join us since we had recently been approved by the French government. This certification was all that was needed for the sisters to work freely in the instruction of youth."[36] Françoise was reluctant to see Julie leave and very much concerned about what she might find in Amiens, and with good reason. On August 19, she openly shared her apprehension about the length of their separation and her desire to see Julie's return to Namur.

> It was with great consolation that we received yesterday your long-awaited letter from Bordeaux, which tells us that you have finally arrived safely, and that you have found there eighteen to twenty members and three hundred children. That seems like a well-fledged brood that won't need a mother much longer. She should return to the little chicks that haven't yet got their feathers. I feel about your absence as I always did when you were away from Amiens; except that I say to myself: this time it will perhaps be a little longer. The good God, who is infinitely good, has let me persuade myself that when you return this time you'll stay for a long time. Whether that's so or not, at least it's true that my weakness needed the support this hope has given me.[37]

Her first extant letter contains those elements that were typical of most of her correspondence: news regarding individual students and sisters as well as items of a more general nature, a report on negotiations with local civil and ecclesiastical administrations and an expression of personal sentiment. Despite the serious nature of much of the content, an appreciation of life's many ironies is usually within reach of her ready wit. "I must tell you, my good Mother, that the day after your departure little Jeannette [a child in the school], to console us for your absence, seized upon a brief moment when she was out of our sight to run off to her home. I think she'll return after the vacation...."[38]

A more serious and ongoing concern would be that regarding the health of a sister who had joined the community in Namur on July 29, just four days after Julie's departure. Elizabeth Leroy, or Sister Anne, had become the headmistress of a lace-making school designed for teaching the older girls a useful skill, since she brought a considerable talent for this trade. "I'm quite well satisfied with the lace maker; she has a fund of good will and virtue and is quite well instructed in religion and the spiritual life....She suffers from some kind of weak spells and her health is very precarious, but she's not confined to her bed."[39] Almost immediately after entering, however, she acquired tuberculosis, a disease that began to progress rapidly. Attentive to Sister Anne's personal needs while wishing to prevent contagion, Françoise soon added the role of nurse to those of superior, founder and organizer of new schools in Namur, teacher trainer and vocation director for new recruits.

Though she had been welcomed warmly in Bordeaux, Julie was initially forbidden by the Bishop of Amiens to reenter his diocese. Learning of the suppression of the Fathers of the Faith on November 1, Julie decided to visit with Father Varin in Paris for their mutual consolation.[40] Depressed by the suppression of his Society, susceptible to accusations leveled against Julie by Sambucy, even he coldly received her. Finally, through the intervention of another friend, Madame Leclerq, and this woman's association with the rector of the Amiens cathedral, Father Duminy, the bishop relented and Julie, now very ill, was permitted to return to the convent there until she had recovered.

The distance between them and the knowledge that her friend had suffered so much misunderstanding and outright hostility to the point that it adversely affected her health, prompted Françoise to include these comments in a December letter:

> We are all very glad to know that you've arrived in Amiens, but we're concerned about your health. It's not surprising after so many fatiguing experiences, that you should feel their effects; what relieves my anxiety is that you'll receive the best of care. I'm writing for the explicit purpose of asking that you send me news of yourself or have someone else do it....
>
> All of us here send you our affectionate greetings and many loving regards to all the family [in Amiens]. Yes, without doubt, we'll place all our confidence in God, especially with regard to present events. Our good God gives me that grace each day to be strengthened in this resolve. I hope, my good Mother, that he'll restore your health for his greater glory. If it should turn out otherwise, don't leave without

me, so that I may be reunited with you either in this world or in the next. All the same, if God wills it, it seems to me that I desire only what he wills.[41]

Julie's health did improve and the bishop again changed his mind in her regard. He now wanted her to resume her role as superior, replacing Mother Victoire, the young religious appointed to this post by Father de Sambucy. The latter was made to cede his title of ecclesiastical superior to Father Cottu. "It seemed as if from now on everything ought to go well, especially since the bishop was treating Julie more kindly, even at times speaking to her in a fatherly way. But these hopeful beginnings did not last. What did last were the unfavorable notions which Father de Sambucy left with him."[42]

Father de Sambucy still considered himself to be the founder of the community and could neither accept the fact that Julie was once again superior nor that he had himself been replaced. At the same time, the bishop was growing impatient with the fact that the Sisters of Notre Dame were still under a provisional rule, and he appointed Fathers Cottu and de Sambucy to finalize one.[43] This they undertook without consulting the foundresses on matters of substance. Tensions between Victoire and Julie became exacerbated, and Father de Sambucy reported to the bishop that this was because Julie was "jealous as a tiger, and that she was always trying to humiliate Mother Victoire, making a living martyr of her." In the meantime, the Sisters of Notre Dame were being asked to take over the school in Jumet, and Julie was to accompany the first sisters to this new mission. Since January of 1808, Françoise had been writing to Julie regarding Jumet and trying to convey the sense of urgency. Sisters of Notre Dame would need to be there by February in order to replace the two departing religious of another congregation. Afraid that her mail from Amiens might again be intercepted by Father de Sambucy, Julie had not been able to inform Françoise of the increasingly tense situation involving herself, the bishop and Fathers de Sambucy and Cottu.

Misunderstandings are unavoidable in friendship, that "gentle struggle" which brings two people together in a deeper and deeper reciprocal sharing of the goods they love.[44] Distance already provided ample opportunity for misunderstanding between the two foundresses, who in early 1808 were only able to communicate by letter. Now Julie was afraid to be too honest and direct in her correspondence. The bishop now forbade her to accompany the first group to Jumet. Françoise wrote: "You make me very unhappy when you tell me that you don't know when you'll be able to come—and it's not the pleasure I'd have in seeing you that makes me say this. Thanks be to God, I've learned to count such things for very little where the glory of God is concerned."[45] Still not able to understand Julie's inability to come, her next letter began:

> I must say, you're treating the matter of Jumet with a great deal of indifference; I was hoping that little establishment would make you decide to come here, and I was thanking Providence, not so much for the pleasure of seeing you, but because I have important matters to talk to you about for the glory of God: some that concern the house at Namur, but also essential matters regarding your house [at Amiens].... You make me very unhappy indeed when you say that you don't know when you'll be able to come. It's not at all the pleasure I would have in seeing you that makes me speak this way; thanks be to God I've learned at your school to prefer the service of my heavenly Father to all the satisfactions of this world. Come, and come as soon as possible; it will be to your advantage. We have to see each other; I can't write to you about these things.[46]

Julie candidly acknowledged the misunderstandings that had insinuated themselves in their correspondence and tried to indicate the type of letter that was needed in order for her to obtain permission from Bishop Demandolx to leave Amiens. "Probably the bishop was afraid that Mère Julie and Mother St. Joseph were planning a secret meeting at Namur, something they certainly were not doing."[47] What he apparently feared, ironically, was that the two foundresses might conspire to move the motherhouse of the congregation from Amiens to Namur. Such a move would relocate the valued financial resources of Françoise Blin de Bourdon and Jeanne de Franssu. Not trusting the foundresses to have an ongoing concern for the welfare of their sisters, no matter where they might be situated, both Bishop Demandolx and Father de Sambucy feared this potential loss of revenues to the Amiens convent. Despite the fact that it was the custom that Julie would assist with a new foundation, and using the specious argument such trips were too expensive, the bishop refused to let her leave the diocese where not long before he had forbade her to enter it. Julie did not succeed either in conveying to Françoise the kind of invitation that was needed, one that she could have shown Demandolx as leverage. In a letter, she admitted that she has had a good laugh with Sister Anastasie over the ongoing miscommunications. This admission prompted a vexed response: "I understood very well what you meant me to understand by your letters; the only thing I don't understand is why you couldn't show [to the bishop] my last one; it seems to me that everyone would find it quite natural for me to think you were indifferent about an establishment towards which I saw no steps being taken....As for me, I have no one with whom to laugh."[48]

Overriding Julie's suggestions regarding her proposed founding sisters, the bishop proceeded to name Sister Anastasie Leleu as mistress of novices for Jumet. Sister Anastasie was the one at Amiens in whom Julie was able to confide, referring to her as her *"petit conseil"* or little adviser. It was Sister Anastasie who then in March personally delivered a letter to Françoise from Julie in which she was at last able to freely unburden herself to her friend. In the meantime, Françoise had experienced the additional sorrow of assisting at the first death of a Sister of Notre Dame. The lace maker, Sister Anne Leroy, died on February 18 after professing her first vows on her deathbed. In the letter in which she communicated this sad news, Françoise reached out to comfort her two good friends in Amiens: "I say to Mme de Franssu all that my heart feels for her, and that is not a little. I meet all of you in the Heart of our Lord; in that way, I'm not absent to anyone. It's especially you, my good Mother, whom I seek in this lovable Heart; you know that my attachment and respect for you can neither change nor vary."[49] Many of her letters contained similar tender messages for her school friend.

Though ill with a very bad cold at the time, Françoise went to Jumet for a couple of days to assist Sister Anastasie and the two other sisters. When the sisters had arrived there "they found, by way of provisions, three sheets, four or five towels, a few earthenware bowls, and little else. Clearly no preparation had been made—they were in need of everything."[50] Françoise wrote to Julie: "My good Mother, I arrived here the day before yesterday and am leaving again tomorrow. I've seen everything, read everything, heard everything, and I'm so full that nothing can come out—I hardly know where to begin." Overcome with the reality of the situation at Amiens, the circumstances at Jumet and her own poor health, Françoise conveyed her faith-filled struggle in this same letter: "Ah! my poor dear Mother, what's all this I've heard and read? Still, none of it astonishes me; rejoice and tremble with gladness: that's the way the good God treats his friends. You may be sure that things will become clear and that a way will open up before you. I admit that I see only shadows at the present time; it's hard to know which way to turn or what steps to take."[51]

To that point, the paternally hospitable Bishop Pisani de la Gaude knew neither the family name of Françoise nor anything of her aristocratic heritage. Upon learning from Sister Anastasie that Bishop Demandolx was appointing Father de Sambucy to visit all the Notre Dame houses after Easter, including the Belgian houses at St. Nicholas, Jumet and Namur, Françoise was concerned about what he might have to say to Bishop Pisani. Now apprised of the true state of affairs in Amiens, Françoise decided it best to confide in Father Minsart.[52] He was the parish priest at St. John and the confessor of the sisters in Namur, a man whom Françoise had found to be full of kindness and goodwill. "The only thing that seems clear to me at all—and Sister Anastasia agrees with me on this—is that I should give Father Minsart some information about the situation before the visit that's scheduled for after Easter....Whatever you think best. I really think it could do no harm; something will happen in minds or events to shed light on the matter."[53] It was decided that the bishop should be told everything since the present circumstances threatened the very existence of the young congregation. As a result, Bishop Pisani became even more deeply interested in the sisters, and he offered his city as a safe harbor. He further encouraged Françoise to go to Amiens for two weeks in order to withdraw Father de Sambucy's power of attorney and to settle her financial affairs.

In another about-face, Bishop Demandolx sent for Julie, kindly asked her about the conditions in Jumet, relented and told her that she should go there. Not wanting to lose any time and fearing another change of heart on his part, Julie was making haste to leave when, quite providentially, she met the notary who had been caring for Françoise's properties. From him she was surprised to be informed that a bid had been made on one of the properties and that Father de Sambucy had demanded secrecy for the time being, a secrecy that annoyed the notary. Julie had just written on April 7, "I have great trouble, my dear, in finding money for habits and for paying off our debts. Think how good the good God is to provide for everything!"[54] Knowing this and that Françoise was sick were reasons enough for her to go to Namur as well as to Jumet.

After doing what she could at Jumet, to the great joy of the sisters who were delighted with her reassuring presence, Julie arrived in Namur to find not only Françoise but two other sisters ill as well. Despite their reluctance to leave at such a juncture, the foundresses set out for France by way of St. Nicolas. There, too, the superior, Sister St. John (Justine Garson) was very sick due to the dampness of the sisters' house. Though city officials had promised to obtain a more suitable lodging for the sisters, nothing had as yet been done. Julie immediately set out to find another house, rented it for a year and took Sister St. John with them to Amiens to recuperate. A letter sent by Bishop Demandolx, which the foundresses received at St. Nicolas, provided a foretaste of what awaited them in Amiens. Again misinformed with respect to Julie and in a fit of irritation, he dashed off a letter which, had its terms been more moderate, might have been deemed a bull of excommunication.[55]

Julie and Françoise reached Amiens on May 5 to the great joy of the community, which felt particularly blessed to have both foundresses with them once again. That same day, Françoise requested an interview with Bishop Demandolx. Saying that he was about to leave for a period of two months, he postponed her request until his return. Knowing that she had been granted but a two-week leave from Namur, Françoise wrote immediately to Bishop Pisani, who kindly responded in a letter dated June 7: "We are accustomed to making sacrifices and submit to being deprived for sometime longer of your example, and virtues, and the fruits of your works of charity....Take care of your health, come back to us as soon as you can. If it is possible, bring your mother general with you. I send her affectionate greetings in the Lord, as I do you, my dear daughter in Jesus Christ...."[56]

Then, too, Françoise was greatly concerned about the sister left in charge at Namur, Sister Xavier (Josephine Evrard). The twenty-three-year-old religious had also been sick when Françoise left Namur for Amiens. In addition to her inquiries regarding the community and school, Françoise remained concerned about the young sister's health:

> How are you feeling, my good Sister Xavier? I always begin with that now because, after the health of your soul, which must come before all else, that of your body concerns me very much. The first, I hope, is increasing and growing stronger, but is the other perhaps decreasing and becoming weaker? If it's the holy will of God, we'll submit to it, but it's certainly his will that we do all that depends on us to keep "Brother Ass" from falling apart.[57]

When Bishop Demandolx did return, his courtesy was met with Françoise's candor. She stated that she believed the problems that they had been experiencing stemmed from the fact that Father de Sambucy "differed from Mère Julie on many points and rarely approved anything she did..., that it would be better if Father de Sambucy had nothing more to do with our community...."[58]

Unfortunately, those counselors of the bishop who supported the foundresses were in the minority, and he appointed the vicar general, Father Cottu, and Father de Sambucy to finalize a rule for the Sisters of Notre Dame. The statutes had been approved by the government and a provisional rule had already been sketched out by the Fathers of the Faith, especially Father Varin.[59] Bishop Demandolx, however, was not in sympathy with the primitive spirit, wanted the sisters to be limited to his diocese and did not want a superior general whose house visitations he considered to be a waste of money.

However, Napoleon, at the peak of his power, had his own designs with respect to religious communities. In 1807 he had demanded copies of their statutes, and he was in the process of amalgamating them: his so-called "Paris Plan." He viewed contemplative communities as completely useless. He regarded the other communities as quite useful to his purposes if they were united in two "regiments"—one for teaching and one for nursing, irrespective of differing rules and characteristic spirit. His religious politics had long been known to be based on three principles: a condemnation of what he termed "monastic laziness"; his refusal to accept any interference from Rome; and his rejection of any scholastic enterprise which would rival that organized by the state.[60] Having heard rumors to this effect, the two foundresses felt it best, given the indefinite nature of circumstances, not to risk further antagonizing the bishop and Fathers Cottu and de Sambucy.

Mother Vincent of the Bordeaux community needed to consult Julie. Decisions regarding the appointment of a superior and a novice mistress as well as that concerning a permanent rule were pending. Having received permission from Bishop Demandolx subsequent to a letter written to him by the archbishop of Bordeaux, Charles-Françoise d'Aviau, Julie left Amiens for Bordeaux on August 1. Hoping that Bordeaux might offer a solution with respect to the nagging question of a rule, Julie thought that perhaps two Fathers of the Faith there, Fathers Lambert and Gloriot, might offer advice and assistance.

During her absence, Françoise dealt with yet another upset in the Amiens community. With no thought of encroaching upon the authority given to Mère Victoire by Father de Sambucy, Françoise succumbed to Victoire's insistent pleadings and gave the instruction in Christian doctrine to the sisters. Though he had placed many restrictions on both foundresses with respect to the Amiens community, he had not absolutely forbidden Françoise to give instructions. But when he learned that she had done so, "the bishop was displeased: he was not exactly partial to Mother Blin."[61]

With extraordinary tact and charity and a friendship anchored in God alone, Françoise Blin and Julie Billiart had reserved to themselves knowledge of their many embarrassments, misunderstandings and outright mistreatment. In July, Bishop Pisani wrote to Françoise from Namur:

> I have been overwhelmed with work, my dear Sister in Jesus Christ–so I am a little late in answering your letter of July 6. I am sincerely glad that you really intend to return to Namur to continue the work of educating our poor girls which you have so happily begun....What causes me regret however is that the foundation at Amiens is in danger; for Amiens ought to be the motherhouse. The bishop will certainly be brought around to your superior general's way of thinking–at least I hope so. As for my diocese, it will always be happy to welcome you–you and Sister Julie and all the companions you bring with you. I only wish we had a larger place for you, but God will find one if it is his will; his will is what we desire....[62]

In August, during Julie's absence, Victoire, being inexperienced and not well educated, had inadvertently said something foolish, causing several of the younger sisters to giggle. Humiliated and acting impulsively, she ran from the house to tell Fathers Cottu and de Sambucy of her perceived slight. While Victoire was absent, Françoise gently rebuked the offenders and, being alone with the group, decided to share with them some of the problems the two foundresses were experiencing:

> Sisters, by now you must realize that something is in the air, a storm is brewing. As you know, we were gathered together to follow our primitive spirit, but the bishop is not at all in sympathy with us. He does not wish us to have a mother general nor does he approve of visits to the secondary houses. And he disagrees with us on many other points which it is unnecessary to mention here. But Mère Julie and I know where we will be welcome if we cannot remain here. Those who love us will follow us.
>
> At this the sisters clapped their hands and without exception exclaimed: "I will go." "And I!"[63]

Julie returned from an aborted trip to Bordeaux after an absence of only five or six days. On her way, she had needed to stop in Paris with some letters for Father Varin. They were written by Father de Sambucy and when Varin read them he began to speak with such severity and vehemence to Julie that she was totally overcome and became ill. He gave as his final word on the subject that Father de Sambucy should write the rule for the Sisters of Notre Dame, that this should be done at Amiens and that she should never again set foot out of the diocese. As a final punctuation mark, he asserted that all the bishops were against the foundresses and that soon the bishop of Namur, too, would see things as his fellow clerics did. Stopping to pray and to confess at the Church of the Visitation, Julie found consolation. Because she was now too ill to continue her travels, she turned back to Amiens. Once there, she learned that Françoise's actions were regarded as disobedience to the bishop and were being treated as a crime. The sisters were deprived of holy communion and were led to believe that the incident was a serious matter of conscience. "It was like walking on a tightrope–the slightest misstep provoked disaster. But it is certain that the bishop's severity did not win anyone's heart; it did, however, bring out the real attachment of the sisters for their two mothers...."[64]

Chapter IV

SUPERIOR OF THE MOTHERHOUSE 1809–1815

As the angel was sent to comfort Jesus in the garden, true friendship aids friends in their suffering for the love of God. A spiritual friend, Francis de Sales explains in the beginning of *The Devout Life,* "should be considered like an angel sent to lead the way to heaven."[1] Without obedience to the divine will until death on a cross, love, according to Saint Francis, is still dominated by selfishness. "Mount Calvary is the mountain of lovers. All love that does not begin with Our Savior's Passion is frivolous and dangerous. How unhappy death is without the love of the Savior and how unhappy love is without the Savior's death."[2]

Having weathered any number of trials and persecutions prior to 1809, Françoise and Julie learned that they were but beginning the ascent to Calvary and that there would be many opportunities for friend to minister to friend as angels in the garden of Gethsemane.

Forbidden to see the bishop of Amiens unless sent for, Julie received such a summons.

> ...Julie was sent for and Mother Blin accompanied her, waiting in a neighboring house to return with her when she came out. This was no idle precaution. When the interview was over, Julie needed someone with her, for she was in tears, something which had never happened before. But this interview, as she

> herself said, was worse than any of the others: the prelate's tones and gestures were so harsh that, though her soul was unshaken, the effects of the shock to her nerves were with her for days afterwards: the bishop's voice kept echoing in her ears....These rebukes lasted a long time, the bishop stamping his foot for emphasis. Mère Julie was too deeply religious not to find a bishop's anger overwhelming.
>
> The two mothers did not go home at once but to clear their minds went for a walk, trying to understand. They thought they could see the hand of God in what was happening....[3]

Apparent in the telling of this incident is the fact that, although Françoise respectfully addressed Julie as Mother and maintained with her a relationship of directee to director, in reality their relationship was one of peers; they were true companions on the journey together.

After she returned from Paris, Julie did as bid and went to Father de Sambucy to begin to work on a permanent rule for the Sisters of Notre Dame. Having most likely been given advance notice of her request, he received her politely. There were about three or four follow-up visits on his part to the foundresses during which "there was a great deal of talk but little real communication."[4] He begged them to speak openly and to commit their ideas to writing. Their frankness produced unforeseen results.

In the meantime, Father Minsart communicated the need to find someone to replace Sister Xavier, temporary superior at Namur, who was now confined to bed and growing daily weaker. He also expressed his desire for the return of Françoise, Mother St. Joseph, the regular superior of Namur. On August 14, he referred to her plans of enlarging the Namur establishment and told her of an old but well-built house with a large garden that was available for rent. Another sister was needed at Jumet, and there were problems in both houses that necessitated a trip on the part of the mother general. Permission was granted and Julie left in October. She was back in Amiens in November, where several sisters were ill as a result of a typhoid epidemic. While almost all had been affected, four sisters were sick for three or four months, and two became mentally disturbed after their long illnesses. Mother Victoire had served ably as infirmarian and had, consequently, asked Françoise to take over the teaching. When the bishop learned of this through a parishioner, he issued an order stating that whenever Mother Victoire could not give the instruction, no one should do so.

Father Cottu gave a retreat during Christmas week at which time the sisters were "troubled by temptations, each in her own way, and all were surprised to find that after the retreat they were worse off than they had been before."[5] Julie took charge of the household duties in order to free the others for the retreat, and Françoise made only part of it. Father Cottu had presented a rule to the two foundresses, who used some of this time during the retreat to confer. Taken in part from the ancient rules of the Sisters of Notre Dame of Bordeaux, this rule had been adapted from the Jesuit rule, since this community had been established by the Jesuits about two hundred years before the French Revolution. Father Cottu had not made the revisions desired by Julie or Mother Vincent of the Bordeaux community: He had not provided for a Mother General or for visits to secondary houses and he had limited the congregation to one diocese in spite of the fact that there were already established houses in other dioceses. Françoise and Julie decided to say merely that some articles needed revision and that, since the present was hardly a favorable time, Father Cottu "should realize that even a year's delay would not be too much, for it was necessary to see how things worked out with the government."[6]

Father Cottu was not happy with their response, saying that such a request was just a tactic for delay and that Bishop Demandolx would never agree to it. The question of the rule had to be settled, preferably by the feast of the Annunciation so that vows could be made at that time. Françoise and Julie did not reply, but on another occasion, Françoise affirmed: "Father, if things keep going from bad to worse with no hope of a peaceful settlement, I promise you I will bring the mother and her daughters to Namur."[7] In the meanwhile, the sisters in Namur had moved into their large rented home, the mansion of the Counts de Quarré, on December 6.[8] On January 5, Julie asked the six older sisters in the community to begin a novena to the Child Jesus, to make special visits to the

Blessed Sacrament in order to have some clarity regarding the will of God in the present crisis. Father Cottu arrived in the early morning of the seventh day of the novena, went to Julie's office and demanded: "Mother, we must come to an agreement. The bishop says he cannot establish a house on nothing. Mother Blin may take it into her head to go off with her income, leaving him to support the sisters, and this he has no way of doing. Unless Mother Blin promises to settle her fortune on the Amiens convent, the bishop will have nothing to do with you; he will take away your chaplain and establish no rules."[9] Leaving her office to find Françoise, and with a gesture of warning as to what awaited, Julie and Françoise together faced the prelate, who repeated his ultimatum. "Mother Blin listened with mixed feelings to the words which seemed to herald her departure from Amiens, feeling more relief than regret, for she was staying only from a sense of duty–her heart was really at Namur."[10]

The two consulted others whom they trusted, such as Father Chevalier, the pastor of Rubempré, and Father Duminy, rector of the Amiens cathedral. The consensus was that the terms which had been set before them were too extreme to be considered and Duminy added that he himself had once been astonished to hear the bishop state: "If Madame Blin wishes to remain at Amiens she will have to sign over her income."[11] Father Chevalier advised Julie to leave at once for Namur and, from there, to write respectfully to Bishop Demandolx saying that, unable to please him, the decision had been made to settle the motherhouse in Namur. After that, Mother Blin and the other sisters could follow. Not convinced that this was the manner to proceed, Julie consulted Françoise, who thought it better not to hasten matters in this fashion, that "such a move was not to her taste."[12] The decision was rendered more difficult by the fact that letters from Namur continued to bring bad news: Sister Xavier was dying; the three young sisters taught all day and then assumed all household chores in addition, a workload that was proving to be impossible. The number of boarders was increasing, and the community, overwhelmed, was so exhausted and discouraged that when they gathered for meals, they were quickly reduced to tears of exasperation. Julie had asked for permission to go to Namur but to no avail. The bishop's response was that, at most, he would only allow Mother Blin to go, an absence the foundresses thought to be too much a risk at the moment.

At the time, Françoise had enough money to cover the expense of a move of the motherhouse to Namur. Her income came to about 3,000 francs. Another 11,500 francs, plus an equal amount from Madame de Franssu, had been loaned to Sophie Barat's congregation for the purchase of their house.[13] The Blin property near Soissons, which had been sold by Father de Sambucy during Françoise's stay in Namur, brought in 28,000 francs, which had been paid in full. Should all of her income go to the house in Amiens, there would not be enough to give assistance to the other small houses when needed. Françoise and Julie went together to explain the situation to Madame de Franssu, who was very much saddened at the prospect that these two whom she dearly loved might leave Amiens for good.

The house in Amiens was leased by Françoise's income in her name, as well as those of Julie Billiart and Anastasie Leleu. Its furniture had been brought by Françoise or purchased by her. If they were they to stay in Amiens, they would either have to submit to the latest ultimatum, confining the Blin income to this house alone and accepting a rule that ran counter to the founding spirit, or live as seculars, since the bishop had stated that he would not allow a priest to say Mass for the sisters.

Clarity with respect to the will of God came in the unexpected guise of a note from the bishop. It had been dictated to Father Cottu and brought by him to Julie on January 12. In essence, the bishop reminded the foundresses that he had rented to them the house they were currently occupying for the purpose of the establishment of a convent for Sisters of Notre Dame. Since, in his eyes, they were leading the sisters by a different spirit, they were free to leave and go wherever they wished. Both Françoise and Julie received this news with a sense of peace, though Françoise was eager for Julie to depart before the bishop should change his mind. Together they came to the decision that Françoise would remain in Amiens until all who elected to go with them had departed. She would also see to it that all household goods, chapel furnishings, bedding and the like were either sent to Namur or sold. On January 14, Françoise wrote to Bishop Pisani to inform him of recent events in Amiens and to ask for the hospitality he had promised to the community. Informing her dear friend, Jeanne de Franssu, of their impending departure was even more painful. Jeanne had hoped to live and die among her friends, Françoise and Julie, who were near and dear to her, in a house that she considered to be her home. Already fifty-eight and suffering from a nervous ailment that made it difficult for her to be uprooted, she had never dreamed that her friends would have to leave Amiens.

Dinner was scarcely over on the afternoon of January 15 when Julie set out with the first group of sisters to leave. Shortly after she left, Françoise wrote:

> Ah! my good Mother, how difficult it is to understand the ways of men—or better, how admirable are the ways of God. On the evening of the day you left, Father Cottu sent Leonard [former lay brother and servant of Father de Sambucy] for Sister Jeanne[14] and me; we were to go to Father Cottu immediately. As it turned out, he had nothing to say to me; but our absence was necessary so that Father de Sambucy might have an opportunity to come and sow terror among the sisters. I could more easily tell you what he didn't say; it was a great error on my part to believe he had changed with regard to us....
>
> I'm very sure the bishop of Namur will receive you well. I have so little anxiety on that score that I still plan to have the coach leave this week with some sisters and Sister Jeanne....
>
> Father Cottu is here for confessions. Several sisters don't want to go to him, and I'm leaving them free about that as well....
>
> One is free indeed, my good Mother, when one seeks only the will of God; I really experience a deep peace, and I believe all this is sent to purify the work. I can't regard all these harassments as an evil, since there is no evil except in sin; yet I still experience exterior suffering; I no longer have an appetite and I don't sleep too well. I'd like to hurry things along in order to be with you soon and to find myself again under the discipline of a more favorable bishop; this one, by the permission of God, is an iron rod that never bends.

> Good Mme de Franssu says she doesn't understand it at all. She's greatly distressed. She sends you greetings. Ask God to console and enlighten her as to what she ought to do....
>
> I hope things will go more smoothly elsewhere for the glory of God, which must be our only goal. I embrace you and assure you of my very sincere and respectful attachment. Pray God that I may not do anything foolish, as I'm quite capable of doing. A thousand assurances of my affection to all my good sisters. How I long to see them again...![15]

Fathers de Sambucy and Cottu put into effect a new plan to try to persuade the remaining sisters to stay in Amiens. They coaxed, threatened and frightened them. Next, the vicar general of the diocese, Father Fournier, accompanied by the rector of the seminary, arrived at the convent. They first went to visit with Jeanne de Franssu and attempted to convince her that Julie was deluded, that she would never succeed and would be back in Amiens begging for forgiveness. Sending for Françoise, Fournier continued his diatribe against her friend in such an unrestrained fashion that she thought "it evident that Satan had something to do with his excess of zeal."[16]

Another trial came again in the robes of a cleric, those of Father Delainville. Tall and imposing in manner, a zealous and powerful orator, he was returning from a mission when he stopped for a visit with Bishop Demandolx. Angry about what he learned regarding the Sisters of Notre Dame in Amiens, he went immediately to the convent where "he expressed himself with all the energy of which he was capable, taking time to quote passage after passage on obedience from scripture and other sources, heaping argument on argument, assuring Mother Blin that Mère Julie was under illusion...."[17] Françoise was overwhelmed and could scarcely get a word in edgewise. "Finally, she stemmed the flood by rising and, speaking with as much respect as she could, said: 'Father, were it only because of your manner of speaking, I could have no confidence in your words. Please pray to God for me.'"[18] Françoise was concerned for the sisters who would be exposed to his vehemence and dissuaded him from preaching to them in the chapel, as he suggested. Delainville then went to Jeanne de Franssu and told her that she was bound in conscience not to approve the "refractory nuns," even though she considered them to be her good friends. He ordered her to show her disapproval on every occasion since their conduct bordered on heresy. "In spite of herself she was painfully bewildered and confused; she could only suspend judgment—neither condemn nor approve—and try to avoid discussion."[19] Providentially, however, a letter arrived from her other good friend, Father Enfantin, "when her distress was the greatest."[20] It was he who had advised her to take up residence with the Sisters of Notre Dame, and this letter from her "angel," as she called him, provided needed comfort. She decided to consult with him, despite the distance that currently separated them, and this decision gave her the hope that restored her peace. She shared this with Françoise, and together they gave thanks to God for communicating his goodness in this manner. Françoise revealed her own distress in a letter to Julie and, though by training accustomed to making preliminary drafts of her correspondence, she was so shaken by this episode that she was unable to adhere to her own discipline as a writer.

> Ah! My good Mother, my good Mother! I've just been through the most frightful ordeal with Father Dalainville; he spoke with overwhelming volubility, hardly listening to me at all. I can't begin to tell you all the things he said. In his view, you are completely deluded. God won't bless your actions; he'd stake his life on it; if he's wrong, may God strike him dead on the spot....He wanted to preach, but fortunately it was near dinner time. With that he went off to Mme de Franssu and upset her; she no longer knew where she stood; he made it a point of conscience for her to tell Mother Victoire that she [Mme de Franssu] must obey her bishop and that she was obliged to remain—that she must declare this to anyone who spoke to her about it. He wanted to assemble everybody. He will return, he will preach. He won't leave us in peace. You know his zeal and his vehemence; he came down on me more forcefully even than the vicar general and all the others.
>
> I'm writing to you to find relief, and so that you'll receive my letter while Sister Jeanne is still there and will be able to send me some words of consolation through her....
>
> It seems to me he's confusing you somehow with priests, who mustn't change their place without being

> ordered to do so by the bishop. Well and good when we have vows; but he doesn't want to hear that.[21]
>
> He says we form a unit, an approved Institute placed under the authority of the bishops; he had a great many things to say about that, but it's the application that is still to be made. He might, I believe, have upset me if we hadn't taken advice beforehand, and if we hadn't been told that they couldn't hold us back by force, that is, that we were free to withdraw without wounding our conscience.
>
> Mme de Franssu was so troubled that she sent for Mother Victoire as soon as he left her. As for me, I'm writing you this letter without stopping to make a rough draft and very soon after the event. Such productions always smack of first impulse, but I needed to let go; I hope you'll approve....[22]

Aristotle had affirmed that, "The very presence of a friend is pleasant as much in good fortune as in bad; by the pleasure one finds in their presence and by the thought of their compassion, our pain is diminished."[23] Julie's sympathetic response to her friend's distress was to write letters of great understanding and counsel on an almost daily basis during these extremely difficult weeks. "Pray much for us–for me," Françoise begged Julie, "I have such need of it. Your letters give me much pleasure; it's not the moment to save on the cost of sending them. I embrace you, my good Mother, while waiting to have the pleasure of seeing you...."[24]

Jeanne de Franssu's temporary withdrawal of sympathetic support was a source a great pain for Françoise. "My good Mother, it seems I'm to be subjected to all sorts of trials! Now Mme de Franssu has joined the fray."[25] Jeanne had found herself surrounded by those who persuaded her that she had the power to keep the work of the sisters at Amiens were she to divert her portion of the money that had been loaned to Sophie Barat's Ladies of Christian Instruction. Then too there were other gifts she had made to the house, such as a ciborium, an altar cloth and a tabernacle. Though she had made no restrictions on her gifts, being deeply attached to Françoise and their community, she pleaded with Françoise: "Please, my dear, leave the tabernacle here for a little while–at least for a few months until we can have another made."[26] Yet, at another time, she said: "I am very glad you have many of my things."[27] Such tensions were resolved when

Jeanne was advised by Father Enfantin not to listen to Father de Sambucy. As well, she and Françoise promised each other not to let trifling issues alter the mutual trust and affection they had shared for so long. Françoise, by nature, was disinterested in anything approaching a dispute over questions of money. She had quite freely renounced her grandmother's rich inheritance. Of the portion of her father's estate that she acquired, she had renounced proprietorship and had become merely the administrator, using this income for the good of the congregation. Understandably, then, disputes over financial matters, whether with diocesan authorities or with her dear friend, Jeanne, were at the very least extremely distasteful but ones that she undertook, when necessary, out of obedience to her spiritual mother and friend, Julie, and in service to her community of sisters.

Adding to the pain of departure from Amiens was the fact that she found it impossible to aptly and charitably explain everything to the Blin family, who naturally saw the closing of the convent and withdrawal from their city as a failure and a disgrace attached to the family name.

Françoise sold all that she could not send on to Namur. With as little disturbance as possible and with the assistance of a workman on the property, who made estimates for the articles for sale, she disposed of everything with two or three buyers. Though she had offered Father de Sambucy the first choice on anything he wanted, he rejected her offer. Behind the scenes, he did ask one of the buyers to purchase certain items for him, however. The accumulated difficulties entailed in preparing for departure, from dealing with churchmen who did all that they could to thwart the other sisters from leaving to the dealings with loans, leases and disposal of saleable goods, weighed heavily. Françoise, nonetheless, gave a faithful rendering of all related details in her letters to Julie. "I have to force myself not to try to escape from here," she wrote at the end of one such letter, "I'm so weary of it all. It seems like a year since you left. Tell my good sisters that I have a great desire to be with them again. His Excellency [Bishop Pisani] is very good to think of me; I express to him my respectful attachment. Good-bye, my good Mother, this is quite enough for one time. I am, with as much tenderness as respect, your daughter, who is very impatient to go and join you...."[28]

Ecclesiastical authorities did everything they could to disaffect the sisters at Montdidier and Rubempré from their foundresses but met with little if any success. Françoise and Julie were steadfast in their efforts to leave each one free to choose as her conscience dictated. In fact, both friends were admirable in their ability to maintain the most delicate thoughtfulness with respect to each of their sisters while they themselves were being so harshly treated. Faithful to her personal rule of life of finding her happiness in attentiveness to the happiness of others, Françoise wrote to Julie, "When you write to me, put in a little word for her [Angelica] from time to time. You know the human heart; it gives her great pleasure, and she's unshakable in her resolve [to remain with the two foundresses]."[29] And Françoise clearly and sensitively explained the situation to the sisters at Montdidier in a letter that remains an important document of justification of Julie's actions.

> I believe it's right to let you know in depth the truth regarding the matters that have given rise to this situation, though not in order to exert pressure on you to leave the place where you are; no, you're perfectly free in this respect, and even supposing that you yourselves should decide to follow our Mother, I would advise you not to be hasty about anything, but to see first if the ecclesiastical authorities persevere in trying to separate you from her and to force you to break off the communication and the submission necessary for real unity.
>
> My dear children, here are the facts: the bishop, through Father Cottu, presented us with Rules and Constitutions that included several passages that were not suitable for us, while others, which we would have wanted, were missing. Nevertheless, we didn't try to explain ourselves at first, because it was useless to do so, since the bishop had had Father Cottu tell us that he would have nothing to do with us and wouldn't give us Rules unless I devoted all my patrimony to the house of Amiens alone, since he wouldn't be able to assume responsibility for the sisters in case I should decide that I wanted to withdraw. Given our present critical

condition, however, no prudent person advised me to accept these terms. Nevertheless, not wishing to annoy the bishop, yet not wishing to accept Rules that were not suited to us, and wanting to have them examined by other persons at their leisure, we felt that in view of these difficulties, we had done the right thing in asking for time. This was interpreted as ill-will, disobedience, and open rebellion, and the bishop at once had his vicar general, Father Cottu, write a note to our Mother which stated that she might withdraw into whatever diocese she saw fit, etc. Father Cottu, in giving her the note, added verbally and still in the name of the bishop, that she was to take all her sisters with her; yet a short time later another order came, stating that Sisters Victoire, Clotilda, and Ciska should remain here....

There is the simple and unadulterated truth; I believe that my sincerity is so well known to you that you will not question it. Sister Marianne will not be surprised at all that; she saw the storm brewing before her departure. For a long time now, *ma Mère* has been the butt of contradictions from men, who, I think, have accomplished in all this the designs of God, who wanted to exercise her virtue; he probably also wanted the change of residence for hidden reasons that are unknown to us, but of which we are able to catch a glimpse, and which may be made clear later. However that may be, here are the dispositions that *ma Mère* manifested while she was still here: to leave all her daughters perfectly free, but to let all those who wish to remain attached to her be firmly convinced that she will not abandon one of them.

It would give me great pleasure to receive news of you before my departure; I've heard that good Sister Angelica has been ill. Give me some news about her and also about yourselves. Believe very firmly that my heart cannot change toward you.

I have received a letter from *ma Mère* in which she instructs me to tell you from her all that you know she has in her heart for the three of you, and which she says will last as long as her life. Let us pray fervently to our Lord that his holy will may be accomplished in us; a little time may bring many changes; God is the Master of hearts. Have patience, and above all do not be too greatly saddened.

> I expect to remain here about twelve to fifteen days longer. Your certificates of Baptism, as well as Sister Marianne's belongings, will be sent this week. I embrace all three of you and remain ever united with you in the Heart of our good Jesus.[30]

By February 20, she had a response from the sisters at Montdidier and reported to Julie, "I've received a letter from Montdidier that's exactly like the others; they want to remain attached to you and are suffering violence."[31] Father de Sambucy had informed the sisters that the bishop had named him as their superior and "father." Françoise's weariness with the entire affair was reflected in one of her last letters written from Amiens: "Good night, my good Mother, I'm going to bed—I really have to; it's been a fatiguing day. When shall I be with you and the good sisters...? I hope to attend Mass at Namur on March 5, and then go to confession. Good-bye, my good Mother. I embrace you with as much respect as tenderness."[32]

The date of departure was fixed for March 1, and Françoise readied the final wagon of goods to be sent on to Namur. She was to travel with the last sister to leave Amiens, Sister Angélique, and one boarder, Félicité Chary, who had begged permission from her parents to follow the sisters to Namur. Desirous as Françoise was to be reunited with Julie and to leave the scene of soul-searing trials, she was deeply saddened to bid farewell to Jeanne de Franssu. She had, of course, invited Jeanne to come to Namur, telling her that the bishop of Namur had said she should indeed come there. But Jeanne, though not adverse to the idea, decided to remain in Amiens while waiting to know the will of God for her and consulting with her spiritual adviser, Father Enfantin.[33] "[I]t was the desolate grief of Madame de Franssu that made her [Françoise's] own tears flow. Still her grief was outweighed by joy at her deliverance and the anticipation of being united again with her mother and sisters."[34] Close relationships, once again, enabled Françoise to continue her journey along life's difficult paths.

> My good Mother, when I think of the sudden consolation I experienced when we parted from each other when you

> went to Bordeaux and I was left at Namur—you know I told you it seemed to me that it was just an ordinary little trip and that we would be reunited; and my sadness, even though it wasn't slight, was completely calmed by this sweet sentiment for which there was no apparent reason; but I see clearly now that it came from God. We are reunited—and we are reunited at Namur, whereas there had been every reason to believe that Namur would separate us forever. I'm still ready to be separated from you for the glory of the good God, but I think he wants us to be very much together, or at least that's what I hope.[35]

Aristotle had taught that if friends could not be present to each other and if communication between them suffered, the friendship would eventually die. Saint Augustine acknowledged how love always desires to be with the beloved, and although he missed absent friends greatly, he took a certain solace in the interior bond of their oneness in God.

> Friends were the only consolation to that longing [to be with Christ], because God dwelt in them, and in their friendship, Augustine was able to somehow rest in Christ's presence, though imperfectly, with them. Spiritually his friends were always present to him, and this was somehow more than bodily presence. It was preferable, nonetheless, to both be with them and to know them with mutual affection and love. He valued their presence highly, read and re-read their letters, and always wanted news of them. Yet still, physical presence was a special solace. He writes many times things like, "I can find no words to express how the intensity of my love enkindles in me the longing to see you." Being present they were able to nourish their friendship in conversation, courtesies, corrections "and by a thousand other most pleasing motions."[36]

Françoise, as she wrote on February 5, was open to being separated from Julie, should that be for the greater glory of God. Yet, it is hard to imagine her joy at being reunited with Julie in Namur as her letter, written almost one month before her departure from Amiens, had anticipated. When she arrived, at last, on March 5, she and her companion travelers were welcomed with sincere affection by the sisters and, most assuredly, by Julie. And while Françoise knew there would be the many little separations that congregational business would require of Julie in her role as mother general, she knew, too, that as superior of the motherhouse, now to be established at Namur, she would regularly enjoy the "special solace" of Julie's physical presence.

By the time of Françoise's arrival in Namur, Julie and the other sisters had already done much to transform their new home, which had been rented just the previous December. Workmen were still on the premises, as they would be for some time to come, but the most necessary improvements to this spacious house in the rue des Fossés, with its many smaller adjacent buildings and spacious garden, had been completed. At about the same time, the house was part of a division of an estate of the countess of Ribeaucourt, who gave the sisters the first option on its purchase. Fortunately, the money used for the purchase came from that part of the Blin fortune that Father de Sambucy had administered and that had, at long last and with much difficulty, been returned. On December 12, 1809, it became the first convent owned by the Sisters of Notre Dame, with the title deed drawn up in the name of Sister St. Joseph Blin. "At the time religious orders were not stable enough to admit of any other arrangement."[37]

With Françoise's return and capable resumption of the office of superior of Namur, Julie was once again free to tend to her visits of the secondary houses or to respond to requests to open new establishments. Indeed, the longest stretch of time that Julie was able to spend in Namur prior to her last illness was but a period of a few months, and Françoise was understandably concerned about each trip Julie took, anxious for that first letter assuring that she had safely arrived. "To go alone on such journeys at her age and in her frail state of health, in public conveyances where she had to hear so much cursing, swearing, raillery, and familiarities, she needed courage and the maturity and religious bearing that were hers. She was over fifty when she began these journeys; her face, though bright and animated, was that of a much older person, and this fact often protected her from insult."[38] The community of St. Nicolas was transferred to more suitable lodgings in Ghent, a city in which two establishments were begun, one in the parish of St. Pierre (1809) and the other in the ancient Cistercian abbey of Nouveau Bois (1809). The first house in the Ardennes at St. Hubert (1809) was founded and another was begun in Zèle (1811), followed by foundations at Gembloux (1813) and Andenne (1813). When Julie was at home in Namur, Françoise spent time in consultation with her each morning before going to the kitchen to assist with the cooking, to the garden to weed and to the boarders' dormitories to make the beds. Always ready to lend assistance wherever needed, she considered no task beneath the dignity of the superior. Certainly, no reference was ever made to her social rank. Sisters who began their association with the community after its transfer from Amiens to Namur were often in the congregation a long while before learning anything about the personal history or family name of their very dignified yet equally self-effacing superior.

Meanwhile, Napoleon was busy with expansion endeavors of his own. Increasingly vexed with the resistance of Pope Pius VII to his nominations for vacant bishoprics, angered by the liberties of the French Church and driven by his desire to take a new wife, Napoleon embarked on a plan to sever connections with the papacy. Because the pope had excommunicated him for seizing the Vatican States, Napoleon ordered his garrison to restrain the pope, remove his temporal powers and leave him with the title of bishop of Rome only. Then, defying Canon Law, the emperor called together the National Council in June of 1811 and demanded that the assembled bishops should confer upon the emperor the complete right of appointment and dismissal of bishops. At the time, the satirical remark circulated that the Holy Spirit would exercise much influence on the Council under the form of an eagle, but little or none under that of a dove.[39] Predictably, the bishops held firm, the Council was dissolved, and several bishops, along with their theologians and chaplains, were imprisoned at Vincennes. Among these were Bishops de Broglie of Ghent and Hirn of Tournai. Their dioceses then were handed over to ecclesiastics named by the emperor himself. Father de Sambucy, who had gone to great lengths to justify his own conduct to the Bishops of Ghent and Namur after the break-up of the Amiens community, insinuated himself into Amiens politics that same year, 1811, and was taken by the imperial police to a Paris prison.

Pursuing a reach that exceeded his grasp, Napoleon undertook a disastrous invasion of Russia in 1812 that left more than 500,000 of his soldiers dead of cold and hunger or slain at the hands of the Russians. Then, in October of 1813, he was crushingly defeated at the battle of Leipzig by a combined European force, just months after he had taken Pius VII prisoner at Fontainebleau. It was there that Julie had had the occasion to visit with the pontiff during one of her final trips to France where, eventually, all the congregation's houses had to be closed or abandoned. The year 1813 closed for Julie with a New Year's greeting from Françoise and dated December 31:

> My dear good Mother, when it's the heart that speaks, it needs no great expenditure of time or effort to express itself. That is why I abandon my pen to it without anxiety; my heart will know very well how to make itself understood by yours, which is always so maternal, indulgent, and disposed to receive favorably the little productions of ours.
>
> Let me say then, my good Mother, that I pray to the Lord at all times, and from the bottom of my heart, that he may bless you abundantly and guide you in all your ways, so that, before your departure from this world, you may make firm the foundations of our Institute. May you leave in it worthy subjects, capable of sustaining it in the purity of its primitive spirit and of guiding it to the end of time if that is the will of the Lord. We must believe that God will be pleased to make our establishment last as long as he sees in it fervor and exact observance of the Holy Rule.
>
> I beg of you to pardon my faults and failings of the past year; they have been numerous, and I have great need of your indulgence. I know well that you have long expected something better from me. I hope that with the grace of God this will be the year. I feel spurred on by something that tells me to advance, that time is flying by and will not return, and that death cannot be very far off for me.
>
> I remain entirely yours in the most sincere sentiments of respect, submission, and love. My good Mother, your obedient daughter and servant,
>
> *Sister St. Joseph Blin*[40]
> Sister of Notre Dame

Early in the New Year, on February 2, 1814, the troops of the European alliance entered Belgium, and the main entrance to the convent in Namur had to be reinforced as protection against marauding soldiers. Napoleon agreed to abdicate by April 13 and to go into exile on Elba, which he was permitted to rule as a sovereign principality. The Treaty of Paris, signed on May 30 by France and the victorious coalition, restored the Bourbon monarchy in the person of Louis XVIII. This agreement reestablished France's boundaries of January 1792, with several modifications. Article VI stipulated that "Holland," placed under the sovereignty of the House of Orange, would be enlarged; the Treaty of London, signed on June 20, reunited Belgium and Holland. William of Orange assumed the functions of governor general of Belgium on July 31, 1814. When the diocese of Tournai was restored to its legitimate and previously imprisoned Bishop Hirn, a Notre Dame convent was founded at Fleurus in June of 1814, shortly after the Treaty of Paris was concluded. This foundation was the ninth of the Belgian foundations and the last established by Julie herself.

The European allies continued to haggle over territorial boundaries and kingships and convened a European assembly in Vienna in September of 1814. The negotiators from the four victorious powers, Castlereagh for Britain, Frederick William III for Prussia, Metternich for Austria and Alexander I for Russia, with France's Louis XVIII represented by Talleyrand, were concerned about creating a balance of power and about avoiding the alienation of any major state. Sessions dragged on into the spring of 1815, and in March representatives to the Congress were appalled to learn that Napoleon had escaped from Elba and was heading for Paris. In the meantime, on May 16, William of Orange anticipated the definitive promulgation of an act by the Congress of Vienna and assumed, on May 16, the title of king of the Netherlands, the amalgamation of Holland and Belgium. Having succeeded once again in coalescing the other European powers as well as in inspiring thousands to follow him, Napoleon crossed the Belgian frontier on June 15 to drive back the Prussian army. At Ligny he managed, as did the French General Ney, to hold back Wellington at Quatre Bras. Napoleon's army pursued Wellington to Mont St. Jean, near Waterloo where, on June 18, Napoleon was defeated. By June 22, he had signed his second and final abdication and was consigned to spend the rest of his life in exile on the island of St. Helena in the South Atlantic. Françoise and Julie had to worry once again about the welfare and security of their sisters in the towns of Fleurus, Jumet and Gembloux, which were overrun by troops. Namur endured the effects of the retreating French army, which entered the city on June 18. "What a sight was this routing of Napoleon's grand army," Françoise wrote, "a frightful rout from which it was never to recover. The unfortunate fugitives did not know where to find refuge or the means of subsistence. It was the same for their pursuers."[41] With characteristic trust in God's providence, she continued her eye-witness account:

> Last of all, after the final rout of Napoleon's great army on June 18, we at Namur experienced great fright, but no real harm. The French soldiers in flight entered the city on the nineteenth. It was then not yet clear whether all was over or what the defeat meant. On the twentieth, early in the morning, the Prussians were at the gates and they did not cease firing their cannons; but the French gave no response, for they had no more ammunition. The Prussian general found it in his heart not to continue to bombard the town, which otherwise would have been completely destroyed; he made this decision because of the good treatment the townspeople had accorded the Prussians.
>
> Toward six in the evening the allies were entering one gate while the French were leaving by the other; and so ended the fighting. All the good people of Namur attributed the protection of the city to the Blessed Virgin and, in thanksgiving, they erected a special altar in the cathedral, sang a high Mass, and held a particularly beautiful thanksgiving service in the cathedral. We ourselves could not thank God enough for protecting us, like a kind Father, from frightful dangers. This is not a story of the war, which is the task of professional writers. It is merely an account of the providence of God, and a tribute of thanksgiving which we wish to pass on to the sisters who will come after us.[42]

Having cared little for the lives of others—of friends, of his soldiers or of those in the nations he ruled—Napoleon was guided by a desire for personal glory. On the other hand, two French women and contemporaries of the French general, Françoise Blin and Julie Billiart, bonded in a friendship that rested on a mutual benevolence, shared the motivating desire of service for the love of God. This sentiment was eloquently summarized in what would prove to be Françoise's last note to Julie, written on December 29, 1815, just a few months before the latter's death. It again took the form of a New Year's greeting:

> My dear Mother in God, I renew at the beginning of this year the sincere wishes I have not ceased to offer since the good God gave me that grace of becoming your daughter in Jesus Christ. I have asked, I ask, and I shall ask without ceasing that you may grow every day in grace, in strength, and in the gifts of the Holy Spirit for your sanctification and for the accomplishment of the work God has put into your hands, so that at your last day you may say with confidence: "*Consummatum est:* all is consummated! I have accomplished by your grace the work you have given me to do; I place it in your hands; may it be cemented in charity and strengthened in unity."
>
> These, my dear Mother, are the sincere wishes of her whose only desire is to live and die.
>
> Your most humble and obedient servant and daughter,
> *Sister St. Joseph of Notre Dame*[43]

Chapter V

MOTHER GENERAL 1816

In December of 1815, Julie suffered a terrible fall that caused such acute pain that she had to be carried to her room. The agonizing pain persisted and, in January, her health began to give cause for serious anxiety. From the outset of her illness, Françoise was at her bedside caring for her, helping her to eat what little she could and reading to her. It was from Julie's room that she maintained her responsibilities as superior. Once, while Françoise was reading to her from the *Imitation of Christ* and though she could not see the words, Julie stretched out her hand to a passage saying, "That is the part; read that." The passage in question was: "'If you carry the cross of Jesus it will carry you and will lead you to the longed-for goal where you will find an end to sufferings, which in this life have no end.'"[1]

Alternately hopeful and resigned to the inevitable, the strain took its toll on Françoise. In February, she had written to Anastasie at Jumet: "I wanted to have something good to tell you, but I've waited in vain; we're not yet over the worst. The cold season delays her convalescence and causes her much suffering. I put out of my mind all thought of danger, and everyone says there is none; but there's certainly suffering...."[2] In March, she wrote: "All of us, sisters and children, are making a novena to St. Joseph to obtain from the Heart of Jesus through his intercession the cure of our dear Mother. This divine Heart cured her, as you know, so that she could begin a work that is as yet only in the formative stage; can he not preserve her to us for its consolidation? Let us hope for everything from his goodness; let us act with courage. If we don't relinquish our hope, the help of heaven will descend upon us; the Lord is trying us."[3] By the end of the month, exhausted and afflicted by an epidemic fever and a severe case of pleurisy, Françoise was obliged to stay in bed. The cofoundress became so ill that she too was administered the last sacraments.

When the friendship is a true one, frankness only serves to strengthen it. As Saint Augustine commented, the greatest lover of all teaches and corrects. Saint Francis echoed the importance of correction, calling it a kind of "circumcision of the heart," which is most effective when another takes the knife to our faults. Such was a characteristic of the strong friendship of the cofoundresses, a characteristic apparent to the very end of the life they shared together. Françoise had said with respect to Julie: "Even when she scolded, resisted, or wounded you, it was impossible not to love her, because she was so loving and lovable, in God and for God, that she knew how to heal the wound she made."[4]

With great difficulty but with a deep desire to be with her friend, Françoise went to Julie's room on April 7. She described her last visit:

> All things work together unto good for those who love God. This truth, I believe, was illustrated by a little incident that occurred the day before she died. In view of the perfect friendship that had always existed between us, this small incident must have served to complete her detachment from the things of the world. I was ill that day, but I dragged myself to her room and sat down in an armchair where I could see her. Her face appeared so changed that I was filled with emotion and, when it was time to leave, I do not know how it happened but I did not as usual go to her bed to say good-night; I went back to my own sickbed, in a little room adjoining hers. The next day I returned for a visit about five in the evening, eight hours before her death. I had my chair moved near her bed.
>
> When she saw me, she shook her finger with just enough strength to say, "God was not pleased yesterday." With no explicit reproach, her word and gesture made clear that I might have done better. Often she took such a way, even when she was ill, to point out a weakness. This time,

> after a moment, she asked, "Will you come back again tonight?"
>
> "No," I said, "my fever has gone up again." Then I kissed her and left. When I saw her again, she was dead.[5]

The sisters notified the cofoundress immediately and she sat for a long while in Julie's room, feeling bereft of the comfort afforded by the physical presence of her closest friend and confidante.

"May God preserve Mother St. Joseph for us," Bishop Pisani said when he learned of Julie's death. "I'm afraid that she will succumb to this terrible blow!"[6] As soon as the news reached Jumet, Sister Anastasie left immediately for the motherhouse in order to offer what assistance she could to Françoise. Profoundly touched, the cofoundress greeted her, as did the other sisters, as a consoling angel. "My dear, dear child, how very much like you. Take care of your sisters."[7] In this informal manner, Anastasie, one of the "two eldest daughters," Julie's "little counselor" and Françoise's "big counselor," was appointed superior of the Namur community.

As for Françoise, she had much to care for: no fewer than eight other sisters at the motherhouse were also dangerously ill from the epidemic. Most of the remaining sisters were overcome by the fatigue of nursing and teaching and by their grief. The eight existing Belgian establishments, with their fifty-eight professed sisters and twenty-five novices, required ongoing attention, and the foundations of the young congregation needed the surer underpinnings of a definitive rule. Nonetheless, Françoise believed in the continued support of her now-absent friend, confident of her heavenly guidance.

One of the first letters of condolence to arrive came from the bishop's palace in Amiens. Bishop Demandolx, ever torn between the opinions of his advisors and his own appreciation of Julie's merits, expressed to Françoise his sincere sympathy for the grievous loss she had no doubt experienced in the death of "your good mother." "You know the tender attachment that I had for her and the high regard in which I held her virtues....Let us always keep before our eyes the examples she gave us and let them serve as encouragement in the trials which we are destined to suffer. I know that I am speaking to Sister Blin, to Sister St. Joseph, to the true friend of Sister Julie...."[8]

Father Thomas expressed his sympathy by writing that he could well believe that "the loss you have sustained affects you more deeply than the danger which has threatened your own life."[9] Condolences came from Father Varin in Paris, who shared with the cofoundress his assurance that her friend would be even more effective for the prosperity of the congregation now that "she is in her heavenly home, in the bosom of God...." Toward the end of his letter, he bolstered her own conviction by acknowledging that "[t]his is a great subject of consolation and of confidence for you who replace her, my dear Mother. Yes, she will be even more useful to you in heaven than on earth; she will make you truly feel the effects of her esteem before God. She will draw down upon you the lights and the graces you need to strengthen and to extend the work of the Lord and all your daughters will recognize with you that they have, in their good Mother, a powerful protectress."[10]

For several weeks, Françoise's condition remained so critical that it seemed she might well join her close friend in death. Then, one evening when the prognosis seemed particularly dire, one of the sisters gathered the boarders in the chapel and with them made the way of the cross. That appeared to many to be the very point at which Françoise began to improve significantly, so that by early May she had enough strength to see the sisters in small groups in her room. On May 21, she was well enough to meet with the community and on May 29, 1816, all the superiors and their assistants gathered at Namur for the first general chapter of the congregation. They spent the first three days in silence and prayer in preparation for the selection of the next mother general.

To her trusted adviser and ecclesiastical superior, Father Médard, Françoise confided her sincere dread at being asked to take up the responsibilities of superior general. Just the same, on June 2, with Médard, the vicar general, serving as president of the proceedings, the sisters unanimously elected their beloved Mother St. Joseph to this post. At the age of sixty, though as stately and dignified as someone much younger, she accepted the position in a deep spirit of humility and obedience, and with a great singleness of purpose.

The erection of a simple stone over the grave of Julie was the first official act of Françoise's generalate. She then made official Anastasie's appointment as superior of the motherhouse and her first counselor, and undertook a visit of all the secondary houses. Having had experience as a young adult in managing the estate at Gézaincourt, she had an experienced sense of administration. Attentive to physical needs and environment—the chapel, household arrangement, classes—she was equally gifted in dealing with her sisters as individuals and brought to the task all the tact, diplomacy, good sense and sensitivity that were part of her own upbringing. Everywhere she went, she went with her friend, and she never let an occasion pass to preface a remark, a request or a plan with the words: "My dear Sisters, Mère Julie, wanted this or recommended that...."[11]

In November of 1815, Julie had entered into negotiations regarding an establishment at Dinant and had visited the city at the invitation of the burgomaster. The following January, arrangements for receiving the Sisters of Notre Dame had been concluded with the city council authorizing an allowance of a thousand francs toward the house and a further thousand francs annually until the house could become self-supporting. Therefore, fulfilling Julie's wish, Françoise wasted no time in sending sisters to Dinant. On July 1, the founding sisters were settled in their new home, and a school was opened there.

As of 1810, the pastor at St. Nicolas in Liège had been begging Julie for a foundation in his city, and her reply to him was that she would like first to see evidence of devotion to the Sacred Heart in his parish. This devotion, dear to both Julie and Françoise, was by now more well-known and practiced in France than in Belgium, and both foundresses worked sincerely to further it in their adopted homeland. The pastor was happy to comply, and by 1813 there was a flourishing Confraternity of the Sacred Heart. Negotiations regarding the proposed establishment resumed in the spring of 1815 but, unfortunately, Belgium was a battlefield at the time. This was another desire of Julie's that Françoise was eager to see realized and, in October, Sister Anastasie went in the name of the mother general to establish the new community there.

Because she was particularly eager to bring to fruition those specific desires of Julie with which she was familiar, Françoise next undertook the drafting of a permanent rule. The provisional one had stood the test of time with prudent adaptations for fifteen years. Thwarted previously by the radical adjustments demanded by Bishop Demandolx and by Father de Sambucy, then by Napoleon's Paris Plan, whereby he projected the fusing of all religious orders into two "regiments" of his empire, the delay had provided opportunity for both foundresses to test the application of the rule to the specific character of the congregation. Françoise began with a systematic study of Julie's government as it was practiced in all the houses. To this end, she asked for each house to send her all the writings of the foundress that they had, along with a listing of the practices regarded in each house as traditional. Françoise spent the summer of 1816 studying the rule outlined by Julie as well as the rules of the chief religious founders: Saints Benedict, Francis de Sales and Ignatius. It was from the latter founder that she borrowed the most, asserting that "the Society of Jesus protected the cradle of the Sisters of Notre Dame."[12] One of the first stated principles, "The Congregation of the Sisters of Notre Dame is governed by a Superior General," was one held firmly by Julie and Françoise; it had contributed to their expulsion from the Diocese of Amiens. The end or purpose of the congregation was stated to be the education of youth with a predilection for the poor of the most abandoned places. Its spirit was characterized by simplicity, obedience and charity. Since the congregation differentiated itself from others in that it was based on the friendship of two women from distinct social spheres, all barriers of class were to be avoided. There was to be none of the traditional distinction between choir sisters and lay sisters, who occupied themselves with mundane household tasks. Julie wanted the sisters to be with the children rather than bound by duties in chapel, praying the Divine Office. Devotion to Our Lady, *Notre Dame,* from whom the congregation took its name, became a focused religious practice. Françoise succeeded in completing the rule for the Sisters of Notre Dame and wisely decided to put it into practice before submitting it for final approval. With the assistance of her council, she began its implementation in the motherhouse, observing and deliberating on its actualization. Subsequently, copies were forwarded to each superior of the secondary houses, who were asked to submit periodical reports on its effectiveness within their communities. Two years were spent in this process of action and reflection.[13] The very process highlighted another principle with which both foundresses were in perfect accord, that of adaptation, in order to maintain a freedom of spirit and an apostolic flexibility.

> For Mère St. Joseph, the writing of the constitutions was an urgent matter to which she addressed herself soon after becoming superior general in 1816. It was an act of faith and worship as well as a family service to the Sisters. Contemporary records describe the intensity of her prayer in the weeks of composition, and her earnest requests for the prayers of the Sisters. She was concerned with a work of God and, when her text was completed, it was the expression of a spirituality as well as of a way of life.[14]

Faithful to her friend's spirit of active contemplation, which Julie described as "rapture of action," Françoise combined the mystical and the practical in her description of the spirituality of the congregation. In this respect, both Françoise and Julie were influenced by the seventeenth-century French School of Spirituality. Saint Francis de Sales had been schooled, like the nobility of his generation, by the Jesuits of the Renaissance, who were predominantly humanists. Their theology was forged by both the threat of Protestantism and the pressing need to show that the honest person, as depicted in classical literature, still needed Christ for happiness. They believed that God was indeed revealed in the beauty of creation, but most of all in the ennobled humanity of a saint. Believing the heart to be the center of human activity, Saint Francis saw that the challenge to confront Protestantism was to lead a devout life outside the protective shelter of the monastery or the hermitage. This called for a new path to holiness, one that combined contemplation and action. And, as he saw it, friendship was to be one of the pillars supporting the living of this kind of life.[15]

As Françoise had provided moral support to the foundress, so her fortune had continued to provide for the material needs of the congregation. When the generosity of a benefactor did not completely cover what was needed for a requested establishment, the Blin inheritance supplied the deficit. And when Françoise's income did not suffice, she drew upon the principle. So it was that, in 1816, she sold the last portion of her patrimony for the good of the institute and used the monies for the purchase of the Abbey of Nonnenbosch (Nouveau Bois) in Ghent.

Françoise had stayed with Julie in that "gentle struggle" which is friendship. She had experienced the joys and the sorrows of this "school of love" and had experienced friendship in its perfection: union in diversity. With her friend, Julie, always in her heart, Françoise was left to carry out the work the two of them had begun. Now, uniquely poised to live as a "community of friends," she and her sisters would learn to an even greater extent that friendship is a school of discipleship in which the friends learn to love all whom God loves.[16]

Chapter VI

FRENCHWOMAN IN A DUTCH DOMAIN 1817–1823

An ordinance had been published on May 10, 1816, that provoked great concern among those who understood its antireligious character. It stated that Catholic worship would continue to be regulated by the Organic Articles and, for most, the notion of the Organic Articles was merely synonymous with the Concordat that had restored religious practice.

Bishop de Broglie returned from exile and immediately began to enlighten the populace. He urged all to refuse to take the required oath of allegiance to the new Constitution and, as a consequence, he was once again banished. While his case was being tried, Bishop de Broglie was in Amiens where, in August of 1817, he tended to his fellow bishop, Demandolx, who died on August 14; Bishop de Broglie celebrated the funeral Mass on August 17. In his absence he was condemned. His image was publicly burned in effigy between two criminals who were being punished for their crimes by public exposure, on November 19, 1817. The symbolism of the event was not wasted on even the simple farmers who had come to the city to sell their produce. The sisters in Ghent, because of their allegiance to Bishop de Broglie, were held in suspicion—this time by King William's emissaries. Fortunately, the townspeople recognized that the sisters were only living as poor women in order to teach poor children of the city.

The clergy of the town continued to be persecuted by the government until their bishop's death in Paris in 1821.

Mother St. Joseph received the news of Bishop Demandolx's death with sincere sorrow and had a Mass said for the repose of his soul. She also asked the sisters of all the communities to say for him all the prayers usually reserved for the death of a member of the congregation. With exquisite charity, not only did she refrain from speaking ill of him and of his treatment of the two foundresses, but she consistently maintained an attitude of deep respect, even veneration, in his regard.

The mayor of Thuin had been corresponding with Mother St. Joseph regarding an establishment of Sisters of Notre Dame in his town, part of the principality of Liège since the ninth century. However, the mother general took great care in the formation of her beloved "little white veils," as she affectionately called the novices, saying that she "would rather sacrifice a class," than risk aborting the religious and educational formation of a novice. Thus, in December of 1816, she had had to respond to Mayor Martin: "I assure you that it is contrary to my inclination to be obliged once more to give you for response the same reasons as of June 12, but I beg you to observe that they must necessarily still exist, since a notable time is required to form young persons capable of fulfilling your views and mine. I cannot even set a date; that depends upon the capacity and progress of those concerned."[1]

"Mère St. Joseph devoted jealous care to the novitiate," noted one of her novices.[2] Following the example of her own mentor and spiritual mother, Julie, Mother St. Joseph wanted to form persons who would have nothing petty about them, who would be both magnanimous and humble. No doubt, her greatest lesson came by way of her own personal example, for the sister novice mistress of the time herself observed that "these young religious were drawn by our Mother St. Joseph to reach for the highest degree of virtue. To see her was to receive a profound impression of a consummate holiness."[3]

She was no less assiduous in assuring their professional formation. To this end, she added to her excellent educational background by studying and comparing various methodologies. As she had with the development of the rule, so she submitted pedagogical methods to an approach of action and reflection, trying and then evaluating them for effectiveness and efficiency. This formation did not end with the novitiate since annually, during the summer months, the sisters from all the secondary houses came home to Namur for retreat and for workshop-like conferences during which all sisters were free to share educational experiences. From this exchange the mother general would develop the plan of studies for the next academic year.

Her interest and concern were not limited to the personal words of encouragement she gave to each as one by one they left the courtyard of the motherhouse at the conclusion of the annual gathering. During the school year, Mother St. Joseph visited the classes, and afterwards she asked the sisters to send her samples of the children's work. In such a way, the young teachers felt assured of their mother's ongoing interest as well as of her exact recollection of the status of each. Indeed, they were astounded by her prodigious memory, which retained details pertinent to the development of each sister. She remembered the specific area in which individuals needed to improve and noted the progress they had made since their last contact.

After Belgium was joined with the Netherlands to form one united kingdom under the authority of the "enlightened despot," William of Orange, tensions between the Flemish-speaking north and the French-speaking south found their origins in a number of areas. One of these had to do with the educational system. In Holland, elementary education had not suffered from long years of neglect as it had in Belgium and, after 1814, the new government was determined to improve and develop a system for the masses. One aspect of William's plan was to provide free education with the creation of fifteen hundred schools but his vision was seen by many to be an infringement on the liberty of the citizens in that it would create a state monopoly with unlimited power in educational matters. Despite her awareness of this potential threat, Mother St. Joseph proceeded with characteristic calm to pursue the educational mission of the Sisters of Notre Dame and, in November of 1817, she was able to respond to Mr. Martin's pleadings for a school in his city of Thuin. The joy was great in the town that autumn day as "[t]he inhabitants, having long awaited the event, crowded the market place where the travelers were to pass. As their carriage made its way through the throng of the curious, Mère St. Joseph, who had come to preside at the foundation, smilingly greeted those to her right and left. The impression made was an excellent one and everyone was delighted so that from the outset a friendly rapport was established."[4]

The looming menace of the government's educational policies was exacerbated by the very real threat of famine. The harvest had failed, the war had depleted the country and the winter had been particularly severe. The years 1816 and 1817 were years of acute scarcity. While some indigent families came for help to Mother St. Joseph, who did what she could to assuage the plight of the poor however it presented itself to her, her nephew, Alexander, was engaged in similar works of charity in Amiens, where he was now mayor. Through his efforts in making known to the king of France the desperate needs of the poor in Amiens, he was able to obtain significant funds from the royal purse for the hungry in his city.[5] For her part, Mother St. Joseph, by economizing and by her foresightedness, was able to procure enough not only for her growing religious family but for several indigent families, as well. That she and her nephew had inherited the family trait and lived up to the adage, *"Bon comme un Blin,"* was definitely not a piece of folklore, but a living tradition.

In May of 1818, two ordinances came like unexpected thunderbolts from the minister of worship, Monsieur Goubau. Henceforth, there were to be no more contemplative orders in King William's realm since he, like Napoleon before him, regarded such orders as completely useless. Like Napoleon, he dreamed of creating a Belgian church independent of Rome. With respect to the teaching congregations, they would be merely tolerated until the Department of Public Instruction had had sufficient time to realize its ambitious plans. Nursing orders were spared since they were deemed to be useful to the government, whose leaders saw that they would never be able to replace the personal services nursing sisters offered. However, even they had to become nationalized and submit their statutes to the king for approval. A plethora of official documents followed the promulgation of these ordinances. Demands were made for numerous detailed statistics. There were any number of forms to be completed and lists of indiscreet questions to which the congregations were obliged to respond. Though this orgy of officialdom found echo in her letters of the period, the mother general of the Sisters of Notre Dame was utterly remarkable in her ability to maintain an inner peace and an outer calm, a calm that edified all who were, along with her, exasperated by the government's attempts to gradually snuff out the religious communities in the realm. "And, my dear," she wrote to the superior at Dinant, "how is it that you haven't thought of speaking to me of the replies you gave to the questions of the government? Send them, if you please, as soon as possible."[6] On numerous occasions, she wrote words of encouragement, inspiring confidence with assurances such as "a regiment that is united and stays close together is impregnable when facing the enemy....We must know how to carry on in good weather and bad, like courageous soldiers of Jesus Christ.... Always be happy and full of confidence in God."[7]

Given the lack of certainty with respect to the future of the existing foundations and their current needs for additional sisters, Mother St. Joseph thought it out of the question that she should begin another school. However, the opportunity to respond to a different sort of need presented itself. In 1819, two young women who came to the provincial of the Jesuits in Holland, Father Wolff, for spiritual direction manifested to him a definite call to religious life. He had long nourished the hope of providing the benefits of a Christian education for the young of his country and, having heard many glowing reports about the work of Julie Billiart, Françoise Blin and their congregation, he made a proposal to the cofoundress. Would she consider providing for his recruits a solid formation in religious life so that they could return to Holland to found a congregation similar to that of the Sisters of Notre Dame? Mother St. Joseph was only too happy to respond in the affirmative and, to facilitate their training, made the decision to have these young Dutch-speaking women spend the first part of their formation period at the novitiate in Ghent. Then, having gained a working knowledge of French and a foundation in the religious life, they would complete their formation under her supervision at Namur. Trust in the potential fruit of this endeavor was apparent in the letter Mother St. Joseph wrote to Sister Marie, the superior of Ghent:

> Let us talk now about our young Dutch girls, who have arrived. I'm glad. If the good God wills to grant it his blessing, that may give rise to a very good work. To achieve this, it seems to me it would be even more suitable to have five or six of them, because, in three or four years, when they have been well formed, they could establish a house of their own, and then receive subjects and propagate themselves as we have done, with the help of the good God.[8]

From 1819 to 1824, seven such young women were formed as religious and trained as teachers. They returned to Holland where they established a community at Amersfoort so that, as a result of Mother St. Joseph's collaboration with Father Wolff, eventually three new religious congregations were begun: the Sisters of Notre Dame at Amersfoort, the Sisters of Notre Dame of Coesfeld, and the Congregation of Jesus, Mary and Joseph of Bois-le-Duc.

The "good weather and bad" seemed to alternate all too frequently for the mother general, with the bad taking ascendancy often enough during her tenure. In 1819, an epidemic broke out among the boarders in Ghent, and one child died. Many others were taken out of the school by their frightened parents. One sister after another fell ill and, after a while, the boarding school, which had been such a flourishing one, began to seem deserted. She had barely broken the news to the superiors at the secondary houses that the loved and respected mistress of novices, Sister Claire Lesergent, had died when she found herself again offering words of consolation:

> My dear Sister Marie, I must tell you first how saddened I was by your last letter; it's always distressing for me to see boarders die in our houses. I'm not surprised that it's a great burden for you. But let us hope the one who has just fallen ill won't have the same fate–that the trouble will end there. Three pupils who have had to leave for the same reason: that's enough to alarm the parents. It's the hand of God that has struck you, my dear Sister Marie, and it's that same hand that

will cure you, for it's the hand of a Father. Have great confidence. It's your turn today; it will perhaps be ours tomorrow.[9]

But, most unfortunately, it was again Ghent's turn to be tried. In the spring of 1820 a fire broke out in a factory that still occupied part of the Abbey premises. It took only a few minutes for the entire structure to be engulfed in flames, and the conflagration threatened the convent itself. The convent roof was burning when, quite providentially, the winds shifted and diverted the flames in the opposite direction. However, several of the sisters suffered from the shock of it for some time. Mother St. Joseph herself appeared to be somewhat winded by the close call, as reflected in her almost breathless enumeration of the possible scenarios that were evaded.

> My dear Sisters, I can't delay uniting myself with you to give thanks to God. If it had happened at night, if the wind had been more violent, if the Holy Angels hadn't inspired those who were trying to put out the fire as to what they should do, and finally if the Heart of Jesus had not been favorable to you, it's a hundred to one that you would have been burned. Tomorrow we'll receive Communion in thanksgiving. I imagine you'll do something similar at the very least. When you've recovered a little, be sure to write me at greater length. I'm anxious to know if the shock may have made some sisters ill—for it's not always in our power to control our reactions as much as we ought.
>
> And you, Sister Marie, did you remain strong? I don't doubt the perfect resignation of your heart, but your weak body may have had to suffer from the shock that inevitably accompanies such events.
>
> I have neither the heart nor the spirit to talk to you about anything else. I ask, and strongly recommend, that you have my respects and thanks presented to M. Lemaire,[10] who was thoughtful enough to write to me before I should learn in some other way what had happened to you.
>
> My love, in God, to all my good sisters. I am all yours in the Lord. It's really good to abandon oneself to God alone! Sister Anastasia greets you as victims escaped from an almost certain death.[11]

This time, a letter alone would not suffice. Mother St. Joseph hurried to Ghent to comfort the community, to help them see that God in his goodness would indeed cause good to come from all they had suffered.

A decidedly bright spot in an otherwise very difficult two-year period was the entrance into the community of the young woman, Thérèse Goethals. The youngest of eight children in a distinguished Christian family, an intellectually gifted individual with a penchant for giving assistance to the poor, she had early in life, like Mother St. Joseph, decided to join the Carmelites. Fortunately, for the Sisters of Notre Dame, the prioress discouraged her by telling her that she thought her destined for an apostolic community. She entered the novitiate at Nouveau Bois in Ghent, took the name of Sister Ignace in honor of her patron in religion and eventually became the one who would follow Mother St. Joseph as superior general. There was to be no doubt that she lived up to her promise of her youth. When Mother St. Joseph said to her, at the time of the selection of a name in religion, that she would confer the name of Sister Ignace on the condition that Thérèse become a second Ignatius in zeal and in virtue, Thérèse replied: "My dear Mother, I accept this mission as a sacred engagement and shall hold myself always obliged to strive to fulfill it."[12]

Early in 1820, the administrators of the Bureau of Charitable Works requested Sisters of Notre Dame for the Girls' Sunday School. Founded in 1645 by Madame Anne de Ruplémont for the purpose of instructing poor children in the catechism, the school was open originally only on Sundays. Over time, reading, writing and arithmetic were added to the curriculum, and it became a day school. Food and clothing were also distributed from the premises. The school was being reorganized, and both Bishop Pisani and Father Minsart promised contributions toward the school's expenses on the condition that the Brothers of the Christian Schools teach the boys and the Sisters of Notre Dame, the girls. In a playful vein, Mother St. Joseph communicated the news to the sisters at Dinant:

> My dear Sister Angela and all my good Sisters, I fear you're weary of waiting for the visit of a certain person [herself, for her regular visit], so for that reason I'm going to tell you a little

> story to dispel your weariness. Some time ago a good and pious lady made a large foundation at Namur for the instruction of children of both sexes. This school, which was called the Sunday School, was entrusted to the care of seculars who are now very old. Recently, the administrators judged it proper to confide the boys to the care of the Brothers of the Christian Schools and the girls to that of the Sisters of Notre Dame....
>
> You'd like to know, perhaps, what mistresses are destined for the Sunday School. It's not an easy matter to make a choice as we haven't many sisters. I'll be obliged to send big Sister A., although she's not yet sufficiently formed to take a class; but the good God will assist her if it's pleasing to him. For the second class we have a good sister novice, who will make her apprenticeship. I hope the good God will bless her. We haven't a single young sister formed at this moment. These good sisters will dine and sleep here at home. I tell you all this, my good Sisters, so that you'll pray that our new apostolate may redound to the honor and glory of God....The [sisters] intend to follow the method used by the Brothers. They're very well satisfied with their mission. Wherever there's question of instructing the poor, the sisters are always delighted and devote themselves to the work with all their hearts. I think I've told you quite a long story, and it's time to finish....[13]

Relations between religious communities and King William's government were about to enter a more tempestuous phase. Another measure was promulgated whereby all religious communities were required to receive royal approbation in order to continue in existence, and vows were not to be made for a period longer than five years. Mother St. Joseph complied immediately by forwarding a copy of Napoleon's signed approbation, along with a favorable testimonial from Bishop Pisani. By July, notification of recognition was granted for the houses of the Namur province only. Not only were the seven establishments in Ghent, Liège and Thuin not officially recognized, but these communities were located in dioceses where the episcopal sees were still vacant, precluding any ecclesial letters of approbation. The See of Liège had been vacant since 1802, that of Tournai since 1819, and Bishop de Broglie was in exile while his vicars general were still in disfavor, having been imprisoned for five months because of their loyalty to him. Further, no additional foundations were to be authorized.

Still another complication muddied the waters. The statutes approved by Napoleon had been hastily drafted by Father de Sambucy, and he had stipulated in one article that: "They are governed in each house by a superior, an assistant and three counselors, elected every three years by plurality of votes, in presence of an ecclesiastical superior."[14] In actual practice, superiors of the secondary houses were nominated by the superior general, and this discrepancy led to confusion and controversy on the part of the governmental authorities. When faced with the issue, Mother St. Joseph simply and honestly replied that the statutes, as presented to the French government, were still tentative and subject to modification after a period of experiment. This battle was won but certainly not the war.

While the decree of 1818 had rendered possible the existence of religious of teaching congregations from 1821 on, under the influence of two ministers particularly, van Driel and van Maanen, and despite the more moderate influence of Goubau, minister of religion, the king became more and more demanding with respect to teaching orders.[15] The assaults now came from two camps: the Ministry of Religion and the Ministry of Education. One decree followed another, each more hostile than the preceding. First, testimonials as to the character and qualifications of teachers were required. In this matter, Mother St. Joseph did not need to worry too much because, from the outset, she had seen to the excellent preparation of her teachers. Then, in July of 1822, another decree announced that there would be severe penalties for any unqualified persons who might be found teaching. This caused concern with respect to those sisters in houses and schools that had not yet received royal approbation. In 1823, religious orders were mandated to render detailed accounts of income and expenses. In 1824, only the government was authorized to determine the number of sisters permitted in each establishment. Quotas allotted were: Namur, fifty, including novices; Gembloux, fourteen; Dinant, twelve; Andenne, five. Accounts were also to be rendered regarding any transfers from one establishment to another, and there were to be no exchanges made between the approved and the unapproved houses. In addition to the paperwork that these measures required, the sisters were being stretched to the limit. Given the quotas, it was virtually impossible to accept new recruits, to replace sick sisters or to send assistance to schools needing additional teachers, not to mention the impossibility of responding to requests for new foundations.

Mother St. Joseph took upon herself the task of preparing the petitions for royal approbation. She was unfailing in her regular correspondence with all her communities, encouraging, empathizing, offering advice. Though the thread of a peaceful and trusting calm is woven throughout all her letters of the period, one written to support a young sister newly missioned to the house at Thuin serves as eloquent testimony to Mother St. Joseph's unique ability to find no concern too small for her sensitive, motherly attentiveness.

> It consoles me, dear Sister Eugenia, to see that you're happy and that the good God is rewarding you for the resignation with which you accepted your hasty departure. You serve a good Master; if you give him something, he returns much more. Be generous and you'll experience this. Try to be always indifferent with regard to the charges, duties, and places to which you are assigned and you'll see the spiritual benefits that this abandonment into the hands of God will bring you. Continue to be open with your superior; this will strike fear into the heart of the devil, who can't endure such openness because he knows that it's the gateway to many graces and that by revealing your temptations to your superior you will find the weapons needed to resist him. Courage, my dear Sister Eugenia; become a good sister. Model yourself completely on God and he will give himself completely to you. To act otherwise would be a great insult to him. As for me, believe that I am your deeply devoted Mother in Jesus Christ.[16]

Since her personal interest was extended to everyone, it is not surprising that she included in a letter to Sister Marie at Ghent, "Joseph, our poor coachman, has died. Since he asked me to recommend him for prayers in all our houses, I hope you will pray for him."[17] Sincere too is a typical note, in a letter to the Superior, with a message for each of the sisters in the house: "Please tell my dear sisters that I don't forget them; it's impossible to forget what is so close to the heart. My constant desire is that they become true spouses of Jesus Christ."[18] No less sincere, as well as humble, is her personal request for prayer: "Please give my best wishes in God to all my dear sisters. Good-bye, my very dear Sister Marie. Pray, pray for me, and write me a letter of consolation; I have more need of it than you have."[19]

It was in the same letter to Sister Marie that Mother St. Joseph had the double sorrow of informing her that Marie's own blood sister, Gertrude Steenhaut, also a Sister of Notre Dame, had died. She was the young Ciska, who had bravely responded to both Father Cottu and Bishop Demandolx with her firm, unshakable, "I will follow Mère Julie," when they insisted she remain behind in Amiens. Sister Gertrude spent half of her thirty short years as a Sister of Notre Dame and had died on May 18 while superior at Gembloux. Consequently, Mother St. Joseph felt both a tender empathy for Marie and her own personal grief at the loss of this young sister who was as dear to her as she had been to Julie.

She sustained another personal loss with the death of her own sister, Marie-Louise-Aimé Félix, before the year of 1821 came to a close. One can only surmise how the accumulation of personal grief along with the persistent concerns relating to the threatened existence of the congregation affected her. Infrequent are the instances of self-reference in her correspondence of the period though, in an unpublished letter to Sister St. John in January of 1822, one feels her deep sense of loss, of personal emptiness. She sought solace in what she knew to be a community of friendship love in God.

> What will I say to you at present, my good Sister St. John? We need to give one another reciprocal encouragement so as to redouble our effort each year to uproot the bad plants which are in us and to graft their fruit for life eternal because we are knocking on the door of eternity, my dear. Let us try not to present ourselves with empty hands. As for me, finding myself closer to the end of life, I feel very destitute; please help me with your prayers and good works. You owe this to

> me, my dear children, and I am claiming it. I've just been warned to keep myself in readiness by the death of my only sister, only slightly older than I, whom God has just called to himself toward the end of December. I recommend her to your charity; what you do for her, I will hold as having been done for myself.
>
> Good-bye, my dear Sister St. John. Let us be very generous this year; we will be rewarded for it. Especially, *let us love very much* and the rest will cost us nothing or very little. Good-bye, my four good sisters. Sister Anastasie is preparing to write to you. Yours in the Lord.[20]

Despite nagging worries regarding the numbers of sisters permitted in each house and the manner of replacing or supplementing according to need, Mother St. Joseph was asked in 1822 to provide two sisters to direct the orphans at the Hospice of St. Gilles in Namur. This request was the direct result of the successful work the Sisters of Notre Dame had done at the Sunday School. Previously, the orphans at St. Gilles were under the care of a congregation of French nuns who were banished from William's realm precisely because they were French. Since there was good work to be continued at St. Gilles, Mother St. Joseph accepted and missioned two sisters in May of 1823. But the ouster of the previous congregation was a particularly ominous sign.

The storm clouds gathered as the establishments of the Brothers of the Christian Schools were suppressed. It seemed to be only a matter of time before Mother St. Joseph's congregation would suffer the fate of some of these other religious communities. But perhaps the biggest blow of all to this heart of hers so open to friendship came from an unexpected source, the death of her very dear Anastasie.

This other "eldest daughter" of the congregation and other daughter from Picardy, France, had been close to Françoise since her entrance in 1804.[21] It was she who had accompanied Mère Julie on the mission given by the Fathers of the Faith at Valery-sur-Somme and Abbeville, shortly after Julie's cure from paralysis. She was the first mistress of novices in Amiens and Julie's "little counselor" there when Françoise was sent to Namur as superior. Anastasie was the first superior named at Jumet and the first assistant to the mother general, after Julie's death. Having been such a stalwart support to Mother St. Joseph as superior of Namur and the mother general's "big counselor" for the preceding seven years, Anastasie's death was felt most deeply because she was a close and trusted friend. The three, Françoise, Julie and Anastasie were bonded by an affinity of character and a mutually profound affection. Late in 1822, Anastasie was afflicted by the typhoid fever that was rampant in Namur, and she was sick for several months. However, in February of 1823, just after the doctors had determined that the critical period had passed, Anastasie took an unexpected turn for the worse and was administered the last sacraments. She was heard to have very peacefully stated: "Whatever God wills; let him do with me as he pleases—I am content." In this disposition, she died around 4 o'clock in the afternoon of February 9 at the age of forty-two. Her last words were: "It is good to be with God." [22] At the time, Mother St. Joseph was sixty-eight years old and keenly aware that her closest ties to the past were now severed with the deaths of both Julie and Anastasie. She had begun the practice of keeping a necrology, noting the passing of each Sister of Notre Dame with the date of death and a few words of remembrance. It was three years before she could make the entry regarding Anastasie, so profoundly was she affected.

> What shall I say of her? What name shall I give her? I will call her Charity, Purity, Meekness, Simplicity, Kindness; for these are her true names since these are the virtues we saw personified in her with a particular brilliance. How many times we thanked God for having given her to us! But, alas, he had only loaned her to us for a little while. This good Father feared that, like weak ivy, we might attach ourselves too tightly to the support He had given us; or, rather, He wished to draw to himself this very white dove and she flew straight to his bosom, because we can devoutly believe her to have arrived there and have confidence that she is still interested in us. Her time, care, and repose were at the service of all, especially of those suffering in mind or body. When there was need, it was not necessary to call her—she ran, she flew. Many are under great obligations to her, and all, all, regret her.[23]

With great sensitivity, measuring her words to the extent she was able, she conveyed to each community the news that she knew would affect them as it had her. One such letter was sent to Sister St. John of the Cross at Thuin:

> My dear Sister St. John, I'm addressing you rather than Sister Marie Therese [the superior] in order to charge you with an assignment that will cause great distress to you as well as to the sisters and to my poor Sister Marie Therese, whose delicate health makes me fear to write directly to her. Ah! my dear Sister St. John of the Cross, enter deeply into the spirit of your name before continuing this letter. The Lord has given us a very bitter cross, and one very heavy for our frailty. But it's he who has done it! Let us kiss the paternal hand that strikes us and will sustain us.
>
> It's been a long time now since our good Sister Superior Anastasia fell ill with one of those frightening fevers you've heard them talk about. I didn't mention it in our houses in order to spare the sisters any anxiety; besides, it didn't seem dangerous. I intended to announce the illness and the convalescence at the same time. But, my dear friend, what sad news I have for you! She was doing better, and suddenly she had a relapse that took her from us. It was on the ninth, at three o'clock in the afternoon. She had received all the Sacraments on the same day, in the morning. That's all I have to say about it; in my sorrow I turn to myself so as not to increase your sorrow. Her death was very peaceful, without agony. She was still smiling an hour before the end.
>
> Set your mind at rest on my account; I'm quite well. The good God, like a good Father, will be my support. Let us lift up our hearts. Don't let us be downcast and we shall draw God's protection down upon us. Let each one, after having paid tribute with a few tears and a legitimate sorrow, cast her heart on God, who is the best of fathers.
>
> I realize, my poor Sister St. John, that I'm giving you a painful assignment. Before carrying it out, pray to God that he may dispose all hearts to receive it; and comfort my suffering, which is greater than all of yours together, by your resignation and generosity in making all the sacrifices he may ask of you. By this means you will draw down his all-powerful protection. Who are we to resist the Lord? He has

his ways, which are unknown to us, and the greatest sacrifices attract the greatest graces!...

I send you all fond greetings in the Heart of Jesus; let us remain there hidden and buried.[24]

The mutuality of affection between the mother and the sisters was evident by the expressions of their personal concern for her welfare. Not afraid to share with them her love, friendship, joys and sorrows, they readily responded in like fashion. And, through it all, the frustrating red tape with the government persisted.

My good Sister Marie Lucie, I have received your sad letter and you must have received one from me at the same time and in the same sad style. I don't know what I said to you, but I undoubtedly told you some of the circumstances surrounding the event that leaves as much to admire as to regret. I probably didn't tell you everything; that will come in its own time. My present concern is to put aside memories so vivid that they present themselves all too often. If I didn't do this, I would do nothing but weep. We must try to close the wound if we're to be in a state to fulfill our duties, for it's only after we've fulfilled them that we'll be able to hope that we, too, may have such a beautiful end. I'm sure that she sees us and helps us; at least it won't be long.

I'm obliged to you for having had some Masses said, and I am deeply grateful to your pastor for all he has done. We know our true friends in life and in death. There are moments, my dear, when I think it's a dream. I can't describe my state, but I'm not ill. What I'm suffering comes from an involuntary action of the soul on the body. I haven't much appetite, and I take bouillon several times a day. I keep up well enough to carry out all my duties.

I'm continually occupied with preparing papers for the government; there's no end to it. I've had to give an account of the qualifications of each sister, and, above all, to designate clearly those who are still novices. They insist on that; I don't know why. Then I have to state the reasons why the sisters who have returned here from the secondary houses have returned and why some have left here and where they have gone. For those I've sent to secondary houses, I must specify the house to which they have been sent. They don't begin by asking for even a half of what they want to know, so when one long piece of work has been completed, it must all be done over again for another part, and that continues for as many times as are required to furnish them with the most exact details. I was still busy with that yesterday, and I don't know if it's for the last time, or where it will end. May the holy will of God be done! He is our Father.

Give loving greetings from me to all my sisters. Don't write without telling me about your eyes.[25] And believe that I am, in the bonds of charity, all yours in the Lord.[26]

After much prayer, Mother St. Joseph appointed Sister Marie Thérèse Vandeputte to the position of superior of Namur and first counselor to the mother general. In a letter to her, Mother St. Joseph had written:

Finally, my dear Sister Marie Therese, I must tell you a thought that pursues me, and that pursues me constantly, without being absolutely decided upon. I expect it will be a great surprise to you, but here it is: I'm thinking of you. It seems to me that we would work together very compatibly; I would find in you attachment, deference, good will and good sense; nothing more is needed; the good God would do the rest. He would give you sufficient health, and I'm persuaded that you would be well received in this house. When your astonishment has subsided a little, you will write to me. I'm confident that the good God will speak to your heart. I don't want to say any more about it today; this is quite enough....Best wishes to you, my dear sister Marie Therese; be sustained in the Lord and fear not.[27]

Mother St. Joseph offered a glimpse into the considerations that entered her discernment in a letter to Sister St. John in April of that year. "She has some resemblance to the precious friend whom I have lost; but her health isn't strong."[28]

Once the decision was final and made official, Sister Marie Thérèse immediately left her post as superior at Thuin and put at the disposal of Mother St. Joseph her considerable gifts of nature and grace.[29] As well, she offered her the sustenance of her own friendship.

Chapter VII

NATURALIZED CITIZEN OF WILLIAM'S KINGDOM 1824

A letter written early in January of 1824 revealed an immediate cause for concern:

> We must pray to God, who knows our needs and the straits to which it has pleased His Majesty, King William, to reduce us by fixing the number of sisters for the houses in this province, *which are the only ones approved,* and by decreeing that all the others shall remain *in statu quo* until we're told differently–and no possibility of replacing the deceased or ill. It's a means of killing us by inches so that there won't be too loud an outcry. May the holy will of God be done in this as in all things. Let us pray earnestly, however, that the Lord may come to our aid. What will become of our motherhouse in these circumstances? Many superiors represent their just needs to me, but I'm not able to help them, and, if we are to judge by the measure taken by the government, things aren't going to improve without the intervention of Divine Providence, in whom we must confide.
>
> Good-bye, my dear Sister Marie Lucie; we must bear our cross all the days of our lives. Believe that I am sincerely attached to you.
>
> P.S. It was our governor who conveyed to us the orders of His Majesty regarding the number of sisters we may have. It's far below the number we requested: Namur 50, including

> the novices, Gembloux 14, Dinant 12, and Andenne 5. I don't know how we'll manage. We must pray that the good God will give us grace and light. Dinant already has twelve and it's certainly not enough. I can't make any decisions or plans at the present moment. No doubt all our other houses will suffer in the same way once they're approved. Moreover, French superiors may no longer teach, and all our teaching sisters are obliged to pass an examination before a Board of Education in order to prove their ability. They must take this examination before making their vows.
>
> Good-bye again, my dear Sister; let us accept the good and the bad as the good God sends them, for we can make all things turn into good.[1]

By July, Mother St. Joseph offered to step aside as superior general in favor of a sister of Flemish origin if that would be for the good of the congregation she dearly loved. She wrote, therefore, to Sister Marie Steenhaut in Ghent that "the French superiors are ordered to become naturalized. I think this costs something–and a great deal. You'd render a great service to the Institute and to me by coming to take my place, if that is the will of God."[2]

The sisters did not, however, accept Mother St. Joseph's proposal so the only other alternative that remained was that she should request naturalization as a citizen of William's kingdom. Already, by July 26, they made their desire known to their mother that she remain in office and, in a letter to Sister Regis, superior at Fleurus, Mother St. Joseph wrote: "I went to see the Governor.[3] He made it clear that the King does not like frequent requests and that it would be best to proceed with the head (speaking of me). I proposed to the sisters, given my age and circumstances, the election of a Superior General from this country; this they did not want. We have, therefore, submitted a petition and we'll see how that turns out. The good God will show us what needs to be done. As for myself, I assure you, my good Sister Regis, that I desire in this as in any other thing, the holy will of God, the spiritual progress of my sisters and their satisfaction...."[4] Given her heritage and social status as a Frenchwoman, as well as the attitude toward William of Orange and his policies on the part of the ecclesiastical hierarchy, this was a very brave and generous action, to say the least.

As if there were not already sufficient crosses for her to bear, she was dealt another blow in learning of the death of her dear childhood friend, Jeanne de Franssu, on March 6.

She then learned that, by decree, the king had ordered that all religious houses not approved by August 1 would be suppressed.

Knowing of the headaches and heartaches to which she was subjected, one is in a position to appreciate all the more the delicate gestures toward each of her daughters in religion, which continued as though none of these vexations were occurring. One such example was Mother St. Joseph's practice of writing to a sister as she reached the site of her first assignment or mission.

> My dear Sister Valerie, it's a pleasure for me to acquit myself of my debts, for it's a custom or a sort of duty that my heart imposes to write to my good children at the time of their first mission. So how could I fail to do so when you've even asked me to?
>
> I must first of all tell you how pleased I am to learn that you're happy in the house and the charges assigned to you by holy obedience; for me this is a source of great joy. And my joy is even greater when I hear you speak like one who shows signs of zeal. I beg the Lord himself to breathe on this new fire, and thereby increase the flame. For when one lacks this little spark of zeal for souls and has to be driven like a machine, it's painful for both parties. At first you do what you can and learn by doing, because practice makes perfect. You're not yet a strong grammarian; that won't come as a surprise to Sister N. Don't let the remark she made upset you. Through humility and obedience, if you ardently desire these virtues and try to be faithful about putting them into practice when you have a chance, the good God will give you, in time, all you need, even humility. This doesn't mean that you won't fail from time to time; don't be troubled when this happens, but rather humble yourself. In this way you'll reap profit from everything, even your faults; all things turn into good for those who love God. What a great honor and what great happiness it is to be called to serve him.
>
> What more shall I say to you, my dear Sister Valerie? I can only reaffirm the great interest I take in your advancement in virtue and also in your good health, for the glory of

God; and then, for this same glory, in your advancement in the "little sciences."[5] May the good God grant you that indefinable quality that is the spirit of the good God and that makes good teachers. It will also be timely to rid yourself of your great sensitiveness. I shall earnestly ask all that for you from the good God. Ask him to grant me all that I need.

Good-bye, my dear Sister Valerie; all yours in the Lord.[6]

A response to the appeal made to King William regarding Mother St. Joseph's naturalization was received. He had personally, on December 27, 1824, signed the document by which the former French aristocrat was officially made a naturalized subject of His Majesty William of Orange. The governor of Namur forwarded to her this document along with a personal message and an exoneration of the usually required fees as his New Year's gift.

The sisters of the congregation had many things for which to be grateful as the year 1824 came to a close: their beloved mother had sacrificed her citizenship of birth in order to remain in office as their superior general; the government had not carried through on its threat to close the nonapproved houses; vocations to the community continued to flourish despite the hostility of the government toward religious congregations;[7] the schools continued to grow. At Namur, alone, there were 400 children in the day or free school and more than 80 day boarders. The number of full boarders had grown to such an extent that the remaining portion of the Boneffe refuge was purchased in order to enlarge the accommodations.[8]

What the sisters, fortunately, did not know as they celebrated Christmas that year was that worse battles were yet to be waged. Governmental vexations were about to become open governmental persecution.

Chapter VIII

STRUGGLE FOR SURVIVAL 1825–1829

Emboldened by the knowledge that the Belgian liberals sided with his policies, King William took more actively hostile measures against Catholicism in his efforts to create a completely nationalized educational system. Having shaped to his design the primary and upper levels and, in an attempt to retain despotic control over the intermediate level, he ordered the closing of all minor seminaries in 1825. Along with this act, which couldn't help but further alienate Catholic clergy, he took an additional step in reestablishing the College of Philosophy at Louvain. It was not long, however, before Belgian Catholics realized that they could bypass this secularized education by attending heretofore Catholic universities. In a calculated sidestep, William then decreed that no Belgians should be permitted to attend these institutions; should they do so, they would be barred from holding public or ecclesiastical offices. Opposition to these measures only succeeded in provoking an angry intransigence.

As a result of suspicion, misrepresentation and ignorance, orders were also given to all provincial governors to undertake a thorough investigation of all convents located within their boundaries. This was to be done with a view to bringing to light "all the mysterious things that took place within the interior of convents."[1] A detailed report was afterwards to be forwarded to the king. In spite of his eighty years and blessed with his highly developed Gallic wit, Bishop Pisani took this last directive with great humor wondering if the royal court wanted to know about time of rising, sleeping, meals and the like. Mother St. Joseph relayed the bishop's reaction to the latest of the king's inquiries, stating:

> I hope nothing comes of it. Upon examination of the matter, I find nothing reprehensible. They didn't indicate the suspected houses; nothing is determined, but, to arouse their suspicion, it suffices only to welcome Sundays a number of youth, instruct them and amuse them, something to which we devote ourselves so that they don't remain totally ignorant and to keep them from doing wrong; but that doesn't please everyone. In truth, I don't know what ill wind has blown. This teaches me that we can't act with too much prudence and that often, while thinking we are doing good, we are really exposing ourselves. This is a very difficult century; we must, therefore, call down the Holy Spirit with the fullness of his gifts, because He alone is capable of directing our ship through these storms.[2]

Whereas the nonapproved houses had been free of the series of repressive measures taken against the approved houses, they too began to experience the vexation of endless red tape. All convents were subjected to frequent on-site visits and to regular checks to see that the permitted number of sisters had not been exceeded. Official texts were published and their use made mandatory. Nonetheless, Mother St. Joseph instructed her local superiors to make sure that any text to be used in Notre Dame schools had the bishop's approbation. Once it had been determined that all teachers were to present themselves for examination, Mother St. Joseph did everything to see that any sister destined for this ministry was sufficiently prepared. To this end, she designated Sister Stephanie Warnier as an official directress of studies with the task of overseeing the sisters' professional preparation. It was a real tribute to her foresight and to Sister Stephanie's abilities that every Sister of Notre Dame who took these examinations met with complete success and obtained the necessary qualifications.

In the midst of her ongoing difficulties, Mother St. Joseph neither forgot the significance of April 8, the anniversary of Julie's death in 1816, nor the various kindnesses large and small extended to her by pupils of the congregation, nor even the graciousness of a remembrance of one small child. A typical example dates from this period:

> J.M.J. Namur, April 8, Memorable Day! (1825)
>
> My dear Sister St. John, I owe all of you–you, your good sisters, your children–many thanks for the good feast of St. Joseph. What I value most are the fervent prayers addressed to this great saint in my behalf. My gratitude extends as far down as your little six-year-old boarder, who promises to say a rosary for me. I have great confidence in that. The purity of childhood is so efficaciously privileged before the Heart of Jesus. Give a special remembrance from me to this dear little one and to all your dear children. Tell them I love them very much in God and want to know that they are all being good.
>
> The inspector came to visit our classes. All went well; we're going to have about fifteen certificates. He said that the moment is not favorable for your naturalization; let us abandon ourselves to Providence. Courage! If the good God is for us, who can be against us? The regulation that limits our number to fifty is very trying. Patience, patience; let us allow God to be glorified in us and through us according to his good pleasure. God is such a good Father; let us never forget it. Courage, my four good Sisters, whom I cherish in the Lord. Let us try to draw closer to God each day by withdrawing from ourselves.
>
> Your very affectionate Mother in God.[3]

The Mother General was now a nationalized citizen but the other French women who were superiors of secondary houses were targeted for expulsion from their posts. As steps were being taken to rectify the situation, Sister Emmanuel, the superior at Gembloux, was given a notice of twenty-four hours that she should leave not only her post, but the town. Once the government had attended to French superiors, it turned its attention to all teachers of French nationality. Again, Gembloux was struck a blow, and Sister Angélique was given orders to leave. Next, Sister Adele, at Andenne, an excellent classroom instructor, had to abandon her position in favor of a native Belgian in spite of the fact that Adele's parents had moved to Belgium when she was about four months old.

The strategy of snuffing out the establishments of religious congregations was on course to succeed, and the inevitability of this process worried Mother St. Joseph greatly. The time had come for alternative strategies.

The viscount Alexander Blin de Bourdon, Mother St. Joseph's nephew, was at the time serving as prefect of the Department of Pas-de-Calais in France. He and the priests of Saint-Omer as well as the bishop of Arras were anxious to see his aunt's congregation back on the French soil from which it had sprung. To this end, they had already obtained, from the minister of ecclesiastical affairs, a promise of approbation on the part of the French king, Charles X. The abbé Joyet, principal of the College of Saint-Omer, wrote in June to inform Mother St. Joseph about a house that he had in mind for the proposed foundation. "Count on my complete support," wrote Alexander to his aunt, "for a project which pleases me both in the interest of religion and because it procures for us the occasion of seeing you once again in France."[4] Given the uncertainty of the congregation's survival in Belgium, Mother St. Joseph began to look favorably and with renewed interest upon this request. Not wishing, however, to make a hasty decision or a decision that did not include consultation with the sisters of French nationality in the community, she quietly investigated the possibility. Should the decision be made to undertake an establishment in France, it might not be without risk to the other houses in Belgium. The Dutch government had already set the precedent of repudiating a superior residing outside the country, as it had in the case of the Brothers of the Christian Schools. France, by way of reprisal, might decide to do the same. Further, William's government did not look kindly on those religious bodies that maintained a close rapport with members on foreign soil. Tensions with the hierarchy of the Catholic Church and, most notably, with the pope aggravated this xenophobic attitude. Indeed, the door to a schism had been opened with the closing of the doors to the minor seminaries.

In an admirable spirit of collaboration, Mother St. Joseph's first step was to solicit the reaction of every one of the French nationals in the congregation. She was resolved to leave the decision to them. Their response was affirmative. Knowing that she would be easily and readily recognized were she to undertake the trip to France herself and wishing to keep the project quiet until closer to the time of a final decision, Mother St. Joseph requested that two other Frenchwomen, Sister Marie Thérèse, her first assistant, and Sister Emmanuel, the superior expelled from Gembloux, make the exploratory trip in her stead. They dressed in lay clothing and returned in July full of enthusiasm for the prospective foundation.

At the close of the annual retreat in September, the sisters celebrated the first profession of several of their number. According to recent regulations, this ceremony was attended by a representative of the government. His name, as civil witness, joined those of the newly professed in the community register of vows, to the added annoyance of those present. In October, the opening of school was accompanied by the most unwelcome news that the Brothers of the Christian Schools had been summarily replaced in their institutions by young, inexperienced recruits from the University of Liège. Learning of this dismissal of the Brothers, and as official guardian of the works of Christian education in his diocese, the vicar general, Father Médard, was profoundly distressed. "If ever anyone interferes with the Sisters, it would kill me!"[5] Though he had not been sick and had said Mass that day as usual, at 3:00 A.M. the following morning, October 14, he suffered a heart attack and died almost immediately. The loss of this protector of the congregation was felt keenly by Mother St. Joseph. He had been such a source of support with the difficulties she experienced on the part of the government and she had always sought and valued his advice. In many ways, his sympathetic presence seemed almost indispensable to her. With reason, consciously or unconsciously, she allied herself to Job when she informed Sister Angela at Dinant of this latest blow. "The Lord had given him to me; the Lord has taken him away. Blessed be the name of the Lord."[6]

Another loss, felt as deeply, occurred shortly after the dawning of the New Year of 1826. On February 23, that staunch supporter and faithful friend of the foundresses and the congregation died–Bishop Pisani. Mother St. Joseph added a postscript to a letter she had been writing to the superior at St. Hubert.

> February 23
>
> What a shock! I've just learned that our saintly bishop is no more! The Lord took him from this world at one o'clock last night. He was quite well when he retired at eleven; at midnight he called his servant. It was apoplexy. He received Extreme Unction and general absolution. Offer for this precious friend of the Institute the same prayers as for the sisters. I'll give you all the details. Pray for His Excellency, and pray also for your old Mother. What a trial! "Lord, I have been submissive to your holy will and I have been consoled."[7]

With the death of this eighty-three-year-old prelate, the whole country of Belgium had but one bishop left, the archbishop of Malines, the prince de Méan, and his health was very precarious. Since 1819, the entire Catholic populace had been made to suffer for its loyalty to Rome by the king's refusal to authorize successors to vacant sees. Ordinations, confirmations and consecrations of altars and sacred vessels could only be effected with great difficulty.

The ten years of Mother St. Joseph's second mandate as superior general was to end in 1826. Now seventy years of age, she hoped, understandably, that the burden of the office would be carried by another, younger than she. She began early to plant the seed of this thought in the minds and hearts of the sisters. "My dear friend," she wrote to Sister St. John in March of that year, "I forewarn you that henceforth I'm going to write short letters, for there's more and more to be done and my capacity is diminishing. That's why you'd all be very wise to elect for yourselves another superior general. This is the year to do it!"[8] Reelected on June 26, she couldn't help but chide one of the superiors in a letter written just two days later.

> You don't take time to say a word about your health. You're so full of enthusiasm about having a new Mother, all rejuvenated, that you can speak of nothing else; you'd think it was something marvelous. It would be better to ask God that no one will discover on my first day that I'm really in my dotage; for that's what would naturally be expected. As for me, I can do nothing about it; if that happens, you'll all be to blame. I wash my hands of it. Nevertheless I beg all of you to

ask of God those graces I need if you're not to have reason to repent.

Good-bye, my good Sisters; I send all of you my good wishes and sign myself once more

Your very humble servant
Sister St. Joseph [9]

The month of October brought the unexpected and unwelcome news that her brother, Louis-Marie-César, had died suddenly at Gézaincourt. Her subdued mention of this sorrow gives the impression of a person almost overcome by the sheer accumulation of sources of grief. "I must also tell you, my good Sister Marie Lucie, that I lost my brother a short time ago. I recommend him to the charitable prayers of all of you; do something for him."[10] Without needing a formal request, however, all the sisters of the congregation accorded to the viscount Blin de Bourdon the same prayerful consideration that it was customary to extend to deceased members of the Institute. In this manner, they wanted their superior general to know that she was "mother" for them in more than a canonical sense and that, as a true mother as well as friend, her family was theirs.

Father Jean-François Pierlot, the forty-second and last prior of the monastery of Oignies, also known as Brother Gregory, had long served as chaplain for the sisters at Jumet. Driven from his monastery at the time of the Revolution, he lived for some time as a member of the secular clergy. During his tenure at Jumet, he had had many occasions to come to know and respect both foundresses of the Sisters of Notre Dame. His friendship for them was such that, at the time of the Napoleonic wars, disguised as a peasant, he braved enemy lines to make his way to the motherhouse in Namur in order to bring reports on the status of the other Notre Dame houses. Thanks to his devotion, Julie and Françoise were often relieved and reassured.

In the thirteenth century, his monastery had been made the repository of a collection of relics donated by Jacques de Vitry. De Vitry had been named cardinal archbishop of Tusculum and, as a high-ranking prelate, bestowed many gifts from Rome as well as from the Orient upon his former monastery, relics of the saints, rich church ornaments, books and a number of apostolic privileges. A Brother Hugo resided in the monastery at Oignies at the time and was an extremely gifted metalsmith who devoted his considerable talents to creating, for the cardinal's gifts, reliquaries of gold, silver and precious stones in the tradition of the great masters of the Meuse district. This priceless collection was hidden during the Revolution by a farmer and his wife who were very fond of the monks. When Belgium was annexed to France, church goods were confiscated and made the property of the state.

After the death of the farmer, the widow Moussiaux wished to unearth the treasure from its hiding place before her death and restore it to its rightful owners. In 1817, in the presence of Father Pierlot, it was retrieved from the masonry, where it had been hidden since 1794, and transferred to the presbytery at Falisolles, where Father Pierlot was pastor. The following year, he presented it to the care of the Sisters of Notre Dame, his good friends, and Mother St. Joseph assured him its safekeeping in the name of the congregation.[11]

Though the nonapproved Belgian houses had been spared the endless barrage of inquisitorial documents that arrived at the approved houses, being the foresighted administrator she was, Mother St. Joseph did not wish to be caught off-guard and had all houses apply for royal authorization. Further, she had asked all sisters who taught, whether in approved or nonapproved houses, to present themselves for the required examinations. Even this ritual varied according to the dispositions of the local officials: In Namur, the sisters were treated with unfailing courtesy; at Liège, the inspector refused to examine the sisters fearing that he might compromise himself in granting the certificate to Frenchwomen; in Luxembourg, the certificate had only a two-year validity, after which the teacher was to be reexamined; in Ghent, though the presiding examiner was a friend of the influential Goethals family, he refused to evidence any particular consideration for Sister Ignace and the sister who was to be examined with her, seeing that they both were given a more rigorous examination than the group of laypersons who were with them.

The expulsions of French nationals had continued with the superior at Fleurus being ousted the preceding April. She was welcomed at Namur by Mother St. Joseph, who then had to worry about the stated limit of fifty sisters for the motherhouse. Providentially, a request was made for sisters to assume the administration of the hospital, St. Jacques. Such charitable work did not strictly coincide with the founding educational mission of the congregation, but it did provide a worthwhile ministry for those French sisters who could not otherwise offer their services to the poor and needy of Belgium. Sister Regis, former superior of Fleurus, and another French sister established the presence of the Sisters of Notre Dame there in October of 1826.

> I'm glad to tell you that our two sisters, Regis and Adrienne, have taken over the management of the hospital of St. Jacques in this city. They're well suited to each other and well suited also, I think, to the place. Their task is to take care of the provisions and supervise the kitchen and the servant who works there. They don't have to care for the patients....They have to dish up the food for each meal; see that the doctor's orders are carried out, and that the diet is followed; be sure that everything is clean and in order; take care of the linen and mend it....The only reason I decided to accept this foundation was the hope of helping these poor patients to attain the state of grace and of teaching those who don't know them the truths necessary for salvation.[12]

Since it is often in the nature of things to get worse before getting better, the government took the further anti-Catholic measure of ordering all chapels to be closed to the public. Within two days, however, the order had to be rescinded because a clever Belgian discovered a legal flaw in the decree. This fiasco added one more item to the laundry list of complaints on the part of Belgian Catholics who succeeded in convincing the king of the strength of their opposition to his repeatedly repressive tactics. William, who once thought a schism would be desirable, began to revisit the question of a concordat with Rome. Initiatives for such a concordat had been made as early as 1823 but failed because of William's persistently exorbitant demands. For his part, Pope Leo XII was more than eager to bring closure to the difficulties of the Church in Belgium, including the number of vacant episcopal sees. In March, Mother St. Joseph wrote to the sisters asking them to "join the Christian world" in a novena to Saint Joseph for the success of such an agreement since "the interests of the Church are our first and greatest interests."[13]

The Concordat was signed on June 18, 1827, and according to its terms: attendance at the College of Philosophy in Louvain would be an option for future priests; bishops would be named by the pope based on a list submitted by the cathedral chapter and submitted to the king for approval; seminaries would be reopened; members of the clergy would swear an oath of loyalty to the king.[14] Leo XII published, on August 17, a papal bull, *Quod jamdiu,* in which he explained the terms of the long-awaited agreement. "You are hearing, no doubt, where you live as it is being said here, that the Concordat has been signed. What will it bring us?," wrote Mother St. Joseph on July 28. "Unquestionably some increase in good and some decrease in troubles...!"[15] But, the ink was hardly dry on the document when the king, in an attempt to satisfy the disapproving Dutch Calvinists and the Belgian liberals, had a circular sent on October 5 to all provincial governors stating that, despite thc Concordat, no change would be made in the educational system. He continued to insist on the importance of his College of Philosophy at Louvain in the training of future priests. The king's confidential note fell into the hands of the journalist de Potter, became public, and ultimately caused a union among liberals and Catholics which would prove to be the eventual undoing of the monarchy. Both factions, liberals and Catholics, had suffered from William's politics of partiality—were not the Dutch, for example, awarded the prime administrative positions? Both groups became increasingly aware that William was preparing for the absorption of Belgium into Holland, religion and language included.[16] The rupture between the government and its Catholic subjects was, as a consequence, complete.

The communities not officially approved began to suffer additional effects of the government's hostility toward Catholicism as, one by one, sisters were expelled from these houses. One, two or even four sisters had to leave Jumet, Fleurus, St. Hubert, Liège, Ghent and Zèle. In all these locations, with the exception of Flanders, local officials forwarded petitions to the king to halt the expulsion order or, at least, to postpone the inevitable. The faith of the mother general sustained her throughout as she redoubled her prayer for the congregation and, during the annual retreat in September 1827, formally consecrated it to another mother whose aid she desperately sought, Our Lady, Help of Christians.

Aid was forthcoming through the De Biolley family in the town of Verviers. The daughter of a respected doctor, Marie Claire, or Mademoiselle Clary as she was called, had for about seven years dedicated herself to the education of the children of the working class, gathering them in her own home and instructing them in catechism and in needlework. After a visit to the school of the Sisters of Notre Dame in Liège, she began to implore Sister Marie Lucie, the superior of that community, to prevail upon Mother St. Joseph for sisters to assist her in establishing such an institution in her home city. A promise was obtained from the mother general, after her personal visit to the town, on the condition that royal approval be granted first. Though her family was highly influential, the king's ministers, along with the monarch himself, were adamantly disinclined to concede, and the family's initiatives were rebuffed. Undaunted, Mademoiselle Clary requested and obtained a personal audience with William and succeeded, in May of 1827, in obtaining a begrudging approbation with a limit of three to four sisters for a period of three years. The king further stipulated that there were to be no additional establishments of the Sisters of Notre Dame in Verviers. Mother St. Joseph wrote to Sister Marie Lucie: "Certainly, no natural considerations would incline me to do so, but I'm confident that God will provide some that are supernatural, and that he will sustain us amid all the difficulties and vexations of such an undertaking."[17] By November, negotiations were concluded and four sisters took up residence in the home of "Sister Claire"—as she had requested permission from Mother St. Joseph to be called.

Understanding that the governmental anticlericalism was not dead with the approval granted for sisters in Verviers, Mother St. Joseph recognized that this same government was also responsible for a police raid on the community of Nouveau Bois in Ghent. Early in the morning, the police descended upon the establishment and expelled four sisters as they were engaged in teaching. The paralysis of the local authorities on behalf of the sisters led to this aggressive implementation of the letter of the law, Mother St. Joseph believed. At the same time, she also recognized additional motivation for gratitude to those authorities that were willing to take risks on behalf of her sisters.

> It was an excellent thought on the part of your civic authorities to request your approbation, for even if they don't obtain it, you're less likely to be subjected to hostile action when it's seen that you have the support of both the public and the civic authorities. We really have no other means of defense. This is proved again by what just happened at Ghent. They notified the superior [Sister Marie Steenhaut], who does so much good, that she must send four sisters away immediately. She was unable to obtain a word of assistance from the governor, who is Protestant, or from the mayor, or from anyone at all. Everyone urged her to submit to the ordinance in order, as they said, to save the community. Sister Marie herself drew up a petition to the king, but since she was not supported by anyone of importance, her petition was ineffectual. The vicar general of Ghent is fearful of what may happen, and he too advises her to obey for the sake of the community. It would have been different if the administrators had shown them some consideration....[18]

The four expelled sisters sought refuge in the *béguinage*[19] and then, dressed as laywomen, accepted the hospitality of a devout Catholic man, Monsieur Gobert. It was he who had assisted the Jesuit Belgian province, at the time of Napoleon, by offering his country estate at Destelbergen as the site of a clandestine novitiate. For three months, the sisters were sheltered in his home and, with his help, occasionally visited their community at Nouveau Bois. Then, they quietly reentered the community on a permanent basis, hoping to stay there undiscovered.

The searches did not cease, however, and with each unannounced visit of the police, Sister Marie Steenhaut, maintained an unperturbed dignity. Once, in answer to queries regarding numbers, she responded with the cleverly equivocal, "Sir, we are still of the same number here." No one thought to question whether "still" (or *"toujours"* in French) pertained to before or after the official injunction![20]

At Jumet, three sisters were dismissed, reducing to two the number of teachers in the boarding school. One of the three who were sent away, Sister Ignace Goethals, was accused of a kind of fanatical conspiracy to which Mother St. Joseph alluded in her letter to Sister Constantine at Jumet. Full of the sound wisdom of a balanced educator, the advice in the letter testified to the good sense that she and Julie saw as the bedrock of their educational methods.

> A gentleman from Namur went to see his sister, Mme N. of Jumet. They had much to say there about you sisters; they said: "Those ladies have some fanatics among them: they form groups among their students and classify them as associates or worldlings; a priest goes there to preach; they talk about the Concordat, etc." I'm sure they say other things too....[W]hat shall we do about it? Shall we cease to do good? No, we were created and born to do that and to cause it to be done insofar as it depends on us. It's only with God and through his help that we succeed; but when there's no real necessity, let us try to avoid all that may cause talk and irritation in this wicked world, which takes evil for good and good for evil, always finding that too much is being done in the matter of religion and not enough in that which leads to perdition. Few children will have enough strength to resist the assaults of human respect; that is why we must be instructed ourselves, and must instruct our pupils as to what is to be omitted and what should be concealed from ill-disposed eyes, especially when they have authority or influence over our weakness; let the pupils learn to distinguish what is of absolute obligation from what is only of devotion, not to neglect the latter, but to know the time and manner of its use. I don't want them to become accustomed, while they're with us, to hanging rosaries around their necks or at their sides during the day. It sometimes happens, I find, that they go that way to the parlor and that people then mock and ridicule them. What effect must that produce? It makes one's heart bleed to consider the shoals that surround these dear children; that of human respect is not the least dangerous, and it's not always best to defy it....[21]

In October, Sister Constantine was also expelled from Jumet. Former pupils helped fill the gaps left by these sisters while Sister Ignace continued to direct the boarding school as she moved from one house to another. She had to be on constant guard in her attempt to evade the surprise visits from authorities coming to check to see that the allotted number in a given community had not been augmented. "We are like earthworms," wrote Mother St. Joseph, "which are cut into little pieces and link together again."[22] In the midst of one of her many trips to a different house, Sister Ignace, dressed as a peasant woman, with heavy sabots, listened as her two male traveling companions discussed in hushed tones a Mademoiselle Goethals, who would not succeed in evading them this time. En route for her intended destination of Jumet, the "peasant woman" disembarked at the next stop and returned to Namur–in effect eluding the anticipated arrest!

Sister Gudule, in Fleurus, where she had replaced in 1826 the ousted French superior, Sister Regis, was accused of having written an antigovernment pamphlet that was sedulously circulated in that city. The pamphlet denounced the "ogre king and his satellites" and exalted their victims as heroes. Seeking in vain to ferret out the source of the document, the commission of inquiry determined, without any real evidence, that the Sisters of Notre Dame were the perpetrators. Only they could have had so aptly detailed governmental wrongs as an excuse for being made scapegoats! Sister Gudule joined Sister Ignace in living a nomadic existence for two years while continuing, as best she could, in her function as superior.

While in one way, their will to live prolonged the agony in the communities at Jumet and Fleurus, the community at Thuin enjoyed relative peace due, primarily, to the efforts of two influential friends, Monsieur Martin and Monsieur Troye. On the other hand, the zeal of these gentlemen to preserve the presence of the sisters for their town was on track to lead to a schism within the congregation. It was their proposal that each of the unapproved houses should seek approbation as an independent entity. The proposition had supporters both within and without the congregation, and Mother St. Joseph viewed it only as a measure of last recourse, a compromise solution at best. "Ultimately, it's only when there's a choice between perishing or remaining very sick that one might choose to remain very sick. But we're not yet reduced to that extremity," she wrote in June of 1829.[23]

Extreme measures were avoided as the political quarrels between the king and his Belgian subjects increasingly distracted his ministers. Catholics, wanting liberty in educational matters, and liberals, demanding freedom of the press, both of whom had been "muzzled like dogs," united, and in November of 1828 formed the "Union of Parties for the Redress of Wrongs." William was forced to negotiate with the papacy regarding the still-vacant sees, and he once again made attendance at the College of Philosophy in Louvain optional.

Wishing to test the temperature of the Belgian populace for himself, King William undertook a tour in June of 1829. In Mother St. Joseph's letters of the period, the king's visits at the schools in Thuin, Jumet, Fleurus and Liège, especially, are closely followed. At each locale, William was most graciously received by the sisters, their pupils, and officials speaking on behalf of the sisters and their work. "You were the first Sisters of Notre Dame the king saw", Mother St. Joseph wrote, enthusiastically, to Thuin:

> [S]o you were likewise the first to win his favor. As he passed through Charleroi, he received a request in favor of our sisters at Jumet; a little farther on, at Fleurus, he met a cloud of children with our sisters. Monsieur de Zualart presented the request of the whole administration. The king thus had occasion to remark the favor in which the Sisters of Notre Dame are held by all the local authorities. He'll go last to Liège and Verviers, where he'll find the same thing repeated. Could all that be to no avail? At least he received it all with good grace and seemed touched. Our sisters think there were tears in his eyes when he received the compliments of our three boarders. A concerted action of this kind was impossible at Ghent and Zele,[24] and St. Hubert was too far away. Patience; God has his moments for everything. Let us pray and do what depends on us, and then remain in peace.[25]

The king then visited the city of Namur on June 16, 1829.

He did a great many things in the short time he was here, including one that we hadn't expected: yesterday, as we were finishing our dinner, Sister Candide came in very calmly and said, "The king is going to come here." We were taken totally by surprise! Then another person came with the same news, and a police officer–so we had to believe it. The sisters got busy cleaning, washing, putting the house in order; it was very dirty because we had been laying in our supply of fuel.

Finally, around three o'clock, about fifteen persons arrived; several were dressed in blue and wore different decorations. Sister Superior and I advanced into the court to greet them. One of the gentlemen pointed out the king to us, saying: "This is the king." "Sire, we didn't expect so great an honor." We invited him first to enter the novitiate, where there were about a dozen sisters, professed as well as novices. He remained standing and asked some questions: "How many are you," etc. That took only a few minutes. One of the gentlemen exclaimed: "You must take us to the children!" We proceeded then to the boarding school, where the boarders were in uniform. They had prepared a short musical program for him. During it, he posed several questions to Sister Superior. Three boarders read him very short compliments, which seemed to flatter him. Then they cried: "Long live the king." He laughed. All in all, he appeared satisfied. We brought him then to the three classes for the poor; he showed much interest and spoke briefly to the gentlemen with him and to the mistresses, and talked to Sister Madeleine in Flemish. He asked her very kindly where she came from. He also asked me where I came from. I had to tell him that I was French, but naturalized by His Majesty. We were quickly at ease and found it easy to talk with him. Now everyone is coming to tell us that the king was very well satisfied with our establishment, that he had spoken of it on several occasions. We decided to write him a letter of thanks for his great kindness. We added to it a supplication–very respectful and full of confidence in his goodness–that he would deign to consider the requests for approbation that would be made by local authorities in favor of the establishments of the Sisters of Notre Dame in different provinces.[26]

No doubt the reception given by the former French aristocrat genuinely impressed the Dutch monarch, for he concluded his inspection by stating to the cofoundress, "Madame, a woman like you ought to live forever."[27] In general, however, the trip gave the sovereign the illusion that the unionist agitation was merely superficial.

A new bishop had been appointed as the government's candidate to the Namur diocese in June of 1828, Monseigneur Ondernard. A courtier, born in France in the same year as Françoise Blin, he was viewed as a man who would be more eager to please the king than Catholics and the papacy. He was consecrated Bishop of Namur on October 28, 1828. In October of 1829, after much hesitation, the king accepted the nominations of bishops for Tournai, Ghent and Liège, and he accorded full liberty to the seminaries. "It's a real twist of fate," wrote Mother St. Joseph, "and only one thing is still lacking and this is the thing we need, freedom of education."[28] The hopes of Belgian Catholics were running high when they were dashed by the royal proclamation of December 11 that the king would retain his monopoly over education. In fact, the concession he had personally granted to Mademoiselle Biolley of Verviers had continued to irritate his minister of the interior, so that he backpedaled by declaring that the sisters sent there were still counted as part of Namur's quota of fifty sisters. "We're still being harassed about our sisters at Verviers. The government wants the sisters there to be counted among the number assigned to here. Our governor advised us to send a petition to the king, requesting from His Majesty that they not be so counted. The petition has been sent and we're waiting for the response. God grant that it may be favorable."[29] Able to prove that the sisters were in the right–"Happily it's a false charge and it's easy to exonerate ourselves"[30]–a cloud of suspicion and petty complaints, nonetheless, followed.

The 1820s would end for the Mother General of the Sisters of Notre Dame in much the same way as it had begun: with hope despite adversity, with a vision for the future though prospects for the future appeared dim indeed. "I repeat the assurance of my affection in God," she wrote at the end of November. "Let us pray with all our might. The moment is critical. The cards are shuffled; who will win the game? It will be those for whom the Lord tips the scale, whether in justice or in mercy, in his severity or in his kindness."[31]

The Belgians grew restive and, proportionately, the Dutch government tried even harder to maintain control. Public manifestations provoked various responses from King William. Concessions were followed by returns to severity. He appeared perplexed and unable to cope, frustrated to perceive widening fissures in his beloved amalgam. "What do they want from me?" he asked his Belgian deputy de Gerlache. "They no longer find anything good in my government...! I am King of the Netherlands; I know my right, I know my duty...."[32] Not unaffected by events in France, where the French were growing impatient with the policies of Charles X, the Belgians in their turn were to find the coming year one of increasingly open conflict with the Dutch government. From his cell in the Petits-Carmes, the imprisoned liberal journalist Louis de Potter directed a letter to the king in which he asserted: "Sire, you are not the master of the Belgians, you are but the first among them!"[33]

Which way would fate twist this time around? Who would win after the cards were shuffled? Belgian liberals and Catholics joined forces. The mother general of the Sisters of Notre Dame encouraged a single-minded focus at the closing of this fateful year. "Let us thank God, my dear, who gives us opportunities to work for souls. We were created only to love and serve God, and we are Sisters of Notre Dame only to procure the greater glory of God and to save as many souls as possible. Let us hope in God, my dear..., and not fear the vexations of men. If we have entire confidence in God, he will take care of us. Ask this for me, and I'll ask it for you."[34]

Chapter IX

BIRTH OF A NEW NATION 1830–1831

With a truly extraordinary spirit of faith, self-possession, love for the sisters and their students and hope for the future of the Congregation of the Sisters of Notre Dame, Mother St. Joseph renovated, bought and expanded despite being assailed from within and from without by war, epidemics, adverse political climate and internal problems. "The more we build, the more our buildings fill up; I don't know when it will be finished," she acknowledged.[1] The ancient abbey at Nouveau Bois in Ghent was purchased; Jumet and St. Hubert were enlarged; improvements were made to the establishments at Dinant and Gembloux and, all the while, enlargements and embellishments were regularly in progress at the motherhouse in Namur. There, additions were made to accommodate the ever growing number of boarders and, in 1828, the chapel was enlarged. "We'll be leaving behind us a lot of confusion in the house here," Mother St. Joseph admitted to Sister Marie Steenhaut shortly before leaving for her visit to Ghent, "[A]ll of thirty workmen are engaged in heightening and enlarging the chapel, which will be like a small church. Mass is presently being offered in the high-ceilinged room of the large building we put up last year; we're taking advantage of the fact that no one lives there as yet to use it while the chapel is being renovated, which would be practically impossible otherwise. I don't know what effect this will have on our purse strings, but I have confidence that Providence will provide since it's for the house of the Lord."[2] In June of 1830, the day school was expanded with an extension of the original building so that the sisters would no longer have to turn away pupils.

Growth took place, as well, in the number of charitable institutions staffed by sisters of French nationality who had been expelled from their schools. The fifth such enterprise was initiated in February, when three sisters took charge of the hospice at Huy.[3] Previously, Mother St. Joseph had thought of the sisters of the congregation as earthworms with the capacity to link back together after having been cut apart. Now, obviously delighted about the sisters' being able to continue in some form of ministry, she evoked another earthy image when referring to the congregation's ability to persist in doing good. "We are, it seems to me, like mice; when one of their holes is blocked, they just get into another."[4]

Unrest in France in the springtime of 1830 became more acute as a result of the reactionary policies of the Prince de Polignac, Charles X's head of state. He had suspended the right of freedom of the press, and the ripple effect was particularly palpable to France's neighbor to the north, where a revolt against similar restraints was being predicted. Political concerns find echo in Mother St. Joseph's worry over the welfare of her daughters in St. Hubert, especially. "But I hope that the storm will dissipate and that our country won't fall prey to all the horrors of war. They say that here things will be arranged in a way to avoid spilling so much blood. May God grant us the grace. Pray well, yes, pray well, little flock and don't be afraid. God first of all, then your Mother is watching over you."[5]

Two years of bad harvests and increased dissatisfaction with the reign of Charles X began to reignite the flames of revolution among the French populace. The suspension of freedom of the press came as a clarion call to rebellion and, in July, a riot broke out in Paris. On the "Three Glorious Days," of July 27, 28, and 29, the insurgents took command of the capital and forced the hand of Charles X, who abdicated. Mother St. Joseph wrote of her concern for the land of her birth:

> You know, doubtlessly, about the carnage in France. Every day, the news changes, and since we only know things by means of the gazettes, you will know as much as we so I

> won't repeat it. They say that the slaughter is over, that the Bourbons have been cast aside and that it is the duke of Orleans who will take the reins.
>
> Oh, what a world! How the good God must be offended and irritated! Where will it all finish? Let us try to do good with all our soul and all our strength and devote ourselves more and more to the Lord. He is the only solid support and the only door to happiness and foolish is the one who seeks elsewhere.[6]

The overthrow of Charles X, in July, affected a number of European countries: Belgium, Poland, Germany, Italy and Switzerland. Only the revolution of 1830 in Belgium, however, would result in complete success. It began on the evening of August 25, at the theatre of La Monnaie, during the performance of Auber's opera, *La Muette de Portici,* a work whose theme recalled that Neopolitan insurrection against the Spanish oppressors of 1647. The tenor La Feuillade's singing of the celebrated "Amour sacré de la Patrie" ("Sacred love of country") gave rise to a stirring of deep and fervent patriotism.[7] The houses of the police commissioner, de Knyff, and of the minister of justice, Van Maanen, were put to flame. On both August 26 and 27, simultaneous uprisings occurred in a number of locations throughout Belgium. A French emissary raised the tricolor from a balcony of the town hall in Brussels; it was quickly and angrily replaced by the former colors of the Brabant[8]—black, yellow and red. Another Belgian flag was paraded through the streets of the city accompanied by cries of "We are Belgian. No prefecture!"[9] Though these outbursts of patriotic fervor were quickly suppressed, the spirit of revolution had taken hold. Aware of events and with a disappointment she could scarcely conceal, Mother St. Joseph canceled the annual reunion for retreat and vacation. Since her own childhood, she had treasured such times of family gatherings.

> I have to make a change regarding the September reunion that won't upset you more than it upsets me. You'll be surprised at my decision, my dear Sisters, if you're unaware of the more or less serious disturbances that are taking place in different localities, particularly in Brussels. On that account, informed persons say that it would be imprudent for us to

> have our usual reunions during the vacation; they're afraid it wouldn't be safe to travel. Don't fear for yourselves or for us. As long as we're at home we're safe, and nothing alarming will happen to us. Let us pray and we may be sure that the good God will assist us in all our needs.[10]

Noteworthy in her correspondence, at this as at other politically charged times, was her restraint. In an era of bitter partisan polemics, when cardinals, bishops, and even parish priests were swept up in the political and ecclesiastical debates, the former French aristocrat consistently contented herself with simply conveying her trust in God's providential care and with encouraging others to do likewise. She expressed her desire that the sisters pray for peace and for the well-being of all.

> I'm sure you're looking for news of us, my dear Sister Leocadie. I hasten to tell you that we've had to spend some rather disturbing nights, but all is quiet now because they've taken care to station guards inside the city as well and because deputies have gone from Namur, Brussels, and Liège to present to the king a number of demands which, if they're granted, will restore peace. If they're not, there's no telling what may happen. The trouble may go on for a long time. In any case, it's not up to us to weigh possible events, but to pray much to the Master of these events to turn them all to his greater glory, to the salvation of mankind, and to their happiness![11]

On August 28, a group of civic leaders took a list of grievances to the town hall in Brussels, and a delegation was dispatched to The Hague. King William sent his son, William, the Prince of Orange, to assess the situation in Belgium and to negotiate. Given the cold and menacing reception he received, Prince William had well been able to ascertain that "the Belgians would not want to be Dutch."[12] In the meantime, by commissioning a delegation of deputies to intercede personally with the king at The Hague, Brussels was deprived of its most influential and moderate leaders and began to fall victim to anarchy. Mother St. Joseph acknowledged their vulnerability to her sisters and described the quite natural human inclination to be fearful with the images of "papier mâché" and "wet hens." "It takes virtue to rise above ourselves and above events," she affirmed. "We must be quite persuaded that it's God who gives this grace, for of ourselves we're only papier mâché and wet hens. Be well convinced of that."[13]

An armed mob demanding bread, work and guns stormed town hall in Brussels on September 19 and, on the evening of September 20, King William sent his younger son, Frederick, emboldened by an accompanying forty thousand troops and twenty-eight canons, to quell the insurrection. The city of Namur, shored by the protection of its fortified citadel, held itself on the alert and in a state of siege.[14] Mother St. Joseph tried to allay fears: "My dear Sister, be at peace about us. We're as well off as is possible in these stormy times. Nothing disturbing is happening; there's police protection here that keeps everything quiet. I was aware of almost all that was happening in your area."[15]

To the strains of *La Muette de Portici* (an ironic response on the part of the Dutch to the music that had provided the initial impetus to rebellion in August!), William's troops entered Brussels on September 23 but were forced to retreat after four days of battle. Their opponents were a leaderless but fearless agglomeration of some eight thousand volunteers from Brussels, Liège, Tournai and Louvain, and their relatively meager munitions consisting of ten canons. Carried along by the surprising success of September, all the Belgian provinces followed the example of the insurrection in Brussels.[16] A provisional government of nine was established on September 26, and Mother St. Joseph made plans to reopen the schools of the congregation. Later referred to as the *"Journées de septembre"* (September 23–26), or the *"Quatre glorieuses,"* the dates marked a definite turn of events for the future of the Belgian nation. Having defeated the more numerous and well-trained Dutch troops who had encamped in the Parc de Bruxelles, the outnumbered Belgian volunteers facilitated the proclamation of independence from Holland, which was made on September 26. The declaration was made formal on October 4. On that same day, another siege was undertaken by the Dutch, and again the Belgian volunteers, though lacking in prior military training, were victorious. The Dutch were able to hold only the citadel of Antwerp and the city of Maestricht. In her letters to secondary houses throughout Belgium, Mother St. Joseph communicated her maternal concern for the safety and welfare of her spiritual daughters. As always, she offered calm reason and reassurance and shared her joy at the promise of liberty after many years of religious repression.

> My dear Sister Marie Lucie, your letter was a great relief to me. I was very anxious to have news of you, for although I have full confidence that the good God will preserve you safe and sound, it's hard not to worry. If I'm right, the worst of the fighting took place a good distance from your house, and if we can believe the rumors that are going around this morning, it has ended now that the citadel has been taken. If that's true, everything will soon be quiet and orderly, as it is here. The fighting here lasted only three or four days, during which we experienced cannonades, fusillades, constant fear of being killed or wounded, all the usual concomitants of war. But now everything is organized and going well. We came through it with nothing worse than our fears. It will be the same with you and with our other houses, which up to now have suffered only the inevitable effects of such a situation. Many rumors are afloat that have no basis in fact.
>
> When it's all over at Liège, write to me so that my mind can be entirely at rest....Fifty boarders stayed here with us. We've postponed the opening of school until the sixteenth, but I doubt that many will return.
>
> You may well believe that we pray for all of you as we do for ourselves. I'm sure you do the same. We must also pray and ask for grace and light for those who will be at the head of the new government that's being formed everywhere. We have a new government and burgomaster. They've just come to our office to request a donation for the wounded of both sides. We gave them forty francs.
>
> My good child, I don't know what else to tell you. Let us have patience and courage. Everything passes in this life, the good as well as the ill. It's only our manner of using them that doesn't pass, or at least that brings its own sanctions. We must strive to draw profit from everything in this way, which is the only true way. What I say to you, I say to our dear sisters. Let us all encourage one another in doing good.

That's the proper kind of fighting for us and it can be very efficacious.

Receive Sister Superior's greetings and mine. I send all sorts of love to my dear sisters and am, with affection in God, your Mother.

P.S. I have just now been informed that your citadel has surrendered; that the general has killed himself. Is that true? We hear so much that it's hard to know what to believe.[17]

Uprisings did continue in various locales. The Dutch returned with an army of twenty-five to thirty thousand men and succeeded in penetrating into the north of Belgium. His army repelled, the Dutch general sought refuge in the citadel at Antwerp, and from there he bombarded the city, causing fires in several of its sections.

After an electoral campaign conducted in October, the Belgians went to the ballot boxes on November 3 and chose those candidates who, while remaining attached to traditional values, were open to those large issues of liberty for which the French had fought at the end of the previous century. The first official act of the new assembly was to declare Belgium's independence "in the fullness of its political and international rights."[18] By December, a kind of normalcy had returned, and before the month ended it was learned that the Brothers of the Christian Schools were to return to Namur. "A truly consoling bit of news, my dear Sister St. John, is that the Brothers of the Christian Schools will return to Namur next January. I'm filled with joy because I really missed them."[19]

Your children are very slow about coming back. All of ours are back already except those from Antwerp and Louvain. We have thirty fewer than before the revolution. That's not surprising. The parents don't dare let them come at such a critical moment. What they say about Antwerp is only too true; entire streets have been burned, and also the warehouse, which is an immense loss. We've had news from parents and from some of the children. Nearly all the women and children have left the city, which put them out of danger personally. But some people, we've heard, have suffered considerable

> losses. We're hoping for fair weather after the storm. May it be God's will that it not be delayed much longer.
>
> Today the new congress is assembling. Let us pray that it will pass good laws and give us a good leader. As for Maastricht, we've heard nothing at all. You are the closest to them; perhaps you know something. If you do, please tell us....[20]

Pope Pius VIII died toward the close of 1830 and, after a long conclave of fifty days, his successor, Gregory XVI, was elected in February of 1831. All church bells confirmed the news, and Mother St. Joseph enjoined upon the congregation a novena of thanksgiving.

As soon as it was safe to travel, Mother St. Joseph sent for all the superiors of the secondary houses. What position would the congregation have in an independent Belgium? What would be its attitude vis-à-vis the new regime? Among the existing foundations a few, such as those at Thuin and Dinant, had schools that had originated at the request of local secondary schools. They depended on them for space and some subsidies, which helped to defray the cost of the free education given to poor girls. Other foundations were not dependent on the local secondary schools and were free to develop according to need and congregational directive, as long as the teachers had obtained their official certificates. In still other areas, and this was the more frequent situation, the schools had been initiated by concerted efforts of the local congregations and clergy. With the exception of a few isolated cases, the Sisters of Notre Dame had complete charge of them and bore all expenses. This fact hadn't, however, prevented the government from imposing its monopoly on them, exercising a surveillance that bordered on espionage. Then, there was the establishment at Verviers known as the Biolley School because of the exceptional nature of its origins. It had been understood that the situation was a temporary one and that the school would revert to the congregation should the political situation change. With the fall of the Dutch government, it too became a Notre Dame school. Mademoiselle Clary, or "Sister Claire" "separated from her beloved companions who constituted her religious family and, without renouncing either the title or rights of benefactress, turned over her spacious building which had become the center of a prosperous enterprise."[21] By the end of 1830, there were twelve Notre Dame establishments in Belgium. The Congregation of the Sisters of Notre Dame counted more than 100 boarders and 40 novices.

After negotiations which lasted for several months, Belgium crowned its new king, Leopold I. Initially, the duke of Nemours, age sixteen and second son of King Louis-Philippe of France, had been proposed. (Louis-Philippe's first son was already sixty!) But those gathered at the Conference of London to decide the affair refused to consent to anyone from the five courts represented at the conference, and the choice ultimately fell to Léopold de Saxe-Cobourg. Another indication of the dawn of a new era was the reestablishment of the Jesuits in Namur.[22]

King Leopold had barely made his entrance into Belgium and sworn fidelity to the constitution on July 21 when a Dutch army of 86,000, under the Prince of Orange, invaded on August 2. Responding to the appeal of the new king of Belgium, an army of 50,000 French came to the assistance of the Belgians, while England intervened at The Hague on behalf of Belgium.

> Like the rest of the city, we too have been making preparations these days to receive the king. This morning, however, the news arrived that he won't be coming because our former King William is attacking Antwerp and Maastricht with his Dutch soldiers and others, so that Belgium's armed forces have to hurry to those places. They didn't expect this strife. Our Lancers have gone and all the soldiers are in movement. What we must do, my dear Sisters, is to raise our hands toward heaven and pray with fervor that our Lord may dispel the storm. How sad it all is![23]

The event, known as the Campaign of Ten Days, let the Belgians feel the joy of victory along with the sting of the moral shame of realizing that they had to rely, once more in their history, on the intervention of foreign powers. Once again, warring troops passed through their country, "the cockpit of Europe." "One thousand five hundred French passed here today and we're expecting more."[24]

After August 22, Mother St. Joseph was able to write, "Thanks be to God and to the French, the roads are safe,"[25] and she was able to call the sisters to the annual retreat at Namur. This gathering of 1831 proved to be one of the most memorable for all; safe, sound and free after the agonizing Campaign of Ten Days. "All hearts beat in unison with gratitude to God. The Dutch yoke no longer weighed on us; we saw opened before us an era full of promise where we could, in peace and without hindrance, develop the work for which each felt renewed strength. There were many novices who received the habit and the well-populated novitiate allowed us to dream of future foundations."[26]

As understood by the foundress, Julie Billiart, the cross was never to be absent from the congregation; in the summer of 1831 an epidemic spread throughout Thuin and claimed the life of the superior there, Sister Leocadie. She had become ill in April and died in September. A young sister of twenty-four, Sister Celine Monseu, was sent to replace her. "You may be sure, my good Sister Celine," wrote her mother in Notre Dame that October, "that your letter gave me real pleasure. I marvel more and more at how good the good God is in adapting himself to our weakness. Since, after all, you're only a child, and the good Master measures all things accordingly, he surrounds you with docile persons of good will, and I'm confident that he'll give you the knowledge and qualities suitable to your charge. So long as we refer to him alone all the honor and glory, his benefits will flow unceasingly. Have complete confidence and make good use of this inexhaustible source of graces and blessings."[27]

On October 14, a treaty of twenty-four articles decided the questions of territorial boundaries and of debts. It was a treaty to which William I would refuse to adhere, and he maintained a garrison in the citadel in Antwerp, straining to the limit the relations between Holland and Belgium. The tension that resulted between these two countries was to last until 1839, and it tested the political savoir-faire of Leopold I. As for the Grand-Duché of Luxembourg, Belgium received the French-speaking portion in addition to Arlon. The German-speaking region stayed with William I, and when Mother St. Joseph wrote to the sisters at St. Hubert in late October, she was still uncertain as to the fate of her daughters within this region. "Everything says that you will stay on our side, this is with the Belgians, at least that's the belief of the moment, which gives me great pleasure...."[28]

In her seventy-fifth year of age, Mother St. Joseph celebrated the twenty-fifth anniversary of her profession and of the congregation's official origin on October 15, 1831. Her body was now somewhat emaciated by all the suffering she had endured, yet her soul had maintained the vigor and beauty of youth. From one day to the next, she and the sisters had been freed from the struggle for basic survival; the celebration was a particularly memorable one enjoyed by the Notre Dame family. Boarders recalled in their festive retellings for all gathered the beginnings of the congregation: the painful times traversed over the course of the past twenty-five years, the promise the future afforded because of the freedom of education so recently obtained.[29] The mother general was for all a living reminder of this past, while she herself looked forward, in spite of her advancing years, to continued progress for the Church and for the Congregation of the Sisters of Notre Dame. "That day," related a contemporary, "our good Mother, with an infectious happiness, made the beginnings of the Institute come alive for us; the joy flowed from her lips to fall in torrents of delight over our souls; we were moved by it and the jubilee *Te Deum* became the spontaneous cry of our gratitude."[30]

Political peace and the integrity of the congregation were assured by the end of November. The liturgical date of the feast of the Presentation of Mary in the Temple, November 21, was adopted as the feast of all professed sisters in the congregation. Mother St. Joseph had already, that same year, designated the month of March as the month to be devoted to Saint Joseph on the part of the entire congregation.

It would seem that there were many reasons for celebration.

Chapter X

THREAT FROM WITHIN 1832–1835

At the beginning of the New Year, 1832, Françoise Blin de Bourdon wrote a letter to her family in France.

> You know that Mère Julie and I arrived in Belgium with a very small family of around 20 persons. The Lord has so multiplied it that we now exceed the number 220 and are dispersed in a dozen places.
>
> Ordinarily, in our houses, there are two well-attended classes for the poor, sometimes more; two classes of day students consisting of children of persons somewhat well-off who pay a moderate fee; then a boarding school, small or large, depending on facilities. In them, we have many older girls. People are generally very pleased with the content of the education received in our houses; indeed, we teach all that one would want today for a young woman.
>
> The Namur house is the largest of all. It is the Motherhouse where we have the Novitiate; at the present we have 35 novices and as many professed sisters. The period of the novitiate is considerably long; since the sisters are, for the most part, destined to teach, they must be well formed in virtue as well as in the disciplines. This requires several years of formation, although it does happen rather often that some come from good families and already well educated. Some of our former students are destined for our vocation and that shortens the work to be done in preparing them.

> Among our sisters, there are many very amiable ones and all, moreover, try to practice the virtues of their state in life. Since the time of Belgium's independence, some attractive establishments have been proposed to us; but I think that it's prudent to wait and to see how things will turn out. In addition, we need well-formed subjects and, more and more, we need money. These undertakings always cost a lot and so I am declining, for the present, all that is being proposed.
>
> What more should I tell you? Mère Julie planted a little vine which I have watered as best I could and the Lord has caused it to multiply to such an extent that its branches extend throughout almost all of Belgium, which is, of course, very small. Nonetheless, I try to keep myself ready for that time when the Lord will call me.[1]

At Namur, the novitiate and boarding school were growing to such an extent that it took on the importance of a parish, and Father de Cuvelier, a vicar of the diocese who had succeeded Father Médard as ecclesiastical superior of the Namur community, appointed Father Jeanmart as special chaplain. The entire country began to expand its intellectual horizons with the advent of the new regime. A veritable renaissance of the arts and sciences caused the mother general to consider the viability of introducing a new curriculum in the schools of the congregation. The wisdom of the day offered the advice that, "art shouldn't be a kind of luxury item for the rich and distinguished, as were oysters and caviar, but an element of the profound life of the nation."[2] The educative value of the arts caused them to find their way into public education. What was seen to be such a bold curricular innovation in religious schools was not introduced without considerable forethought. For Notre Dame this meant a deviation from Julie's own limiting of the disciplines to be studied in order to put emphasis on the basics. Incurring the criticism of some of the more conservative members of the congregation and the charge of succumbing to a spirit of worldliness, Mother St. Joseph did what she could to allay fears, reminding the sisters that, since the decision was hers, she carried the burden of responsibility for its outcome. Knowing better than anyone the spirit as well as the letter of the thought of her dearest friend, Julie Billiart, Françoise had the foresight to know that a teaching body claiming to prepare its students for their future could not cling to history, even its own. However, not yet willing to counter Julie's injunction against having lay teachers in the boarding schools, she was prepared to see that sisters were trained accordingly. In May, she sent a circular to the secondary houses announcing the new program of studies permitting the teaching of drawing and instrumental music. Many, including Sister Ignace, named superior at Jumet the preceding year, were disturbed by the divergence from the rule of 1818 that had reflected Julie's prohibition against such subjects. With understanding and true wisdom, Mother St. Joseph wrote to Sister Ignace on August 10.

> I'm not surprised that you're worried about the new project; it cost me as much and more; it took two long conferences with Father Méganck[3] to reassure me. As for you, I urge you to have a conference with him next time you come here. All I wish to say to you today, for your peace of mind, is that you won't be personally responsible for the consequences of this arrangement; it's an external regulation that doesn't affect the rules governing our religious life and that I can change without anyone's consent when I think it's for the greater good. As for its causing dissipation in one or other of the sisters, I believe there's little to fear: our sisters will bring to it a spirit of sacrifice; it seems, moreover, that they'll spend only a fixed time on it, in a place as secluded as possible, and at hours when the other children are busy with needlework. You must admit that the plan to which the founder and foundress gave the first inspiration has, in the natural course of events, become completely outmoded.[4] We have founded only large houses instead of small ones of two or three sisters in country places; the Ladies of the Sacred heart, to whom we were supposed to leave the higher branches, are all at a distance from us, etc. It's an elementary principle, my dear Sister, that when the purpose for which a law was made ceases to exist, the law itself is abrogated.[5]

In June of 1833, the consecration of the next bishop of Namur, Monsignor Barrett,[6] brought four other bishops, visiting the city for the celebration, to the motherhouse. "[They] honor us with their visit," Mother St. Joseph wrote to Sister Marie Lucie.[7]

With a typical admixture of joy and sorrow, many in Belgium again suffered from an outbreak of cholera. The disease raged throughout the country and did not spare any social class. "My plans are being thwarted by illnesses that don't seem to pass quickly–or perhaps quickly enough," wrote the mother general to Sister Aloyse, superior at Verviers, on July 27, 1832. At one point, particularly, the mail brought frightening news to the Namur boarders. The boarders' imaginations were so affected that one girl after another identified the symptoms in herself. Since the headmistress was not able to calm them, she sent for Mother St. Joseph. Being at the same time consoling mother and credible doctor she reassured them. "Don't be afraid, little flock, the cholera is not visiting either the Sisters of Notre Dame or their pupils because the Heart of Jesus is watching over them." They were so reassured by these words of the respected and beloved mother general, confirmed a witness, that there was no longer room for fear in their hearts. "If the issue of the cholera did remain with us, it was in order to pray for its victims, a duty which had been pointed out to us as the most serious obligation of the moment, and one which we truly desired to fulfill."[8] Sisters and students of the community were indeed spared from the cholera's devastating effects.

That same summer, King Leopold I paid a royal visit to Namur and he and his retinue were accorded the same gracious reception as had been given to William I only three years previously. He was enthusiastically welcomed by all the students decked out in the national colors. The boarders, gathered in the assembly hall, sang to him as the occasion required.

> By way of news, I'll tell you that we had the honor of receiving the king here yesterday morning; we had, I think, a good eight hundred children lined up in the courts and gardens; we had waited for him in vain all the day before; but in the end it was worth the trouble and we had not regrets. You can't help admiring his gentle, peaceful manner; unhurried, quiet, thinking of everything, taking a lively interest in all that is good.[9]

Given the continuing polemics in official Church circles regarding the religion of the new monarch and the attitude toward Protestantism characteristic of the age, the mother general was considerably broadminded by contrast: "Ah, what a pity, how regrettable, that this man who is so virtuous isn't a Catholic. You must pray so much to the good God that he'll grant him this grace; pray with all your hearts, my good Sisters."[10] Apparently, King Leopold was impressed, and upon his departure he said, "I will return." And, indeed he did. The following year, in September 1833, he returned accompanied by his queen, Louise-Marie. Herself a French princess by birth, the queen too was quite favorably impressed with "the French ladies" and indicated that she would like Sisters of Notre Dame for any Catholic school that she might establish in Brussels. Despite the appeal of the queen's request, Mother St. Joseph graciously abstained from such a commitment at that time, given the needs for additional teachers in the already existing houses and the dearth of teachers whose formation was completed. Subsequently, however, the royal wish was fulfilled, and Notre Dame schools were established in the capital city and its suburbs. While taking his leave, the king reiterated his promise of the preceding year and assured Mother St. Joseph that he would take her congregation under his special protection, especially its motherhouse.[11]

The congregation earned royal favor but had lost a devoted friend with the death the previous March of Father Thomas. His death occasioned a touching note from the other of the "first fathers in Jesus Christ" to the congregation. Father Varin was at the room in Laval where Father Thomas had just died and discovered a note of thanks written by Mother St. Joseph in response to greetings Father Thomas had sent her for the feast of Saint Frances of Rome on March 8. Moved by the memories of the foundresses, which her note revived, Varin wrote: "Your whole family is singularly dear to me and so it is with great consolation that I learn from time to time that it is blessed by God and that it is working usefully for His glory."[12] The sincerely affectionate vote of confidence bolstered the spirit of the mother general who, in turn, asked the sisters to remember him and Father Varin.

> Pray for our good Father Thomas. In addition to receiving Holy Communion, let each one do whatever else her devotion may suggest. Just think! In M[arch], after three years of

> silence during which I thought he was dead, I received news from him and sent him mine. Now I hear that he has died and, at the same time, I receive from our first Father, who knew us so well, a very tender assurance of his own affection and of his approval of our manner of living and acting. I assure you that it gave me very great pleasure to have news of him. Father Thomas has gone to receive the reward for all he did for God and for the good of souls.[13]

A similar letter, yet one with significant variations was sent to Sister Ignace. In a humanly understandable need for affirmation of what was a risky decision, Mother St. Joseph conveyed to her Father Varin's endorsement of the direction taken by the congregation to keep abreast of educational trends.

> I don't know whether you noticed an extraordinary touch of Providence. Father Thomas wrote to me after three years of silence; I received the letter on March tenth; he received my reply on March fourteenth while he was still in good health; Father Varin happened to be at Laval; he read my letter and shared its contents with all his companions. This letter contained a long account of our present situation, even that we are teaching music, piano, etc. Yet you see the joy and satisfaction that Father Varin expresses to me; there's no question of thunder or malediction. Good Father Thomas died on the twenty-third of March. Admire, admire God's loving attention to the needs of his weak creatures.[14]

Another loss deeply affected the cofoundress with the death, in November of 1833, of Father de Cuvelier, the ecclesiastical superior to the community, who had followed Father Médard. While these two had been solid supports for Mother St. Joseph, the successor to Father de Cuvelier, though supportive, would prove to be much more rigid in his dealings with the congregation.

The annual gathering for vacation and retreat at Namur that September reflected the health of the congregation as thirty novices made their first profession of vows and twelve postulants were received. The school at Noveau Bois had enrolled its one-hundredth boarder while that at Namur, overflowing with students, was being enlarged with another floor. Already the sisters at Verviers had taken over the administration of a large orphanage founded by the Biolley family.

But in the background of all this observable prosperity of the congregation was the development of an internal plot that would threaten its very existence. Not too much unlike the misunderstanding with her spiritual daughters at Ghent, especially, over her freer interpretation of the provisional rule and the implementation of Napoleon's *Universal Catechism,* which caused Julie such sorrow just prior to her death, so some of Mother St. Joseph's spiritual daughters were to be the source of great pain to her during the last decade of her life. What could be said, however, to be of a distinct difference was the deliberateness of intent in the latter instance.

Sister Marie Thérèse, Mother St. Joseph's first assistant and the superior at Namur, had never enjoyed very good health. By 1833, illness indicated that she might be incapacitated for a considerable length of time and it was thought advisable to name a subassistant in the interim. Mother St. Joseph looked to a young professed sister at Namur, Sister Borgia. She had been one of Namur's boarding students before entering the community and was formed under the first directress—a highly gifted teacher—Sister Gertrude Morel. Even as a student she had demonstrated significant promise, and whenever Sister Gertrude was to be absent, which had occurred frequently enough during her later years, Sister Borgia was asked to stand in as her replacement. It seemed only natural that when Sister Gertrude died, Sister Borgia would be appointed as the new directress. What hadn't been sufficiently noticed, however, in Sister Borgia's obvious talents and in her apparent devotedness was her driving personal ambition.

One of the boarders during Sister Borgia's tenure as directress was a young woman who had confided to the popular teacher her own desire to become a Sister of Notre Dame. In 1830, this former boarder did enter the community and became known as Sister Francis Xavier. After her profession she was sent to Thuin. Once there her heretofore latent hysterical tendencies and delusions induced a kind of pseudomysticism. Her extravagant behavior became extremely detrimental to the small community at Thuin as well as an almost impossible challenge for the young superior who replaced Sister Leocadie in 1831, Sister Celine. Sister Francis Xavier was recalled to Namur and assigned a teaching position in the boarding school under Sister Borgia's direction.[15]

The directress, flattered by the adulation and confidences of her former student, began to resent the suspicions surrounding Sister Francis Xavier and took up her cause, defending her as misunderstood and undervalued. As subassistant to the mother general, Sister Borgia went to great efforts to rehabilitate Sister Francis Xavier in the eyes of her superiors so that more and more came to view with compassion the young "prophetess," as she gradually came to be known.

Strange physical symptoms emerged from unknown causes. Sister Francis Xavier was alternately blind, deaf, deprived of the use of certain senses, paralyzed in certain limbs. Moods shifted accordingly. Doctors, baffled by the mysterious illness, and clergy, some of whom were lauding her virtue, came and went.

Her visions told her a reform was needed in the congregation. Among the believers were counted, in addition to Sister Borgia, flattered by the role assigned to her in the reform as indicated by these visions, about eighteen others, novices and professed alike, particularly those teachers noted for their intellectual gifts. Sister Vincent, the directress of novices and, consequently, along with Sister Borgia, a counselor to Mother St. Joseph, was one of these so-called "reformers." The plan consisted, first of all, in replacing Mother St. Joseph, a goal that seemed to them readily attainable given the mother general's weakness due to her advanced age. The new regime would then divide the congregation into two castes: choir sisters—an intellectual elite who would form the corps of teachers and local superiors—and lay sisters, charged with the domestic duties. The order of teaching priorities would be completely upended: Whereas the congregation had been founded, principally, to teach children of the poor by means of free schools and, secondarily, to maintain day schools for the middle class and boarding schools for the upper class, the reformers would reverse this hierarchy with emphasis placed on boarders from society's leisured class while reserving only modest space for teaching the poor. Day schools, populated chiefly by children of the bourgeoisie, would be suppressed entirely.

In 1834, as the Church in Belgium was soliciting funds for the founding of the Catholic University of Louvain, to which Mother St. Joseph enthusiastically encouraged all convents of the Sisters of Notre Dame to contribute annually according to their means, plans for the proposed coup were put in motion.

Five children from the countryside, seen as being too simple for the aristocratic allure that the boarding school was taking on, were dismissed in May, for rather specious reasons. Mother St. Joseph made brief reference to this event when she wrote to Sister Marie Steenhaut on May 15. After congratulating Sister Marie on the enrollment of the one-hundredth boarder at Ghent, Mother St. Joseph cautioned that this number may be sizeable enough since much vigilance and prayer were demanded in maintaining such a large group of students. The schools must avoid having those few "scabby sheep" who might "spoil the others, causing them to lose their innocence, good religious principles or spirit of subordination."[16] In this context, Mother St. Joseph told Sister Marie that they had just expelled five such boarders from Namur, obviously taking as fact the interpretation of events as related to her by Sister Borgia.

By July, a young professed sister, who was proving to be intractable to the reformers' plans, was accused of disturbing the others by her confiding to them her own temptations and desolation. She was transferred to Ghent. In September, the directress of novices accused several novices of insubordination, and on these grounds they were dismissed from the congregation. In fact, they too had not been amenable to the reform and maintained a loyalty to the traditional spirit. These events were occurring while Sister Marie Thérèse's illness was most acute, causing Mother St. Joseph to rely heavily on the advice and opinions of her other counselors. As she wrote to Sister Marie Lucie in September:

> Sister Superior is rather ill with a fever and an upset stomach; pray for her, and for me, who am not feeling any too well either; but I'm keeping on my feet. Both you and we must try to strengthen ourselves by having confidence in God; that is often what we lack. We're too wavering, yet the

> good God exercises us in many ways to strengthen us. Let us try then to enter into his designs; this is the grace I wish for you as well as for myself, who feel such great need of it.[17]

The reformers grew emboldened by their successes. Mother St. Joseph's second term of ten years was to end at the conclusion of 1835 and, according to the visionary, Sister Borgia would lead the congregation to the new order of things. Not able to wait to effect their reforms and, inspired by Sister Francis Xavier's revelation that the day school was being seriously contaminated by a supposed lack of morality on the part of some of its middle-class students, it was deemed that this school should be closed immediately. Sister Borgia insisted on this course of action after relating to the mother general that she had thoroughly investigated the situation and that her investigation yielded alarming results. Mother St. Joseph, finding it difficult to believe that such was actually the case, decided to defer the matter to Bishop Barrett. Out of deference, the families of the students were told that the school was being closed for the sake of a complete reorganization. The event caused a scandal in the city, though many attenuated their judgments by openly declaring that the mother general of the Sisters of Notre Dame was obviously in her dotage, an interpretation fueled by comments made by the reformers. The beleaguered mother wrote to Sister Ignace:

> Something very sad has just happened here; we've been obliged to dismiss our two large classes of externs; that, you may be sure, is causing much criticism in the town. We've made a pretext of intending to reopen later after some reorganization, but that's not the real reason; you can easily guess it, but we couldn't announce it. We came to this extreme measure only with the advice of the bishop and other wise persons. Doubtless not all of these children were guilty, but when only a small part remain innocent, the whole is soon corrupted. It's really necessary for the mistresses to exercise a great deal of surveillance, zeal, and prudence. Don't speak openly about this to everyone at your house, only to those for whom it may be useful for their instruction.

Let us pray for one another; I have great need of prayers on my own account.[18]

April had not come to an end when similar charges were beginning to be made about the boarding school. The presumed delinquents were expelled one after another so that, in about six weeks, one-third of the pupils of the boarding school had been sent away. By way of contrast to these events, how much Mother St. Joseph appreciated the gesture of a child in the boarding school at St. Hubert was quite apparent: "You have some very precious fruit in your boarding school, my dear Sister Maxine," she included in a letter to the superior, Sister St. John. "A little ten-year-old asks me to receive her as a postulant. Her little letter is charming in its simplicity. Tell her I send her the blessing she asks, and that I'm already her Mother and she is my daughter and that she may come to Namur when she has grown a little taller."[19]

Solace also came in the form of unburdening herself to Sister Ignace at Jumet:

I tell you in a whisper—and you have perhaps had an inkling of it—that something is fermenting in our house. It's being done quietly, but the sisters are disturbed and tormented—at least some of them are. As for me, I pray, I observe everything, and I await from the Lord a solution with which I can try to cooperate insofar as he gives me the grace. What is certain is that everyone wants what is good. A certain occurrence has already heated matters again, namely, that eight boarders have been sent away for the same cause. What an affliction that is. However, I can't condemn the action after the information that has been given to me and that I believe to be very true.

I hadn't really planned to tell you all that, but it came to the tip of my pen and I'm not sorry to have said it. You will pray for your old Mother, who finds herself at her age in such strange circumstances, and who, over and above all that, must console, support, and distract our poor sister superior, who has really only me to render her this service....

My love to the sisters, and believe that I am, as always, all yours in the Lord.[20]

Recriminations on the part of the parents of those students unjustly accused made the affair public. Accusations were leveled against Bishop Barrett who, it was said, caused the superiors to obey his orders. Since he was ill and out of the city, two of his vicars general, Fathers Poncelet and Collard, arrived at the motherhouse to consult the superior general. It did not take them long to ascertain that she was anything but senile, as was rumored. On the other hand, they felt that she had placed too much trust in her assistants at Namur and urged her to carry through with her own investigation into the matter. Indeed, some of the superiors in the secondary houses had either suspected or received accounts of the actual situation at the motherhouse. Judging it their duty to write to Mother St. Joseph on the subject, some sent letters on the matter, letters that were intercepted by Sister Borgia. Mother St. Joseph began her own investigation as requested and, contrary to the persistence of her counselors, she put a temporary end to the dismissals. On June 1, she gave Sister Ignace an update on the situation in the school and described the factions into which the community was by now openly splitting, factions that were becoming apparent at meetings of the community. She saw that she was no longer the uncontested mother of all the sisters. This partial defection deeply wounded her sensitive and affectionate heart, yet her grief never held the slightest tinge of bitterness. "I saw our good Mother," testified a witness to these events, "at the time of her great sorrow, sad and calm as befits one at the foot of the cross."[21] She had begun to realize that she may well need to replace Sister Borgia:

> ...a sort of schism is being formed in the community among the sisters, some taking one side, some the other....It's certain that a remedy must be found, and a common bond that will strengthen the entire edifice; our dear sister superior [Sister Marie Thérèse] thinks, and I am of her opinion, that someone should be appointed in her place. It won't be Sister Borgia. That's not my intention. Although she may have many good qualities, she lacks certain essential ones. Sister Celine is too young, she wouldn't be accepted by all the sisters, and then she has poor health. Devote yourself to prayer, and I'll do the same. The whole house is praying, making novenas for me, for my intentions; perhaps at Pentecost the Holy Spirit will let us know what we should do; I hope in his goodness. Abandonment, a spirit of sacrifice—

> these are the dispositions in which we must try to place our souls, our minds, our wills, and our whole selves.
>
> My old head is really too tired to write more–and with it an aching heart; but I hope the Lord who is so full of goodness, will have pity on me and on this house, and that he'll come to our assistance.[22]

On June 13, Mother St. Joseph invited the entire congregation to join her in an extraordinary novena to the Sacred Heart. On June 16, she wrote a compelling and touching letter to Sister Ignace in which she relayed her decision regarding Sister Marie Thérèse's replacement:

> [M]y dear Sister Ignace, it's not just me whom you must blame if I look to you in my need. There's a saying that "the voice of the people is the voice of God," and I've heard that among sisters it's being said, "If only we had Sister Ignace!" You understand that it's not all of them who are saying this–that a certain number of them may be saying something else; in fact, I must tell you that there's some diversity of opinion; to what may that not lead if I don't call the whole to unity? Don't imagine that the work is very difficult, but we mustn't allow the evil to take root while we nourish ourselves on hope. Come, come! Invent some pretext for making this little trip, and believe that I am suffering, troubled, overwhelmed. I am also your very affectionate Mother, whom you must like a good daughter, try to relieve.[23]

A letter followed to the community at Jumet which attempted to prepare them for the move of their beloved superior: "This is to remind you that you are Sisters of Notre Dame, and that it's on great occasions that we manifest our courage. No weakness, I beg of you. After some tears and sighs given to sentiments of a just gratitude, you must rise higher and understand well that God and the Institute must prevail over all else....*Sursum corda,* my dear Sisters; lift up your hearts and believe how much it has cost my maternal heart to have to afflict you."[24]

The appointment of Sister Ignace as superior of Namur and first assistant to the mother general was welcome news to most. However, it was a decision that pushed Sister Borgia, expecting to be named to that post herself, into open revolt. Mother St. Joseph tried to reason with her but to no avail. Threatening to take at least eighteen sisters with her, Sister Borgia did leave but accompanied only by Sister Francis Xavier and the latter's blood sister, Sister Marie Xavier. In response to a sister who had earlier encouraged severe measures, Mother St. Joseph had affirmed: "If even one of my daughters should be guilty, I wouldn't want her to feel like an orphan."[25] Truly, in that school of discipleship, which is friendship, she had learned to love all whom God loves!

On June 25, the day of Sister Borgia's departure, Mother St. Joseph called the sisters together for an assembly at Namur and urged charity toward the repentant sisters. A few days later, at a subsequent gathering, the mother general made what was to be her last open reference to the situation: "Your sisters are coming back among you," she said. "Receive them with love and kindness. They have suffered; they have so generously done reparation that they are worthy of the predilection of the Heart of Jesus and of yours. Excel in that delicate and gentle kindness that assuages all pain and that loves more, because one has suffered more....You protest that you want to console me: if you are sincere, love one another as your old Mother has loved you all. Forget everything and be henceforth but one heart and one soul."[26] Her interpretation of events was characteristically and unfailingly charitable.

> My dear Sister Marie Lucie, I think you're somewhat prepared for what I'm about to tell you. There has been a great revolution here. It broke out, I believe, when I had Sister Ignace come to the motherhouse as assistant and Sister Borgia found herself consequently supplanted in many areas. As you may well suppose, my reasons were good. But my action threatened to undo this sister's plans, which were nothing short of a reform of the Institute. Finding herself thwarted in these plans, she immediately made the decision to leave the Institute. Sister Marie Xavier and her sister, Sister Francis Xavier, followed her two days later. A relatively large number of other sisters, among them many young ones, were also supposed to leave with them. The carriages had been ordered and everything was planned, but the *good* God in his mercy allowed us to be warned in time to prevent such a foolish action. They're repentant now and doing penance. I say "foolish action" because it's a

sin of delusion rather than of malice that leads to all such grand projects of reform.

All those things so contrary to the Rule, to obedience, and to the vows they had made were the fruit of the revelations of Sister Francis Xavier. She's a very trying person, who did us much harm without intending it; I always mistrusted her sanctity since she never set foot in chapel except to receive Holy Communion and assist at Mass, and was often absent even for these. Although she was in good health, it had been a long time since she had appeared in chapel any more frequently than that; nor had Sister Borgia, but she at least had the excuse of weak nerves. Sometimes we deceive ourselves in an effort not to make rash judgments.[27]

By August, Mother St. Joseph was able to invite the sisters, as was customary, for the annual vacation and retreat. "Come, all of you, all of you, to make a good retreat. The *Veni Creator* will be recited on the first of September in the evening and the retreat will begin on the second. We'll try to make such a good retreat that it will dispose us for any sacrifice....To tell you something about the distressing affair that we're trying to forget, I'm happy to say that all is very calm in the house; everything has returned to normal!"[28] So determined to both forgive and forget, she made no further allusion to the heartbreaking months she had endured. The Annals of the Motherhouse confine the entire incident to a simple and discreet mention and any related correspondence was filed with the notice that it was confidential and to be seen by future mothers general only.[29]

Her attention went next to the parents of the dismissed students. In justice, she wanted their rehabilitation to be accomplished with all due speed and publicly, since their dismissal had received public notice. A special invitation was issued by those in charge, and all but very few of the students returned. One testified later:

For my part, invited on the morning of July 2, I returned to the boarding school before dinner that evening. Good Mother St. Joseph, to whom each returning student presented herself, received me with such tenderness. Tears obscured her vision, but that didn't prevent her from recognizing her child. The very effect of her maternal look made me consider what I had suffered as nothing. I don't know how it happened, but the past was quickly forgotten. A new life animated the school....With maturity, I appreciated even more the extraordinary veneration in which we students and our families, along with the entire city of Namur, held Mother St. Joseph. Without this universal esteem, without this reputation for holiness which surrounded her, the Institute would never had triumphed over this terrible trial.[30]

Chapter XI

WOMAN OF INFLUENCE 1836 AND BEYOND

Once the community had regained its customary harmony and stability, Mother St. Joseph sought to reinforce this positive spirit by instituting monthly community days of recollection along with regular occasions for celebration. The feast of Saint Stanislas, Polish nobleman and bishop who had been dedicated from birth by his parents to the service of God, was to be observed as the feast of the novices. The Presentation of Mary was designated as the feast day of all professed sisters, and superiors were assigned their own feast. Beginning with the recitation of Vespers the evening before, these celebrations were marked by familial expressions of affection and appreciation, by laughter and good cheer. New Year's and the feast of the Three Kings added additional holidays and, as long as the practice was feasible, the schoolchildren, young and old, participated in the festivities.

On Laetare Sunday of 1836, March 13, Bishop Dehesselle was consecrated bishop of Namur, replacing Bishop Barrett, who had died the previous year. Having studied as a seminarian in Namur, Bishop Dehesselle was well known by the Sisters of Notre Dame because he had served as a pastor in Liège. His kindness to the community was such that, years later, Sister Ignace compared his solicitude for Notre Dame to that of Saint Francis de Sales for the Order of the Visitation. Mother St. Joseph eagerly awaited his arrival in Namur for his installation. "Our bishop hasn't arrived yet," she wrote on March 2 to Sister Aloyse, superior at Verviers. "We're eager to see him as soon as possible. As for us, there's no doubt that we can go to him with confidence. All is at peace and in order by the grace of God, who has permitted a great calm to succeed the storm."[1]

Age was beginning to take its toll on the mother general, and her regular correspondence with the secondary houses became less frequent, the letters less lengthy. "Despite the difficulty I have in writing because of my hands, my dear Sister Constantine, my heart urges me to it so strongly that I can't resist."[2]

Nonetheless, that April, she felt strong enough to make her annual visitation of the houses in the province of Hainaut. Leaving Namur in the care of Sister Ignace, she and Sister Marie-Thérèse made the trip by public stagecoach over long and difficult roads. One of the sisters of Thuin, present for the reception, expressed the feelings of all gathered there that spring day. "We were sad to see her suffering from such a tenacious rheumatism. We found her much aged and were fearful of not seeing her anymore. No one spoke openly of these somber projections but she divined them. At the time of her departure, seeing us grouped around her in a very moving silence, she enjoined us to remain good religious and good Sisters of Notre Dame until death, in the manner of Mère Julie."[3]

Mother St. Joseph reassured the sisters of God's care for the congregation and used the examples of Sisters Anastasie, Marie-Thérèse and Ignace as evidence of his providence. Had not God blessed the community with their leadership just when it was most necessary? The moment of separation was still painful, and many tears were being furtively wiped away when, perceiving them, Mother St. Joseph playfully chided: "Let none of my daughters be weaklings!" However, deeply moved herself, she quickly boarded the waiting coach and, for a last time, blessed them and said, "My dear children, love one another." It was indeed the final farewell for many of those present that spring day.[4]

The death of the last friend to have known Mother St. Joseph from her first days in Namur transpired on May 11. Father Minsart had been, along with Bishop Pisani, a welcoming protector and he had provided ongoing support from 1807 to his death in 1836. To him Mother St. Joseph had always been very grateful—

for his spiritual advice, his wise counsel in business matters and his indefatigable energy on behalf of the congregation. His departure was but one more painful break with the past.

One of the new bishop's first official functions as ecclesiastical head of the Namur community was to preside at the general chapter. From May 16 to 18, the superiors gathered at the motherhouse for the election of the mother general. Despite reminding them of her advanced age and increasingly apparent physical weakness, Mother St. Joseph was unanimously reelected. Significantly, another change had been determined during this chapter. Henceforth, the term of office of the mother general was not to be a temporary one of ten years but one that would last for the duration of her life. A true vote of confidence in Mother St. Joseph's leadership, it was a decision that was seen to give the office additional authority and permanence. At no time in the future of the Institute could such a history of intrigue and divisive partisanship, as was so recently and painfully experienced, repeat itself.

At the time of his annual visit with his aunt, Alexander Blin de Bourdon was struck by the obvious changes that had occurred by the summer of 1836. Though still remarkably young at heart and lucid of mind, physically his aunt had weakened to such an extent that, upon leaving, he was fearful that that would be their last meeting.

In the fall, the trustees of the Namur hospices, with the full support of Bishop Dehesselle, requested that Mother St. Joseph send Sisters of Notre Dame to administer the hospice at Harscamp. Isabelle Brunell, the widowed countess of Harscamp, had died childless in 1806 and bequeathed a considerable sum for the purpose of establishing a home for elderly indigent. One stipulation of her bequest was that this home be staffed by religious. Despite repeated requests, the intervention of the minister of the interior and a trip to Paris on the part of one of the executors, the comte de Croix, religious orders in France had been able to give only vague and heretofore unrealized promises. The success of the Sisters of Notre Dame at both St. Gilles and St. Jacques caused the trustees to go to the superior general of these sisters with their appeal. She graciously acquiesced. On October 8, three sisters undertook this new mission, the last to be directly established by Mother St. Joseph.[5]

As her nephew had observed, Mother St. Joseph's heart remained younger than her failing body. She suffered more acutely from rheumatism, especially in her hands and wrists, yet her New Year's greetings reflected her continued desire to communicate her affection for her sisters despite her physical infirmities.

> My dear Sister Aloyse and all my dear Sisters of Verviers, I desire at the beginning of the year to write you with my own hand a little note that will come straight from my heart, for it's to tell you that you are as dear to me in this year of 1837 as you have been in all the preceding ones. Then, too, I recommend myself to your prayers and good works. I have great need of this assistance. My heart would like to say much more to you, but my hand tells it that this is enough. All yours, your Mother.[6]

In the meantime, negotiations regarding a possible foundation in Bastogne were reopened. Designated the "Paris of the Ardennes," it would be another century before the city would become well known as the locus of the last and one of the bloodiest battles of World War II, the Battle of the Bulge. Mother St. Joseph had herself made a trip to Bastogne in 1824, a year after the first request was made, and it was King William's refusal that had caused the deferral of her promise. On November 3, six sisters accompanied by Sister Ignace, in the mother general's stead, boarded a stagecoach with their personal effects as well as household items that had been contributed by the existing establishments.[7] Because of the length of the journey to the Ardennes, the little group stopped in Dinant, where they were warmly greeted by the community as well as by the local authorities. One of the officials, Monsieur Roubaud, gave a welcome address in which he alluded to the parable of the workers who were needed in the vineyard of the Lord.

At daybreak, they resumed their journey. This time, however, a private carriage barely large enough to comfortably hold six adults without baggage awaited them. The travel time was all the same agreeably passed as the little band prayed, sang, enjoyed one another's company and paused to rest the horses. At

St. Hubert, the driver stopped before an inn, but the sisters were understandably reluctant to leave all their belongings unattended in the carriage and, after a wait of four hours, the driver returned as he had promised with fresh horses. The trip was resumed around ten in the evening and, by three in the morning, the tired group reached Bastogne. It was only in the morning that they realized that, apart from the beds in which they had slept, the house, though spotlessly clean, was completely devoid of any furnishings. Thanks to the ingenuity of the sisters and the generosity of the townspeople, school was opened on November 15 with a full complement of children in the school for the poor. As there were twice as many day pupils, a second room was quickly readied. Six resident students formed the initial nucleus of the boarding school. Sister Ignace stayed with the community for about two weeks before returning to Namur to resume her duties at the motherhouse.

Constantly challenged to maintain quality establishments and to provide adequate formation of the new recruits, Mother St. Joseph was still moved by the needs presented to her. One such plea was made by a Father Grosjean, president of the seminary in the neighboring town of Philippeville. In March, Sister Ignace visited in order to make necessary advance preparation and on May 20, she accompanied three sisters there.

One improvement that had been desired since the sisters assumed direction of St. Gilles was a separate building to house the orphans who were lodged there with the elderly. The monastery abandoned by the Carmelite friars of Namur became available, but purchase of the property was out of the question since the price was a prohibitive 80,000 francs. Not deterred, the sisters decided to obtain from public charity what they could not garner from the trustees of the hospice. A subscription list was begun in 1832 headed by Queen Marie-Louise herself and many benefactors followed her lead. Monies were still needed and the sisters asked special permission of Mother St. Joseph to be permitted to beg from door to door, an undertaking which had not been a practice in the congregation. Permission granted, they solicited funds in this manner for several months, collecting another 11,000 francs. The total acquired now came to 40,000 with an additional 40,000 still needed. Seeing their dedication to the orphans of St. Gilles, the trustees unanimously voted the remainder. The building became the property of the hospices in November of 1835 but, because of delays for various formalities and remodeling, it took until October of 1837 for the orphans to finally move to their spacious new accommodations.

Consoled by the prospect of a nearby presence of her beloved Carmelites, Mother St. Joseph helped to welcome a community that had been banished from Douai. With the assistance of Bishop Dehesselle, who facilitated their relocation in his diocese, the nuns were eventually housed in a building in the shadows of the Cathedral of Saint Aubain itself. Able to empathize from experience with their situation, Mother St. Joseph did all she could to help them feel at home in Belgium and saw that their meals were prepared until they were definitively installed in their new home. While waiting, they stayed with a Madame Kinet and daily, as they came to the motherhouse of the Sisters of Notre Dame for a meal, they stopped by the community room to greet their welcoming sisters in religion.

Mother St. Joseph had suffered a setback with a severe recurrence of rheumatism during the preceding winter. It had then abated that summer only to recur more acutely in October. Those around her knew she that she had to be suffering greatly and were in utter admiration of her constant serenity and cheerfulness. "The more one lives with this good mother, the more one appreciates her virtues," wrote Sister Ignace. "Always the same serenity, the same peace, the same resignation. She senses that nature is growing weaker and she praises the Lord for it. She asks me to tell you that she blesses you all very affectionately and that she wants you to pray for her"[8] In December, Sister Ignace wrote to Sister St. John: "In spite of her continual suffering, she is always cheerful and very amiable, as she will be to the end. Oh! What a saintly soul! She edifies us by the example of all her virtues."[9] The sisters stormed heaven to obtain a cure and knowledge of the nature of their prayer caused their beloved mother to plead for an amendment: "If the Lord were to listen to you, I would still be here in a hundred years. Ask rather, please, that I might have the desire of a child to go to see her heavenly Father, the desire of an exile to return home."[10]

On the feast of the Ephipany, 1838, the mother general summoned her forces to join the community for the traditional celebration. Whether by happenstance or by means of an understandable ploy, she was the one to find in her piece of cake the hidden token and was proclaimed queen of the feast, according to the traditional French manner of observing the holiday. She accepted the circumstance with good grace proclaiming, "I willingly reign over you because you wish to be the beloved spouses of Our Lord Jesus Christ."[11]

At about the same time, a mother of two of the Flemish novices arrived to visit her daughters. Though she was cordially received by the first assistant of the mother general, she declared that her joy in the visit could not be complete without having seen the mother general herself. "And I have come from so far and will have to return without having seen the mother of my children?"[12] One of her two novice daughters, after a brief consultation with her sister and confident of the graciousness of the mother general, hazarded a trip to Mother St. Joseph's room and a knock on her door. The bold undertaking produced the desired result, as Mother St. Joseph came to the parlor and welcomed this generous mother who had given two of her children to the congregation. She thanked her for her sacrifice and spoke so encouragingly that the Flemish mother left utterly delighted with her visit. "I go home completely satisfied," she said to her daughters, "because I am leaving you in good hands. Your Mother General is a saint. Yes, I have seen a living saint and I will proclaim it everywhere and will never forget her."[13]

In the middle of January of 1838, Mother St. Joseph took to the bed from which she was not to rise again. On January 15, she wrote what is her last extant letter: "My dear Sister Marie Lucie, by this little note I want to assure you and all my good sisters of Liège of my affection. I can't express myself at length, but very few words are needed to tell you that I am, and always will be, Your entirely devoted Mother in our good Savior, Sister St. Joseph."[14] Her only other concern, in addition to assuring the sisters of her affection, was that she should die truly poor. For this reason, and so as not to be too much a burden to the sister nurses who were already caring for a number of sick sisters, she suggested that she be moved to Harscamp. The chagrin and vehement rejection reflected by Sister Marie Thérèse, to whom she confided this suggestion, was such that Mother St. Joseph did not pursue the notion. One thing of which she did wish to be reassured, however, was that everything she had possessed was indeed turned over to the congregation and that she would die without having anything which could be called her own. Had she not begun her apostolic life with an act of consecration on February 2, 1804, and recorded in her journal of that same day, "I will live poor, I will love the poverty of Jesus Christ in order to merit being the servant and mother of the poor."[15]

On the morning of February 2, Bishop Dehesselle came to administer the last sacraments. Mother St. Joseph renewed her vows and asked pardon of the sisters for any harm she might have caused them and begged them to obtain for her, "from the goodness of God, the grace of a holy death."[16] Peaceful and lucid, she responded to the prayers being offered. In the afternoon, she asked to see all the sisters for a last time during a free moment after the noon meal. She looked lovingly at the group silently assembled at her bedside and, in a very weak but expressive voice, emphasizing each word, said: "My dear children, I thank you for the affection you've shown me. Always love and respect your superiors. Remain united in heart and soul. Observe your rule and God will bless you, each one in proportion to her fidelity." She then raised trembling hands to heaven as if to ask God's blessing before making a very distinct sign of the cross over her daughters. Profoundly moved, the sisters withdrew, proceeding one by one past her bed. She recognized and smiled a goodbye to each sister as she passed. Those who had been in the community the longest were the last to leave, bringing tears to the eyes of their customarily dignified and calm mother general.[17]

Bishop Dehesselle came again for a final blessing on February 8. On February 9, he brought holy communion for the last time to her for, while the chaplain was reciting the psalms from the Office of Virgins and saying the words, "I rejoice in the things that were said to me, we shall go into the house of the

Lord," Mother St. Joseph passed away peacefully and imperceptibly. "Is it true," one sister lamented, "Is it true that our good Mother is no longer with us?"[18]

The body of the beloved mother, sister and friend was carried in procession to the convent chapel the following afternoon, where blessings were administered by the attendant priests. Afterwards, the procession continued to the novitiate, causing some to wonder about the delay of the burial. Speculation was that the three-foot snowfall was responsible. What the majority of the community did not know was that, at around eleven in the evening, Françoise Blin would be taken to the garden chapel to be buried beside her dearest friend, Julie Billiart.[19]

On Monday, February 12, a solemn requiem was offered in the parish church of St. Joseph. In attendance were represented the entire social spectrum. All had come to pay tribute to this noble woman who had sacrificed homeland, family, fortune and social rank in the service of Christian education. Everywhere people repeated, "Mother St. Joseph was a saint, a saint has just died."[20] Bishop Dehesselle addressed the bereaved community with words of consolation and of hope:

> We have every reason to hope that she has obtained her recompense; God has received her into his bosom. She has not died, she lives in God. She also lives among you, by her virtues and her benefits. Never forget, my dear daughters, the part she has had in the foundation of the Institute. Without her, your congregation would never have existed; she was the worthy collaborator of Mère Julie. While remembering one you can't forget the other because they were never separated. Yes, you can without fear of being deceived, say of them what the Church sings of Saint John and Saint Paul: They are united for eternity![21]

His words bore testimony to the perfection of true friendship as lived by Françoise and Julie. Together, they had grown into that union to which Saint Francis liked to refer, quoting from Saint Paul, as the "bond of perfection."[22] Sharing this bond of perfection, God drew them together, first to bear the fruits of the foundation of the congregation of the Sisters of Notre Dame and in time, through the process of purification, to a unity in detachment, to a true unity in diversity. Their friendship's very raison d'être, its limits and its orientation were wholly in God, as they assured each other in various ways again and again, in thought, word and deed. It had permitted each to exercise to the fullest extent her personality, thereby bringing out the best in each while, at the same time, enabling each to participate in the other's qualities.

Françoise Blin de Bourdon's influence extends to the present through the life of the congregation she had helped to establish. From the small seeds planted, first in Amiens, France, in 1804, and then in the diocese of Namur in 1807, fruit has been harvested worldwide. It was from Antwerp, Belgium, in 1840 that her spiritual daughters, the Sisters of Notre Dame, first became missionaries to the New World, setting sail for Cincinnati, Ohio. Others would follow for mission territories in Britain (1845) and in Africa (1894). Today, Sisters of Notre Dame can be found on five of the world's seven continents. Unquestionably, her story is the story of a loving woman's potential for influencing the course of history through the way of friendship.

NOTES

Acknowledgments

1. "She esteemed the congregation as she would her mother and she loved it as her child. She devoted herself to it, body and soul." Françoise Blin de Bourdon, *Mémoires* (Rome: Tipografia P.U.G., 1978), p. 380. Translation is my own.

Preface

1. *The American Heritage Dictionary: Second College Edition* (Boston: Houghton Mifflin Company, 1982).

2. Paul J. Wadell, C.P., "Friendship: Pastoral-Liturgical Tradition," *The Collegeville Pastoral Dictionary of Biblical Theology,* Carroll Stuhlmueller, C.P., et al., eds. (Collegeville, Minn.: The Liturgical Press, 1996), p. 351.

3. Julian Haseldine, "Friendship, Equality and Universal Harmony," *Friendship East and West: Philosophical Perspectives,* Oliver Leaman, ed. (Surrey, U.K.: Curzon Press, 1996), p. 202.

4. Wadell, "Friendship: Pastoral-Liturgical Tradition," p. 352.

5. From *Confessions I, I/Oeuvres...IV*, p. 187, quoted in Terence A. McGoldrick, The *Sweet and Gentle Struggle: Francis de Sales on the Necessity of Spiritual Friendship* (Lanham, Md.: University Press of America, 1996), p. 67.

I. To the Manor Born: 1756–1794

1. Fighting started once again in 1756 among those European powers who wished to take control of the continent: Austria, Prussia, Russia and France. This time the European states divided themselves into two blocks: Austria, France, Russia and Sweden against Britain,

Hanover (a German state) and Prussia. Lasting for seven years, it ended only when a new czar, Peter II, came to power in Russia. He wanted peace, and the treaty that ended the fighting was signed in Paris in 1763. In the meantime, and in addition to losing land in Canada and India to Britain, France's livestock was depleted, its soil was starved, it was near bankruptcy commercially and the government was inefficient and corrupt. It would not be until the era of Napoleon that France would fully recover from the effects of the Seven Years' War.

2. John McManners, *The French Revolution and the Church* (New York: Harper and Row, 1969), p. 5.

3. Ibid., p. 12.

4. Ralph Gibson, *A Social History of French Catholicism: 1789–1914* (London: Routledge, 1989), p. 1.

5. Taken from the *Souvenirs de Mademoiselle Ursule* and quoted in Clara Tomme, S.N.D. de N., *Histoire de la Vénérée Mère Saint-Joseph* (Marchienne-au-Pont: L.Téchy-Tomme, 1920), pp. 10–11. This and all subsequent references to this invaluable resource are my own translations.

6. Ibid., pp. 12–13.

7. Ibid., p. 12.

8. The formation of good wives and mothers was Madame de Maintenon's idea of a good education. Because she distrusted the corrupt society of late-seventeenth-century France, she preferred to have boarders who would be separated from their families. During their stay at Saint-Cyr, usually between the ages of seven and twenty, the girls were not permitted to have any home vacation, and visits with families were restricted to only thirty minutes every three months. "Founded in 1686, the Maison Royale de Saint Louis was at first a secular institution for impoverished noble girls where Mme de Maintenon's *bel esprit* mingled with a certain religiosity. Believing in women's inferiority, she aimed to form girls into good but secular Christians, hard-working [and] capable of fulfilling their duties as wives and mothers according to their station. Hoping to provide good husbands for all her girls, she 'trained her pupils in the domestic arts, the techniques of household management and finances....' Moral education took precedence over intellectual education: the formation of character and the development of a sense of responsibility were theretofore most important. Mme de Maintenon's ideal woman was sensible, modest, discreet, and one who knew how to listen...The curriculum at Saint-Cyr included reading, writing, arithmetic, grammar, the lives of the saints, music, drawing, dancing, practical crafts, needlework, and sewing. Omitted were novels, physical and

natural sciences, ancient philosophy, history—except for the lives of a few great men." (Jeanne Masteller, *"Education of French Women in the Seventeenth and Eighteenth Centuries"* [master's thesis, Wright State University, 1986], pp. 50–51.) At Saint-Cyr, the programs varied according to age: from seven to twelve: reading, writing, arithmetic, grammar, catechism and the scriptures; from twelve to fourteen, history, geography, mythology; from fourteen to eighteen, French, musical culture, dance and religious instruction; from sixteen to twenty, religion, music, French and discussions of moral problems.

9. From *Témoignage de la Soeur Reine,* quoted in Tomme, p. 17.

10. Tomme, p. 18.

11. Bishop de la Motte was born in Carpentras, January 13, 1683, and educated by the Jesuits in that city. Not wishing to partake of "worldly glories," he entered with the Trappists at Sept-Fonds. However, due to the unanimous desire of the clergy as well as the nobles and other people of his province, he resumed his position outside of the monastery. He was appointed bishop of Amiens in 1733. He said that he had not expected to be *"Monseigneurised"* so soon and that he would not yet assume the title. His sincere objections were not accepted and, en route to his new post, he made a stop in Versailles to greet Cardinal de Fleury. A minister to the court, de Fleury asked him if he had traveled far: "Without needing to travel too far, in two days, to the two ends of the world: that of 'la Trappe' and the Court." See Cristiani, L., *Madame de Franssu, Fondatrice de la Congrégation de la Nativité de Notre-Seigneur. (1751–1824)* (Avignon: Aubanel Frères, 1926), p. 24; translation my own.

12. Pope Clement XIII (1758–69) instituted this feast on February 6, 1765. The devotion draws upon the popular sense of the heart as the seat of a person's inner life, an important emphasis in Salesian spirituality. The maxim that guided Francis de Sales and that became the motto of the Visitation community, which he founded with Jeanne de Chantal, was *"Vive Jésus!"* It was to be engraved on one's heart as the inmost and vital core of personhood. The devotion was bequeathed to the Society of Jesus by its founder, Ignatius of Loyola (1491–1556). John Eudes (1601–80) composed a Mass and Office of the Sacred Heart, and the private revelations of Margaret Mary Alacoque (1647–90) at Paray-le-Monial (1673–75) promoted the devotion and shaped its practice. By this devotion, Jesus Christ is venerated as the Word of God incarnate and his physical heart united to his divinity is seen as the symbol of his redemptive love. In 1765, the bishops of Poland were allowed to celebrate the feast of the Sacred Heart, which

was extended to the universal Church in 1856. It is celebrated on the Friday after Corpus Christi. A significant devotion during this period in history, it is said to have brought consolation to Louis XVI while he was imprisoned. As one of his last acts, he is said to have consecrated himself and his kingdom to the Sacred Heart before he was guillotined. Unfortunately, the devotion became politicized when it was almost exclusively associated with conservative royalists during the counter-Revolution.

13. Tomme, pp. 20–21.

14. The Ursulines had been founded by St. Angela in the early sixteenth century. The principal work of this society was the Christian education of young girls. It was the first religious order of women to have education as its special aim. Girls were educated in monasteries, but no prior religious society had been created to conduct schools. While it is true that the first Ursulines devoted themselves as well to "pious works," it was to reach young girls that Angela Merici introduced into her rule visits to the sick and the poor. See Marie de St. Jean Martin, O.S.U., *Ursuline Method of Education.* (Rahway: Quinn & Boden, 1946), pp. v–vi.

15. See Martin, ibid., for a complete treatment of this topic.

16. Tomme, p. 24.

17. Quoted in Will and Ariel Durant, *The Story of Civilization: Rousseau and Revolution* (New York: MJF Books, 1967), p. 97.

18. Recounted by her nephew, the viscount Alexandre Blin de Bourdon, and quoted in Tomme p. 32. With respect to the friends of Madame Elisabeth, a biographer notes: "Madame Elisabeth was so kind to those about her, but all her life she continued to practice prudence in choosing her friends....In return for the friendship that she gave, the holy Princess, without doubt, desired affection, but the appreciation that she always preferred was that of good conduct in those she loved. 'If you place any value on my friendship, please believe that it is to your becoming conduct that you owe it.' Or: 'If I but know that a person behaves as she should, my friendship is requited.'" See Yvonne de La Vergne, *Madame Elisabeth of France.* Cornelia C. Craigie, trans. (London: B. Herder, 1957), pp. 53–54. In her biography, Noelle Destremau cites a prayer recited each day by Elisabeth while she was held prisoner at the Temple, a prayer that testifies to her faith in and abandonment to the will of God. See *Une Soeur de Louis XVI: Madame Elisabeth* (Paris: Nouvelles Éditions Latines, 1983), p. 9. Indeed, Pope Pius VII is quoted as saying, while residing at the Tuileries, Pavillon de Flore, where Elisabeth was also lodged: *"J'habite l'appartement d'une sainte"* ["I am living

in the apartment of a saint"]. (Ibid., p. 10). Madame Elisabeth was guillotined on May 10, 1794, at the age of thirty. Another prayer attributed to her, in addition to the act of resignation referred to above, is located in the biography by Monique de Huertas, *Madame Elisabeth: Soeur de Louis XVI* ([Paris: Librairie Académique Perrin, 1995], p. 421). It is a devotional prayer to the Sacred Heart and was confided by Elisabeth to her good friend Madame de Raigecourt before the departure of the latter in 1789, along with other émigrés.

19. The Dauphin Louis de France, the father of Louis XVI, died in 1765. At that time Louis-Auguste, age eleven, became heir to the throne.

20. John Lough, *An Introduction to Eighteenth-Century France* (London: Longmans, 1960), p. 196.

21. Durants, *Rousseau,* p. 99.

22. The parish priest at Gézaincourt, the Abbé Bray, would later testify that Françoise had the habit of spending long hours in prayer after daily Mass, for which she herself prepared the altar. She would spend entire Sundays in church, decorating the altar and preparing the sacred vessels for the ceremonies. She organized beautiful processions to celebrate the feast of Corpus Christi, practicing the children for the procession and teaching the girls to sing with devotion. She set up a repository in the manor house and decorated all the village wayside altars. Villagers noted that she embroidered magnificently and carefully tended the priestly vestments. "Her name was synonymous with charity," they affirmed. From the *Témoignage de M. l'Abbé Bray, curé de Gézaincourt,* quoted in Tomme, pp. 41–42.

23. Blin de Bourdon, Françoise, *Écrits spirituels* (Namur, Belgium: General Archives, Sisters of Notre Dame), BC 272.

24. See Tomme, p. 48.

25. Alan Forrest (*The French Revolution and the Poor* [Oxford: Basil Blackwell, 1981], p. 5) supplies these details with respect to the diet of the mass of the people: "The normal peasant diet can be briefly summarized, consisting primarily of cereals, usually in the form of bread, though often supplemented by various forms of gruel. The basic hot dish of the day was *la soupe,* of which, once again, bread was the staple component, with the result that bread was the basis of every single meal the peasant consumed. It was, of course, variously supplemented, by milk products, by some fruit and vegetables, sometimes by fish which supplied the bulk of the protein since meat was very rare indeed. Wine or cider would accompany some meals, but even in wine-producing areas the crop was for sale and not primarily for the local people."

26. See Durants, *Rousseau*, chap. 37, especially.

27. George Lefebvre, *The Great Fear of 1789: Rural Panic in Revolutionary France*, Robert Forster and Orest Ranum, eds. (Baltimore: Johns Hopkins University Press, 1977), pp. 12–13.

28. André Dumont was born in Oisemont, in the department of the Somme, on May 24, 1764. During the Terror, thinking he needed to "run with the wolves," he was given to inflated discourse in order to appear more fearsome than he really was. In actuality, the guillotine was less busy in Amiens than it was in other cities of France, and Dumont admitted, after the period of the Terror had passed, that he had caused "more ink than blood" to spill (Cristiani, pp. 61–62; translation my own).

29. A Madame Carpentier, an octogenarian in 1879, recalled clearly that during the height of the Terror, Mademoiselle Blin was hidden in an attic in the Carpentier home when Monsieur Blin was taken away by revolutionaries. Later, when Monsieur Blin returned to Gézaincourt, he presented Madame Carpentier's father with a gift to thank him for his devotion in a time of adversity. Tomme, p. 54.

30. Tomme, pp. 55–56.

31. From the *Mémoires de Soeur Stéphanie Warnier*, quoted in Tomme, p. 56.

32. Ibid., p. 58

33. Quoted in Tomme, p. 59.

34. See Tomme, p. 505.

II. For Carmel Bound: 1794–1803

1. Quoted in Tomme, p. 60.

2. "If, when the Revolution is over," Joseph Lebon had said, "we still have the poor with us, our revolutionary toils will have been in vain." McManners has offered the following explanation for the erratic nature of this revolutionary official, appointed to the department in which the Blin de Bourdon family resided: "In the days of the Thermidorian reaction he seemed doubly sinister as a terrorist, for he had made arrangements at Arras to give émigré property to the poor. At his trial Lebon claimed that there had been a continuity between his life as an Oratorian and his work as a terrorist–'I derived most of my revolutionary maxims from the Gospels which, from beginning to end, preach against the rich and against priests....' Lebon was only a moderate de-Christianizer. He detested priests, and tried to force them to marry by the threat of conscription, but he did not close churches and he tried to ensure

that clerical pensions were paid. Perhaps the ultimate explanation of his mingled harshness and sympathy is found in his private life—his mother's insanity, brought on, he believed, by the fulminations of the orthodox clergy, and his brief, idyllic marriage to his cousin, Elisabeth Régnier." See *The French Revolution and the Church.* (New York: Harper & Row, 1969), p. 91.

3. Tomme, p. 62.

4. The story of the Carmelites of Compiègne bears retelling. In that city, the Committee of Surveillance indicated that the former nuns, supported by their *dévotes,* were maintaining their communal life and rituals. The committee suspected that they were in criminal correspondence with "fanatics" in Paris. In July, 1794, the Carmelites were tried by the Committee of Public Safety and accused of hiding arms in the convent. One of their number drew out a crucifix and said, "here are the only arms we have ever had in our house." Arrested, brought to Paris and condemned for treason, the Carmelites sought to use their time in prison to convert their guards and their fellow prisoners. Marie de l'Incarnation, the natural daughter of the Prince de Conti, was absent from the house when the group was arrested, and for years afterward she wandered around France as a refugee. She reentered the Carmel at Sens in 1823 and recorded various eyewitness accounts of her sisters' end. They had recovered enough of their habits to go as nuns to the guillotine. As they mounted the tumbrils, they began to sing. The crowds of Paris were abashed. Onlookers testified to the silence as the chanting nuns were driven through the streets. Even the rattling drums that customarily accompanied the death of an aristocrat were silenced. The prioress received permission to shepherd her flock before her and each nun renewed her vows and asked the prioress for permission to mount the scaffold. The novice went first, singing the "Laudate Dominum." A Sister Julie, who had so feared the scaffold, refused her family's attempt to free her. "We are the victims of this age," she proclaimed, "and we should sacrifice ourselves for its reconciliation with God." See Jo Ann Kay McNamara, *Sisters in Arms: Catholic Nuns through Two Millennia* (Cambridge: Harvard University Press, 1996), pp. 561–62.

5. Tomme, p. 62.

6. The countess (?–1796) lived in Paris with her husband and three daughters. She spent her summers in the environs of Cuvilly, where her father, Charles Adrien Prévot, count d'Arlincourt, sometimes joined her. Through Father Dangicourt, she and other pious ladies of the neighborhood frequently visited the invalid Julie Billiart.

The count d'Arlincourt so admired Julie that he included her in his will. In May of 1794, he and several other farmers general of the revenue were executed, and in July of the same year Count Baudoin followed. See Françoise Blin de Bourdon, *The Memoirs of Mother Frances Blin de Bourdon,* Thérèse Sullivan, S.N.D., trans. (Westminster, Md.: Christian Classics, 1989), p. 233.

7. See Roseanne Murphy, S.N.D. de N., *Julie Billiart: Woman of Courage* (Mahwah, N.J.: Paulist Press, 1995), for a more complete background.

8. Nonjuring priests were those who had refused to take an oath of allegiance to the Civil Constitution of the Clergy. This constitution, voted in on July 12, 1790, and reluctantly sanctioned by King Louis XVI the following December, attempted to limit interference on the part of the Holy See in Rome in French Church matters. Essentially, it aimed at making the clergy of France an official body of civil servants in the service of the State. The ministers of religion were to be remunerated by the State and all had to be elected to their positions: the bishop by the electoral assemblies of the department and the parish priest by the assembly of the district. Assistants could be selected by the parish priest. Because relations with Rome were already strained and because the Civil Constitution implied that bishops and parish priests could be elected by assemblies that included non-Catholics, the Civil Constitution was condemned by Pius VI (1775–99) in March of 1791. In the meantime, many republicans suspected the nonjuring or refractory priests of being in sympathy with the royalists and, therefore, enemies of the revolution.

9. Madame de Pont l'Abbé spent the summer months at Gournay-sur-Aronde, near Cuvilly. While there, she had the custom of engaging Father Dangicourt, the pastor of Cuvilly, as tutor for her son. This priest had introduced her to Julie Billiart.

10. Blin, *Memoirs,* p. 4.

11. Félicité supported herself and her aunt through her lace making, an industry that employed the largest numbers of women in northern and central France and in the country as well as in the towns. Its value lay almost entirely in the handiwork and was a livelihood highly dependent on the dictates of fashion, "a luxury industry with an aristocratic and an international clientele." On the eve of the Revolution, lace making was the most flourishing female industry in France, even if the lace maker received but a pittance for the labor that would often ultimately take her sight. By the 1790s there was an almost uniform drying up of luxury industries, many of them the preserve of women. This was

due partly to the emigration of a wealthy clientele, partly to the suspension of international trade and partly to the emergence of much more austere fashion. For example, the lace industry depended on fichus, cravats, ruffles, petticoat edging, the paraphernalia of a girl on a swing in a *fête galante.* See Olwen Hufton, "Women in Revolution," in *French Society and the Revolution,* Douglas Johnson, ed. (London: Cambridge University Press, 1976), pp. 149, 150, 154.

12. McGoldrick, p. 65.

13. Françoise's ministrations to Julie reflect the Lucan ideal of friendship. Luke's lack of a unified "philosophy" of friendship distinguishes him from ancient authors on the topic. St. Luke, in his focus on utopian allusions, appeals to the friendship tradition to question the cultural expectation of giving for a return. He challenges the ethic that limits reciprocity to a selfish aim and he does this by suggesting how Lucan Christians can become friends across status divisions, thereby extending the normally practiced conventions of friendship. The stories of Barnabas and others in Acts show cases where individuals retained their property until there was need. After voluntarily selling it, they donated the proceeds to the community for the welfare of its members by means of a ritual gesture of placing the proceeds at the apostles' feet, a gesture more clearly depicted in some translations. Whereas authors like Aristotle and Cicero used the friendship maxim to uphold the social order of their day, Luke wanted the status people of his community to transfer some of their benefits to those without status, through the institution of friendship, which normally would have kept the two societal levels separate. In other words, Luke used an institution very familiar to people of means, friendship, to get them to share their possessions with those without means. Friendship between nonequals was possible, but then it took on the trappings of patron-client relationship and the expectations changed. See Alan C. Mitchell, "The Social Function of Friendship," in *Journal of Biblical Literature* (111/2): pp. 257–72.

14. McGoldrick, p. 174.

15. For this and other reasons, I object to Jo Ann Kay McNamara's perspective on the initiation of the relationship between the foundress and cofoundress of the Sisters of Notre Dame de Namur wherein she states: "Women, who worked for a living as servants, like Margaret Hallahan, or were, like Julie Biliart [sic], self-employed as dressmakers, cultivated relationships with influential women or clergy through charitable work and secured their patronage while advancing into the religious life." Such a rendition gives the impression of manipulation on Julie's part.

The friendship of Françoise Blin and Julie Billiart was one of definite mutuality, a choice that both women made. Further, at the time of their meeting and through the early years of their friendship, Julie had no clear idea of founding a religious congregation for which she needed to secure patronage. See McNamara, p. 619.

16. Antoine Thomas (1753–1833) was born in Normandy, France, on September 23, 1753. He was a teacher at the Sorbonne and vicar at St.-André-les-Arts in Paris, a priest known for his erudition as well as virtue. He refused to take the constitutional oath and was imprisoned at Arras and condemned. Serious illness delayed his scheduled execution, and he was subsequently liberated after the death of Robespierre. Continually pursued as a refractory, Father Thomas exercised his ministry secretly in Amiens. A Father of the Faith as of 1803, he became a Jesuit in 1814. See Blin de Bourdon, *Memoirs,* pp. 285–89.

It would be simplistic to draw clear-cut lines between those members of the clergy who took the oath and those who did not seeing them only in terms of a loyalty or a lack thereof toward the Church. One social historian, Ralph Gibson, sees the distinction largely in terms of a referendum on post–Council of Trent (1545–63), or Tridentine, Catholicism.

"Those who rejected the oath were, by and large, those who accepted a hierarchical Church, in which authority cascaded down from the Pope and the bishops, and in which laymen had no authority at all. Timothy Tackett has made a fascinating study of the justifications that *réfractaires* offered for their rejection of the oath; he observes that a great many of them 'viewed their predicament through the optic of a rigidly disciplined and hierarchical church, particularly as that church had been reordered and restructured after the Council of Trent and the Catholic Reformation.' They felt that the oath was part and parcel of a wider attack on hierarchy, through lay election, a role for the lower clergy in the government of dioceses, and so on. (This was no doubt one of the reasons why the bishops were almost universally hostile to the oath.) Those who swore the oath, the *jureurs,* tended by contrast to see themselves less as authority figures and more as priests operating in a lay community; they seem to have shared, in varying degrees, the Enlightenment ideal of the 'citizen priest'....There was an interesting minority, however, for whom the acceptance of the oath was motivated in part at least by an uneasiness about the dominant model of Catholicism under the ancien régime." See Gibson, *A Social History of French Catholicism: 1789–1914,* pp. 38–39.

At best, motives were mixed and often included "the logic of the cooking pot," since those who refused the oath were initially denied employment, whereas the material benefits of the reform were intended as a measure of long overdue justice. "Reasonable incomes and a chance of rising to the very summit of the hierarchy were to be the lot of clergy of the new Constitutional Church...." See John McManners, *French Ecclesiastical Society under the Ancien Régime* (Manchester, U.K.: Manchester University Press, 1960), p. 267. For others, it would simply be too hard to leave their people, their work and the niche in life that they loved. Further, the taking of the oath depended to a great extent on where one was located in France and reflected the attitudes of the local populace. "To understand the decision of a parish priest one needs to study, not only his own career, but also the revolutionary record of his family and relations, the opinions of his parishioners, and the state of local popular feeling for or against the Revolution." See McManners, *The French Revolution and the Church,* p. 54. In towns, generally "the oath was refused, and while one reason may be found in the superior education and theological enlightenment of the urban priesthood, probably more weight should be put on its greater cohesion. An isolated country curé would come into town to consult his oracles...." See McManners, *French Ecclesiastical Society,* p. 270. Seminaries and faculties of theology were united in opposition to the oath, as were communities of nuns. They shared a desire for orthodoxy and were determined to have no communication with schismatics. In some instances, the oath was taken with certain reservations, stated or implied, to ease the conscience; in others it was taken in the honest belief that the Civil Constitution would not be condemned by the pope since the question of its canonical approval had been under negotiation for several months. Of the 130 diocesan bishops of France, only four took the oath and, perhaps not surprisingly, Talleyrand was of their number. Over time, more aggressive steps were taken against the nonjuring priests. They emigrated in large numbers and, after 1792, if found in France, faced the guillotine or deportation to French Guyana. Some stayed behind in hiding.

17. Louis de Montfort, one of the saints of the seventeenth-century French School of Spirituality, had stressed the importance of devotion to the mother of God in the spiritual life and taught that "devotion to Mary 'is necessary, simply and solely because it is a way of reaching Jesus perfectly, loving him tenderly and serving him faithfully'" Quoted in Patrick Gaffney, S.M.M., "Louis-Marie Grignion de Montfort," *Alive for God in Christ Jesus: A Conference Exploring Contemporary Influences from the French*

School of Spirituality (Buffalo: St. John Eudes Center, 1995), p. 207. Marianism was strong in the eighteenth century, especially among women. It became even more so during the Revolution, among *sans-culotte* women who related to the suffering mother of God, who also lost her son in a good cause, and even more so among the counterrevolutionary women. "As the Roman Catholic faith progressively became a fortress faith it was driven back into the home and hence largely into the hands of women. It became a faith based on the rosary with its ten Hail Marys for the one Our Father. The rosary was the perfect expression of a fortress faith. It offered the one means whereby the simple and illiterate, stripped of a priesthood and the familiar rituals of church ceremony, could maintain contact with their deity and could do so collectively. The congregation was replaced by the smaller unit of the family or the work group gathered, perhaps for a *veillée*....The recitation of the rosary, for centuries encouraged by churchmen, now gained new significance as the expression of a corporate faith" See Olwen Hufton, *Women and the Limits of Citizenship in the French Revolution* (Toronto: University of Toronto Press, 1992), p. 108.

18. Quoted in McGoldrick, p. 65.

19. Letter 1, July 15, 1795, in *The Letters of St. Julie Billiart,* Sister Frances Rosner, S.N.D. and Sister Lucy Tinsely, S.N.D., trans. (Rome: Gregorian Press, 1974), p. 20. This and all subsequent references to the letters of Julie Billiart will be taken from this edition and will be indicated by date only. There is no extant correspondence from Françoise Blin from this early period, her first extant letter being dated August 19, 1807.

20. Billiart, *Letters,* around August 1, 1795.

21. Ibid., July 15, 1975.

22. McManners, *French Revolution and the Church,* p. 118. The courageous minority, primarily women, who attempted to open the available church buildings found them to have been sold, demolished or in a dangerous state of ill-repair. As Boissy d'Anglas had declared in his speech the day his decree was passed: "The best way of slaying the Church is to grant it a disdainful toleration" See C. S. Phillips, *The Church in France: 1789–1848.* (New York: Russell & Russell, 1966), p. 31. Notwithstanding, the Thermidoreans, those responsible for the overthrow of Robespierre and his Jacobins, had unwittingly assisted in the revival of religion and, more specifically, in the reconstruction of the Catholic Church, by withdrawing patronage of a state cult and pronouncing *"la liberté des cultes"* [freedom of religion]. See Olwen Hufton, "The Reconstruction of a Church 1796–1801," in *Beyond the Terror,*

Lewis G. and C. Lucas, eds. (London: Cambridge University Press, 1981), p. 36. The effect produced a remarkable revival in both the constitutional and nonjuring Churches. Nonjuring priests were now immune from prosecution as Catholics but still held suspect as royalist sympathizers. Émigré priests returned in masses. Not all authorities were pleased with this turn of events, but there was widespread pressure on them to allow it. Both the constitutional clergy and the "*réfractaires*" were active and many of the faithful did not seem to have been bothered by this fact, "so long as services were held and religious baptism, marriage, and burial were available. There seems to have been much less enthusiasm for catechism and confession, both key elements of Tridentine Catholicism; what people wanted was not to be indoctrinated and controlled, but a religion concerned with parish life (centered on church services) and rites of passage." See Gibson, *A Social History of French Catholicism,* p. 46.

23. "*Nonante cinq,* as 1795 was referred to in popular lore, was dubbed by Richard Cobb as the year of the loss of illusions. By this he meant that there was an official abandonment of the pretence that government policies had been sound or had worked but for the opposition of a dissident minority. Colin Jones called it the year of the U-turns. Policies to which there had been an apparently total and explicit commitment since 1790, such as the right of the poor–specifically defined–to state assistance, were dropped without any real dissent. The politicians opted, at least temporarily, for religious tolerance: they opened the prison doors and they stopped pretending that the state could succour the poor and extolled the virtues of *bienfaisance individuelle*" [private or individual exercise of works of charity]. See Hufton, *Women and Limits,* pp. 134–35.

24. Billiart, *Letters,* October 21, 1795.

25. Ibid., February 1796.

26. Blin, *Écrits;* translation my own.

27. Billiart, *Letters,* February 1797.

28. Ibid., February 4, 1796.

29. Ibid., February 1796.

30. Ibid., February 1797.

31. Ibid., February 1797.

32. Doubtlessly, this is a reference to the highly popular spiritual classic commonly attributed to Thomas À Kempis, *L'Imitation de Jésus-Christ,* much in vogue in the spirituality of the time.

33. Blin, *Écrits.*

34. Ibid.

35. Billiart, *Letters,* March 1797.

36. Blin, *Memoirs,* p. 6.

37. Ibid.

38. Quoted in Tomme, p. 107.

39. Will and Ariel Durant, *The Story of Civilization: The Age of Napoleon* (New York: MJF Books, 1975), p. 184.

40. Joseph-Désiré Varin (1769–1850) was born on February 7, 1769, in Besançon, the youngest of three children of the president of the Parlement in that city. His parents gave him the name of one of their lands situated on the frontier with Switzerland, de Solman, by which he was often called.

In spite of his penchant for hunting and for the army, he studied for the seminary at Saint-Sulpice in Paris and was in his second year of theological studies at the beginning of the Revolution. Among his fellow seminarians were the princes Charles et Maurice de Broglie, the latter the future bishop of Ghent, de Villèle, future archbishop of Bourges, Eléonor de Tournely, and Etienne de Sambucy. He sought refuge in Switzerland with his family and joined the army of French princes concentrated near Coblentz.

Eventually, he was tempted to remain in the army and was distracted by a variety of diversions. Then, in May, 1794, he received from Louvain a letter that caused him to reflect more seriously about his commitment. He learned that the young priests, Charles de Broglie and Eléonor de Tournely, along with two others, wanted to begin a religious congregation, the Society of the Sacred Heart of Jesus, with the goal of reestablishing the Society of Jesus, which had been suppressed in 1773, and they invited him to join them. Greatly affected by their invitation, though still pursuing a military advancement, Joseph Varin hesitated. On July 18, 1794, he spent some time in prayer over the matter; he later learned that, on July 19, having been arrested after her return to France, his mother went to the scaffold praying for her son's vocation. He joined the new community, which established itself at Leuterhofen and followed closely the rule of the Company of Jesus. Their numbers grew dramatically.

Ordained in March of 1796, Varin became superior of the order, at the age of twenty-eight, at the death of de Tournely in July of 1797. In August of the same year, the Fathers of the Faith in Rome, founded by Father Paccanari, who had had the same intention of resurrecting the Society of Jesus, learned of the existence of the Fathers of the Sacred Heart and proposed a fusion of the two communities. After a period of mutual correspondence, the proposal was accepted, and Paccanari was made superior general. As of April 18, 1799, both congregations became known as the Fathers of the Faith.

At the time of his visits to Father Thomas in Bettencourt, Father Varin made the acquaintance of Julie Billiart while she was still bedridden. It was he who drew up the first provisional rule of the Sisters of Notre Dame. See Blin de Bourdon, *Mémoires,* pp. 382–85 and Cristiani, pp. 96–102.

41. Madeleine Sophie Barat (1779–1865) founded the Society of the Sacred Heart or *les Dames du Sacré Coeur,* in 1800, with the assistance of Father Varin, who was recommended to her by her older brother, Louis, a nonjuring priest at the time of the Revolution. Louis devoted himself to the ministry in the diocese of Paris and brought his gifted sister to the capital as a student and collaborator. He eventually joined the Fathers of the Faith and served as his sister's spiritual director with Jansenist rigor. The Amiens foundation of the community dates from 1801. Dedicated to the education of girls, the Society became known in the United States as of 1818 for the education of the daughters of the wealthy. Father Varin frequently sent the young religious superior, Madame Barat, to Julie Billiart, twenty-eight years her elder, and to Françoise Blin for guidance. As he wrote to Sophie Barat on July 1, 1803, "Go see the good Julie and Mademoiselle Blin and tell them that I will write to them soon, that I think about them every day." See Jeanne de Charry, R.S.C.J., *Joseph Varin S.J.: Lettres à Sainte Madeleine-Sophie Barat (1801–1849)* (Rome: n.p., 1982), p. 33; translation my own. Since the designation *Sacred Heart* was rendered suspect by the followers of Napoleon, the official name of Barat's congregation was, at the time, *les Dames de l'Instruction chrétienne,* or Ladies of Christian Instruction.

III. En Route to Namur: 1804–1808

1. Blin, *Memoirs,* pp. 7–8.

2. Victoire Leleu (1780–1823) was born at Chépy, near Abbeville. Knowing that his sister wanted to become a religious, her brother, Louis Leleu, introduced Victoire to Julie. She became Sister Anastasie, accompanied Julie on the missions at Valery-sur-Somme and Abbeville shortly after Julie's cure from paralysis and played an important role in the early years of the congregation. The first superior at Jumet, Soeur Anastasie became Mother St. Joseph's (Françoise's) assistant and the superior at Namur in 1816, after Julie's death. Julie often

referred to Soeur Anastasie as her *"petit conseil,"* [little counselor or adviser] and to Françoise she was *"mon grand conseil."*

3. It was under the guidance of Father Enfantin that Jeanne de Franssu, Françoise's good friend, would found in 1813 the *Congrégation de la Nativité de Notre-Seigneur* at Crest, a little village of the Drôme.

4. Blin, *Memoirs,* p. 10.

5. Blin, *Écrits.*

6. Ibid.

7. Ibid.

8. Blin, *Memoirs,* p. 11.

9. Blin, *Écrits.*

10. Ibid.

11. Phillips, p. 84.

12. Jean-François Demandolx was born in Marseille on September 20, 1744. At the time of the Revolution, he refused to take the oath of allegiance to the Constitution and sought refuge in the mountainous southwestern part of France, in Italy and in Germany. After the period of religious persecution, he returned to France, where he was named vicar general to the archbishop of Paris, Monseigneur de Belloy. Shortly afterwards, he was named bishop of La Rochelle and consecrated in Paris on February 2, 1803. Once at Amiens, he felt that his greatest challenge would be to reunite the still hostile juring and nonjuring secular clergy. Assessed initially by Julie and Françoise to be a "good and saintly prelate," he proved to be overly susceptible to the suggestions of his fellow priests. His erratic behavior seems to be due, in large part, to the fact that he was suffering from an incipient brain tumor that caused his death twelve and one-half years after his installation in Amiens.

13. Tallett relies on the Langlois study (see n. 14) when he cites that "[f]our hundred female *congrégations* were created between 1800 and 1880, and nearly one-quarter of a million women became novices in this period." See Frank Tallett, "Dechristianizing France: The Year II and the Revolutionary Experience," *Religion, Society, and Politics in France Since 1789,* Frank Tallett and Nicholas Atkin, eds. (London: Hambledon Press, 1991), p. 23. McNamara offers the following as a partial explanation of the phenomenon: "The congregation came close to capturing that elusive chimera, an order founded and administered by women. As secular women wrestled with the conflicting claims of family and society, sisters in religion experienced an ongoing ideological conflict between the humility and obedience expected of daughters of the church and the independence and authority of activists within

the women's sphere, sometimes far in advance of their secular contemporaries. Their feminine culture conflicted with a masculine culture of authority and obedience." See *Sisters in Arms,* p. 612. She also offers these characteristics of a *congrégation* to distinguish them from the historic monastic communities of nuns: "A congregation usually consisted of a number of small communities growing up in a single locality. A common novitiate in a common motherhouse formed their charism, that spiritual and vocational character that expressed itself outwardly in tailored devotional practices. A superior general coordinated a rule of life for all houses, which would enshrine their aspirations and guarantee their continuity....[T]he congregation developed a flexible and united sisterhood from a disparate set of local ties." See *Sisters in Arms,* p. 603. Rapley explains the controversy surrounding the establishing of *congrégations:* "In the course of the three centuries since Trent, the Catholic Church has succeeded in establishing a harmony between the contemplative and the active religious life....This only happened, however, after the day had been carried, in numerical terms, by the active orders. Throughout the nineteenth and twentieth centuries, the active congregations grew while the contemplative orders did not. By 1969, only 10 percent of all female religious in France were contemplatives. In the Old Regime the order was reversed: the *congréganistes* were always in the minority. In the seventeenth century they were still newcomers, in a society that was suspicious of change. In consequence, they had to build defenses, against attacks on their legitimacy, against the draining away of their best subjects into 'real' religious life. The quarrel between the active and the contemplative orders was continuous and, sometimes, bitter....[R]esistence to change was particularly strong in France, where the continuing power struggle against the Protestants prolonged the siege mentality of the sixteenth century well into the seventeenth. The first active congregations aroused sharp controversy when they sought dispensation from formal vows and strict clausura. The Council of Trent had forbidden religious women to leave the grounds of their monastery without express approval from their bishop....Novelty was heresy....In most quarters, the Church's need to rechristianize its people was not considered sufficient cause for any change in the monastic discipline of women." Elizabeth Rapley, *The "Dévotes": Women and Church in Seventeenth-Century France* (Montreal: McGill-Queen's University Press, 1990), pp. 168–69.

14. See Rapley's *The Dévotes* for an interesting history of this struggle. See also Claude Langlois, *Le Catholicisme au féminin: Les congrégations françaises à supérieure générale au XIXe siécle* (Paris: Les

Éditions du Cerf, 1984), for additional perspective on women's attempts to govern themselves in the face of adverse ecclesial and political circumstances.

15. These latter would pronounce their first vows on March 27, 1806, five months after Julie, Françoise, Victoire and Justine.

16. On June 19, 1806, the French government approved the statutes of the Sisters of Notre Dame. Then, on March 10, 1807, they were confirmed with Napoleon's signature while he was camped at Osterode.

17. Because the Society of Jesus was still suppressed and any references to it aroused suspicion, Julie continued to be called by her baptismal name for most of her religious life.

18. The plight of *enfants trouvés,* the myriads of children abandoned or left without parents for one reason or another, is undoubtedly one of the saddest stories of eighteenth-century France. Forrest, Hufton and Badinter, among others, have dealt extensively with this issue. Infant mortality rates as well as the number of deaths among those children who did end up in institutions are staggering by any measure. These children fared no better in the latter part of the era than they had before 1789. As Forrest states: "Throughout the years from 1795 to 1800 the whole structure of charitable provision for *enfants trouvés* seemed on the verge of total collapse. Occasionally belated money grants from Paris were received, and a threatening crisis passed once more. Or local short-term expedients might be tried, like the decision of the authorities in Metz in Year VI to pay their *nourrices* by selling off *émigré* lands, or the quite arbitrary distinction made at Bagnères whereby only those nurses caring for children under the age of seven would be paid, on the somewhat unscrupulous grounds that the hospital would lack the skills and resources to look after very young children if they were handed back. But the service was constantly tottering on the brink of disaster. For the *nourrices* were being treated very shabbily, their relative ignorance and isolation being played upon mercilessly by a government which could afford to regard them as a lower priority for scarce funds than the war effort or the requisitioning of food for Paris." See *The French Revolution and the Poor,* p. 131. Lack of space in institutions, too few personnel, overcrowding, rampant disease, scarcity of food and clothing (children were frequently made to stay indoors simply because they did not have the clothing to go out into the fresh air) were but a few of the related problems. It perhaps goes without saying that, lacking necessities, the education of these children was merely a distant dream.

19. Blin, *Memoirs,* p. 12.

20. Blin, *Écrits.*

21. Both the Blin de Bourdon town house and that of the Croquoison (de Franssu) family were nearby in the Faubourg-Noyon and were part of the parish of Saint-Michel.

22. Blin, *Memoirs,* p. 13.

23. Ibid.

24. Tomme, p. 136.

25. Testimony of Sister Stephanie Warner and quoted in Tomme, p. 137. Jesuit connections to the *congrégations* can be found almost everywhere and many of the religious orders consciously designed their communities as feminine complements to the Society of Jesus. One sister was to have said, "It was the blessed Father Ignatius who encouraged me to take up the teaching of girls." These congregations drew from the Society, not the subject matter taught, which was at the time considered to be too sophisticated for girls, but the educational methods, that is, discipline and pedagogy. Gradually, the religious women added to their curricula and strove to develop a more feminine pedagogy. (See Rapley, chapter 7, "Development of a Feminine Pedagogy.") Emulation and imitation played important roles in this pedagogy.

26. Pierre-Charles-Marie Leblanc (1774–1851) was born at Caen, Normandy, of a family of rank and fortune. At sixteen he was aide-de-camp to the marquis St. Simon, but when the Revolution drove the princes of the royal family into exile, he went with them. Having determined that the military life was not his calling, he went to Louvain to seek a profession and there met Xavier de Tournely. He accompanied Xavier on a visit to his brother, Father François Eléonor de Tournely, who with Father Charles de Broglie had established a house of the Society of the Fathers of the Sacred Heart on the outskirts of the city. After making a retreat, he joined the Society and remained in Belgium until the invasion of the French army in 1794, when he left with the group for Germany. On May 16, 1799, he was ordained and later, with the other members of the Society, joined with the Fathers of the Faith. In 1802, he had temporarily replaced Father Varin as superior in Paris when the latter was summoned to submit the statutes of the Society to the minister of religion. See Blin, *Memoirs,* pp. 260–63.

27. Louis-Étienne de Sambucy de St. Estève (?–1848) had been a seminarian at Saint-Sulpice with Joseph Varin, François Eléonor de Tournely and Charles and Maurice de Broglie, all of whom were under the direction of the well-respected Monsieur Emery. There they formed a group to encourage one another in theological study and in mutual

efforts to become good priests. After Sambucy was ordained and affiliated with the Fathers of the Faith, he became a professor at the college of the Faubourg-Noyon in Amiens. Initially appointed as confessor to the Sisters of Notre Dame, he was soon thereafter named ecclesiastical superior. As Françoise herself wrote in her *Memoirs:* "It must be acknowledged that Father de Sambucy had the intelligence and knowledge of social manners that would befit the head of an academy; but a house like ours with an aim so different needed someone with quite different qualities. After all, no one has a gift for everything. Mère Julie, who was manifestly chosen by God for the position she held, sometimes said: 'Father de Sambucy has many fine qualities, but he is not the man for our work. He is not the one we need.' Father Varin was of the same opinion. He told Mère Julie: 'Mother, I know he is not the person you need, but I have no one else to give you. You must do the best you can'" (p. 20).

28. Monseigneur Charles Molette, longtime church archivist in France, adds an interesting sequel to the Sambucy story. After attempting to alienate their communities from both Sophie Barat and Julie Billiart in 1806 and 1809, in 1819 he repeated his efforts by attempting to replace Jeanne-Antide Thouret, foundress of the Sisters of Charity of Besançon, with a superior completely submissive to his authority. This community ended up by locking out the foundress, and the majority who remained faithful to her became the congregation known as Charity of St. Jeanne Antide. It is noteworthy that all three foundresses who had dealings with Father de Sambucy were subsequently canonized!

29. Charles-François-Joseph Pisani (1743–1826), marquis de la Gaude was born in Aix-en-Provence the youngest of an illustrious family that had given two doges to Venice. Having completed his studies in law, he became a lawyer and then a member of the Parlement of Provence. He was engaged to a Mademoiselle d'Entrecasteaux, who died shortly before the wedding date. Subsequently, he had decided to become a Franciscan when his maternal uncle, the marquis de Reboul, who was bishop of St. Paul-Trois-Châteaux, persuaded him to become a secular priest. In 1783, he was named bishop of Vence. Refusing to take the constitutional oath, he was ordered before the revolutionary tribunal. Being close to the border, he escaped and sought refuge in Rome where he wrote his "Lettre pastorale de l'évêque de Vence sur l'obéissance au Souverain Pontife." After the signing of the Concordat of 1801, he went to Paris where his friend, Portalis, who had served with him on the Parlement at Aix, was the new minister of religion. Portalis introduced Bishop Pisani to Napoleon. Having heard of Julie and Françoise through the Fathers of the Faith, he invited the Sisters of

Notre Dame to begin an establishment in his episcopal city in 1806, and in 1807 the first foundation of the congregation in Namur was made on the rue du Séminaire. Bishop Pisani de la Gaude became a faithful friend and supporter of both of the foundresses. See Blin de Bourdon, *Memoirs,* pp. 275–76.

30. For more about this community in Bordeaux, see Rapley, chapter 3, "The Teaching Congregations of the Counter-Reformation (1598–1640)."

31. Blin, *Memoirs,* p. 15. What Françoise was inadvertently describing in explaining the unity that existed between herself and Julie what was Cicero had called *consensio.* "Friendship," he had said, "is indeed nothing other than *consensio* in all divine and human things with benevolence and affection" (quoted in McGoldrick, p. 48). Difficult to translate, the term can be rendered as a complete and absolute understanding accompanied by a mutuality of feeling. In other words, it is an accord or harmony of feelings and understanding between those who seek goodness (see McGoldrick, pp. 48–49).

32. Blin, *Memoirs,* p. 21.

33. The house was so named because it had been built by Cardinal de Bérulle who had studied with the Jesuits before founding the Congregation of the Oratory. It was then occupied by the college founded by the Jesuits before their suppression and maintained by Father Sellier in their tradition until the Revolution dispersed teachers and students. Subsequently, it was entrusted to Father Varin, superior of the Fathers of the Faith. Julie and Françoise had been thinking of obtaining this house for their congregation. For them, it had the added attraction of being very close to the Blin town home.

34. "As they freed themselves from a badly defined limbo between clergy and laity, women religious moved into the very center of religious public life....No longer recognizable as nuns in the traditional sense, many religious came to call themselves 'sisters,' while their superiors gave up the old aristocratic titles in favor of 'Mother.'...Strengthened by their new prominence in the world at large, they were more articulate in expressing their own goals and convictions than they had been in the established churches of the *ancien régime.*" See McNamara, p. 602.

35. Thérèse Boutrainghan was only about twenty-one years of age at the time. Françoise and Julie always wisely preferred someone older and of greater maturity for such a position. Further, Thérèse had been a domestic servant before entering, and Father Varin had counseled Julie and Françoise, for reasons of credibility, not to accept such in the congregation since the sisters were to be educators. It was Father de

Sambucy who had her enter the congregation and, having such a high opinion of her, named her superior. She subsequently left religious life. See Blin, *Memoirs,* p. 238.

36. Ibid., p. 17.

37. Blin, *Selected Letters,* to Mère Julie Billiart, at Bordeaux, August 19, 1807.

38. Ibid.

39. Ibid.

40. The imperial police under minister Fouché had been intercepting Father Varin's mail. They were suspicious of his activities and, consequently, were attempting to implicate him in some plot against Napoleon. Napoleon himself was worried about a resurgence of the Jesuits, expelled in 1764, and refused to let them reenter France. He admired them greatly, however, for their strict organization as a dedicated guild of teachers. "The essential thing," he wrote (February 16, 1805), "is a teaching body like that of the Jesuits of old" (Durants, *Napoleon,* p. 265). Napoleon's ideal of absolutism held suspect the existence of any other type of power or organization, especially one that had ties to Rome. Consequently, the Jesuits and those thought to be aligned with the Jesuits were outlawed. Had not Napoleon's own minister of cults, Portalis, written in a report dated 1803, "The Fathers of the Faith are only Jesuits in disguise."? It little mattered that Napoleon tended to confuse the Jesuits, the Fathers of the Sacred Heart and the Fathers of the Faith. The fact was that, until the end of the empire, the members of these congregations were dispersed and pursued by the police. See Jean Lacouture, *Jésuites* (Paris: Éditions du Seuil, 1991–92), vol. 2, p. 38; translation my own. In November, the Society of the Fathers of the Faith was dispersed, each priest being required to return to his own diocese. Ironically, this dispersal only facilitated the development of new apostolic works throughout France. On the other hand, the Society of Jesus had been re-established in the kingdom of the Two Sicilies in 1804. It had been the new Pope Pius VII's intention since 1800 to reinstate the Society completely. (See Alain Woodrow, *The Jesuits: A Story of Power* [London: Geoffrey Chapman, 1995], p. 87.)

41. Blin, *Selected Letters,* to Mère Julie Billiart, at Amiens, December 17, 1807.

42. Blin, *Memoirs,* p. 29.

43. Ibid., p. 31.

44. See McGoldrick, p. 201.

45. Blin, *Selected Letters,* to Mère Julie Billiart, at Amiens, February 6, 1808.

46. Ibid., February 14, 1808.

47. Blin, *Memoirs,* p. 34.

48. Blin, *Selected Letters,* to Mère Julie Billiart, at Amiens, undated, 1808.

49. Ibid., February, 25, 1808.

50. Blin, *Memoirs,* p. 36.

51. Blin, *Selected Letters,* to Mère Julie Billiart, at Amiens, April 1, 1808.

52. Nicholas-Joseph Minsart (1769–1837) was born in Linsmeau, Belgium. He had been an ordained Bernardine monk of the Abbey of Boneffe with the name of Dom Jérôme. After the pillaging, burning and selling of monasteries during the Revolution, the monks had been dispersed. Some of them had been taken as hostages, as was he. He was detained and strictly guarded at Mons for four months. At the end of the period of persecution, he enrolled at Louvain to study theology with Monsieur Devenise. When Devenise was called to Namur by the bishop to reorganize the seminary there, Father Minsart followed him and was named vicar (1806) then pastor (1808) of St. John the Evangelist Church in Namur. A trusted advisor to the Sisters of Notre Dame as well as a great source of moral support, it was he who located the property on the rue des Fossés for the young community, the property that was subsequently to become the site of the motherhouse. Responsible for building and restoring several churches, among which features the Chapel of Our Lady of the Ramparts in Namur, he later became pastor of the parish of St. Loup in 1813 and died in Namur. See Blin, *Memoirs,* pp. 268–69.

53. Blin, *Selected Letters,* to Mère Julie Billiart, at Amiens, April 1, 1808.

54. Billiart, *Letters,* April 7, 1808.

55. Tomme, p. 163.

56. Blin, *Memoirs,* pp. 54–55.

57. Blin, *Selected Letters,* to Sister Xavier Evrard, at Namur, June 23, 1808.

58. Blin, *Memoirs,* p. 43.

59. It is estimated that Napoleon gave official approval to about one thousand religious institutions by means of imperial decree from 1804 to 1814. The real explosion in women's congregations began after the Concordat and, more specifically, after 1808. At that time, they were reauthorized and even encouraged by both civil and ecclesiastical hierarchies. As Hufton states: "The decision to return to *bienfaisance individuelle,* to provide charity, to maintain the hospitals without effective

state monetary support, and to proclaim the need for home relief agencies created a space. To fill it was needed a personnel dedicated to fundraising who would work for relatively little and who could enter without flinching the hovels of the poor. Revolutionary rhetoric had not succeeded in providing willing women—the only people capable in the conditions of the day of assuming such work." See Hufton, *Women and Limits,* p. 144.

60. Lacouture, *Jésuites,* vol. 2, p. 38.
61. Blin, *Memoirs,* p. 50.
62. Ibid., pp. 55–56.
63. Ibid., p. 52.
64. Ibid., p. 53.

IV. Superior of the Motherhouse: 1809–1815

1. Quoted in McGoldrick, p. 183.
2. Ibid., p. 203.
3. Blin, *Memoirs,* p. 51.
4. Ibid., p. 54.
5. Ibid., p. 67.
6. Ibid., p. 62.
7. Ibid.
8. This old mansion of the Counts of Quarré was located on the site of the Boneffe abbey refuge, or monastery shelter, in the fortified town. It was the property of the Cistercians from 1463 to 1710. The main house with the garden was sold in 1710 and passed to the Counts of Quarré at the end of the eighteenth century. Françoise gives an account of its providentially designed sale to the Sisters of Notre Dame in her *Memoirs,* pp. 129–30.
9. Blin, *Memoirs,* pp. 62–63.
10. Ibid., p. 63.
11. Ibid.
12. Ibid., p. 65.
13. Julie and Françoise had been thinking of obtaining this house for their congregation. For them, it had the added attraction of being located just across the street from the Blin town home.
14. Jeanne Godelle entered when she was over thirty years of age. Well educated, with maturity of judgment, she was appointed by Julie to the office of mistress of novices at Amiens and then at Namur. Subsequently, she was named the first superior at the new foundation in Zele in 1811.

15. Blin, *Selected Letters,* to Mère Julie Billiart, at Namur, c. January 15, 1809.

16. Blin, *Memoirs,* p. 83.

17. Ibid., p. 92.

18. Ibid., p. 93.

19. Ibid.

20. Ibid., p. 94.

21. Because of the precarious state of religious orders with respect to Napoleon's Paris Plan, the bishop did not at present insist that the sisters make vows. As for the Sisters of Notre Dame, given the situation in Amiens, they were careful not to ask to make them for the time being. This, and the fact that there was not yet a permanent rule, facilitated their departure.

22. Blin, *Selected Letters,* to Mère Julie Billiart, at Namur, January 19, 1809.

23. Quoted in McGoldrick, p. 15.

24. Blin, *Selected Letters,* to Mère Julie Billiart, at Namur, January 30, 1809.

25. Ibid., February 1, 1809.

26. Blin, *Memoirs,* p. 96.

27. Ibid.

28. Blin, *Selected Letters,* to Mère Julie Billiart, at Namur, before February 14, 1809.

29. Ibid., February 10, 1809.

30. Ibid., to the Sisters of Montdidier, February 14, 1809.

31. Ibid., to Mère Julie Billiart, at Namur, February 20, 1809.

32. Ibid., February 22, 1809.

33. Ibid., February 4, 1809.

34. Blin, *Memoirs,* p. 101. Later that year, Jeanne wrote to Françoise to share with her that she had made "certain plans" that she hoped would be realized the following spring. Due to illness, however, she had to postpone her intention of beginning another religious community. With the assistance of Father Enfantin, her "angel," the Congregation of Sisters of the Nativity, which still exists, was started in 1813 at Crest. For her biography see, L. Cristiani, *Mme de Franssu.*

35. Blin, *Selected Letters,* to Mère Julie Billiart, at Namur, February 5, 1809.

36. Quoted in McGoldrick, pp. 87–88.

37. See Blin, *Memoirs,* p. 131.

38. Ibid., pp. 109–10.

39. Quoted in Tomme, p. 195.
40. Blin, *Selected Letters,* to Mère Julie Billiart, December 31, 1813.
41. Blin, *Memoirs,* p. 196.
42. Ibid., p. 198.
43. Blin, *Selected Letters,* to Mère Julie Billiart, December 29, 1815.

V. Mother General: 1816

1. Blin, *Memoirs,* p. 202.
2. Blin, *Selected Letters,* to Sister Anastasia, Superior at Jumet, February 9 (?), 1816.
3. Ibid., March 12, 1816.
4. Blin, *Memoirs,* p. 204.
5. Ibid., p. 203.
6. Tomme, pp. 199–200.
7. From the Annals of the Motherhouse, quoted in Tomme, p. 200.
8. Quoted in Tomme, p. 205.
9. Ibid.
10. Ibid., p. 206.
11. Ibid., p. 212.
12. From the testimony of Sister Reine and quoted in Tomme, p. 228.
13. The rule was, subsequently, submitted to Bishop Pisani of Namur, who officially gave his approval on September 8, 1818. Papal approval was accorded by Pope Gregory XVI on June 28, 1844. See Tomme, p. 235.
14. Sister Mary Linscott, S.N.D. de N., *This Excellent Heritage: An Introduction to the Constitutions of the Sisters of Notre Dame* (N.p: privately printed, 1995), p. 15.
15. McGoldrick, pp. 130–35.
16. Paul J. Wadell, C.P., "Friendship: Pastoral-Liturgical Tradition," *The Collegeville Pastoral Dictionary of Biblical Theology,* Carroll Stuhlmueller, C.P., ed. (Collegeville, Minn.: Liturgical Press, 1996), p. 351.

VI. Frenchwoman in a Dutch Domain: 1817–1823

1. Blin, *Selected Letters,* to M. Martin, Mayor of Thuin, December 7, 1816.
2. An observation made by Sister Marie Cornelia, one of the pioneers of the California foundation. Quoted in Tomme, p. 238.

3. Testimony of Sister Vincent, novice mistress, and quoted in Tomme, p. 239.

4. From the Annals of the Thuin foundation, quoted in Tomme, p. 247.

5. Bibliographic entry on Monsieur Blin de Bourdon from the *Physiologie de l'Assemblée nationale de 1848* and quoted in Tomme, p. 245.

6. Blin, *Selected Letters,* to Sister Angela Witmeere, superior at Dinant, September 26, 1818.

7. Blin, *Lettres,* to the sisters of Thuin, May 10, 1820. Unpublished and untranslated; translation my own.

8. Blin, *Selected Letters,* to Sister Marie Steenhaut, superior at Ghent, November 17, 1819.

9. Ibid., December 9, 1819.

10. A merchant in Ghent who rendered many services to the sisters there.

11. Blin, *Selected Letters,* to Sister Marie Steenhaut, superior at Ghent, June 26, 1820.

12. Quoted in Tomme, p. 265.

13. Blin, *Selected Letters,* to Sister Angela Witmeere, superior at Dinant, February 17, 1820.

14. Tomme, p. 271.

15. See Alois Simon, *Le Cardinal Sterckx et son Temps (1792–1867)* (Wetteren: Éditions Scaldis, 1950), p. 67.

16. Blin, *Selected Letters,* to Sister Eugenia Fermine at Thuin, October 27, 1820.

17. Ibid., to Sister Marie Steenhaut, superior at Ghent, March 31, 1821.

18. Ibid., to Sister Marie Thérèse Vandeputte, superior at Thuin, May 9, 1821.

19. Ibid., to Sister Marie Steenhaut, superior at Ghent, May 19, 1821.

20. Ibid., to Sister St. John, superior at Dinant, January 24, 1822. Unpublished and untranslated; translation my own.

21. In a letter of September 27, 1815, Françoise had written to Anastasie: "We're the two eldest daughters, who have seen and known the beginnings. It's not easy for the others to know how to appreciate our Mother as we do; but you know, as I do, that she was fashioned and prepared long beforehand and in an admirable manner for the work she's doing, and anyone who is willing to consider this work as a whole will see that it has been abundantly blessed in spite of all the harassments that human ignorance and weakness as well as the malice of the

devil can contrive." This was during a particularly difficult period for Julie when some of her own daughters questioned her willingness to adapt the rule to circumstances. They did not understand that the rule was, at the time, meant to be a provisional guide until a final one was completed. *Selected Letters,* to Sister Anastasia Leleu, superior at Jumet.

22. Quoted in Blin, *Memoirs,* pp. 266–67.

23. Quoted in Blin, *Memoirs,* pp. 263–67, and as quoted from the Register of the Deceased Sisters of Notre Dame, in Tomme, p. 281.

24. Blin, *Selected Letters,* to Sister St. John of the Cross Mallart, at Thuin, February 11, 1823.

25. In a letter to Sister Marie Lucie on February 19, 1823, Mother St. Joseph refers to Sister's loss of one eye.

26. Ibid., to Sister Marie Lucie Lavoine, superior at Liège, February 14, 1823.

27. Ibid., to Sister Marie Therese Vandeputte, superior at Thuin, March 6, 1823.

28. From a letter to Sister St. John of April 4, 1823, and quoted in Tomme, p. 282.

29. It was of Sister Marie Thérèse Vandeputte, the fourth superior general, that it was noted: "She esteemed the Congregation as her mother and loved it like her child; one can say that she devoted herself to her body and soul." From the Register of Deceased Sisters of Notre Dame in the Namur Archives and quoted in Tomme, p. 282.

VII. Naturalized Citizen of William's Kingdom: 1824

1. Blin, *Selected Letters,* to Sister Marie Lucie, superior at Liège, January 14, 1824.

2. Ibid., to Sister Marie Steenhaut, superior at Ghent, July 10, 1824.

3. Monsieur d'Omalius de Halloy, governor of the province of Namur and a man very favorably disposed toward the Sisters of Notre Dame.

4. Blin, *Lettres,* to Sister Regis, superior at Fleurus, July 26, 1824. Translation my own.

5. Secular subjects as opposed to the "great science," or study of the faith.

6. Blin, *Selected Letters,* to Sister Valerie Jacquemart, at Jumet, November 11, 1824. Born in Liège in 1801, Sister Valerie made her vows on September 12, 1826.

7. In a letter of April 1822, Mother St. Joseph had written to Sister Marie Lucie that there were 200 sisters in the congregation. And in her correspondence with Sister Marie Thérèse, she had written in July 1822, that there were 50 sisters at Namur.

8. See Tomme, p. 283.

VIII. Struggle for Survival: 1825–1829

1. From the Archdiocesan Archives at Namur, quoted in Tomme, p. 286.

2. Blin, *Lettres,* to Sister Angela, superior at Dinant, January 20, 1825. Translation my own.

3. Blin, *Selected Letters,* to Sister St. John Cardon, superior at St. Hubert.

4. From the letters of the viscount Blin de Bourdon in the Namur Archives and quoted in Tomme, p. 292.

5. Quoted in Tomme, p. 295.

6. Quoted in Tomme, pp. 296–97.

7. Blin, *Selected Letters,* to Sister St. John Cardon, superior at St. Hubert, February 22, 1826.

8. Ibid., March 28, 1826. At the time, the superiors and older sisters participated in the election of the superior general. On June 26, these sisters assembled at Namur and elected Mother St. Joseph for another term of ten years. She was elected on a "unanimity of votes, minus one, which was her own." From the Annals of the Motherhouse, quoted in Blin, *Selected Letters,* p. 365.

9. Ibid., to Sister Leocadie Hubin, superior at Thuin, June 28, 1826.

10. Ibid., to Sister Marie Lucie Lavoine, superior at Liège, October 23, 1826.

11. This collection is considered to be one of the finest ecclesiastical treasuries in Belgium today. Two of the magnificent pieces, many of which bear extremely delicate chasing with foliage and sometimes little hunting scenes, are a cover of a gospel, or "Evangelarium" of 1230 from Trier, decorated with enamel work, and the goblet of Gilles de Walcourt of 1238. The collection is officially designated as one of the "Seven Wonders of Belgium." There are a number of engraved articles of surpassing beauty: a jewel-encrusted cross, plates or patens for the sacred host, articles of wrought metal fashioned with such artistic talent and religious fervor that they were already regarded as masterpieces in the

time of Hugo von Oignies. They serve as an example of the perfect, unquestioning faith of his era.

12. Blin, *Selected Letters,* to Sister Marie Lucie Lavoine, superior at Liège, October 23, 1826.

13. Blin, *Lettres,* to Sister Angela at Dinant, March 20, 1827. Unpublished and untranslated; translation my own.

14. Georges Dumont, *Histoire de la Belgique* (Bruxelles: Éditions Le Cri, 1995), p. 418.

15. Blin, *Lettres,* to Sister Leocadie, superior at Thuin, July 28, 1827. Unpublished and untranslated; translation my own.

16. Dumont, p. 420.

17. Blin, *Selected Letters.,* to Sister Marie Lucie Lavoine, superior at Liège, July 23, 1827.

18. Ibid., to Sister Leocadie Hubin, superior at Thuin, April 21, 1827.

19. A Belgian phenomenon, Beguines date back to the twelfth century. This lifestyle gave to unmarried or abandoned women, women left on their own as a result of wars or the Crusades, and who sought a life of religious devotion, the opportunity to ally themselves to a secure and respected community without having to take religious vows. Consequently, they were allowed to own personal property. Originally from poor families and women for whom no dowry could be provided, the Beguines' main task was to wash wool and prepare it for the weavers, causing beguinages to be located near watercourses. Later, because of their popularity, women from all classes of society joined them, and they devoted themselves to the care of the sick or earned their bread by making lace. The head of the community was referred to as the Great Lady. They lived in small, individual houses protected by an enclosure, which also contained a church and an infirmary. At times, a larger building would shelter about ten Beguines. The first beguinage was that of Lambert-le-Bègue, in Liège, founded in 1173. See *Belgium: Abbeys and Beguinages* published by the Belgian National Tourist Office, Brussels, for the Year of Abbeys and Beguinages, 1973. A recommended recent publication, *Brides in the Desert,* by Saskia Murk-Jansen (New York: Orbis Books, 1998), deals with the origins, development and spirituality of the Beguines.

20. Quoted in Tomme, p. 313.

21. Blin, *Selected Letters,* to Sister Constantine Collin, teacher at Jumet, April 23, 1827.

22. Blin, *Lettres,* to Sister St. John, superior at St. Hubert, October 31, 1827. Unpublished and untranslated; translation my own.

23. Blin, *Selected Letters,* to Sister Leocadie Hubin, superior at Thuin, June 20, 1829.

24. In these cities, the local authorities were not so helpful to the sisters.

25. Blin, *Selected Letters,* to Sister Leocadie Hubin, superior at Thuin, June 20, 1829.

26. Ibid., to Sister Marie Lucie, superior at Liège, June 17, 1829.

27. From *Testimonies of Contemporaries* and quoted in Tomme, p. 322.

28. Blin, *Lettres,* to Sister Marie Steenhaut, superior at Ghent, October 7, 1829. Unpublished and untranslated; translation my own.

29. Blin, *Selected Letters,* to Sister Marie Lucie, superior at Liège, February 16, 1829.

30. Blin, *Lettres,* to Sister Marie Steenhaut, superior at Ghent, July 8, 1829. Unpublished and untranslated; translation my own.

31. Blin, *Selected Letters,* to Sister Gudule Dubois, superior at Fleurus, November 11, 1829.

32. Dumont, p. 424. Translation my own.

33. Ibid., p. 425. Translation my own.

34. Blin, *Selected Letters,* to Sister Angela Witmeere, superior at Dinant, November 27, 1829.

IX. Birth of a New Nation: 1830–1831

1. Blin, *Lettres,* to Sister Marie Steenhaut, Superior at Ghent. December 1, 1829. Unpublished and untranslated; translation my own.

2. Blin, *Selected Letters,* to Sister Marie Steenhaut, superior at Ghent, April 25, 1828.

3. The others were at Thuin and Zèle, along with St. Gilles and St. Jacques at Namur.

4. Blin, *Lettres,* to Sister Ignace, headmistress at Jumet, February 9, 1830. Unpublished and untranslated; translation my own.

5. Ibid., to Sister St. John and the Sisters of St. Hubert, April 23, 1830. Translation my own.

6. Ibid., to Sister Leocadie Hubin, superior at Thuin, August 3, 1830. Unpublished and untranslated; translation my own.

7. See Henry Dorchy, *Histoire des Belges des Origines à 1991* (Bruxelles: De Boeck, 1991), pp. 137–39.

8. Province in the center of Belgium formed by part of the former duchy of Brabant. It is separated by a linguistic frontier with Flemish

being spoken to the north and Walloon or French to the south. Brussels is located in this area.

9. Dumont, p. 429.

10. Blin, *Selected Letters,* to Sister Angela Witmeere, superior at Dinant, August 27, 1830.

11. Ibid., to Sister Leocadie Hubin, superior at Thuin, September 2, 1830.

12. Dorchy, p. 138. Translation my own.

13. Blin, *Selected Letters,* to Sister Leocadie Hubin, superior at Thuin, September 2, 1830.

14. Dorchy, p. 139.

15. Blin, *Selected Letters,* to Sister Aloyse Servais, superior at Verviers, September 25, 1830.

16. Dumont, p. 435.

17. Blin, *Selected Letters,* to Sister Marie Lucie Lavoine, superior at Liège, October 6, 1830.

18. Dumont, p. 439.

19. Blin, *Lettres,* to Sister St. John, superior at St. Hubert, December 17, 1830. Translation my own.

20. Ibid.

21. From the Annals of Verviers, quoted in Tomme, p. 333. Translation my own.

22. See Camille-J. Joset, S.J., "L'origine des Facultés de Namur 1831–1845," in *Études d'Histoire & d'Archéologie namuroises,* for a detailed account of the founding of Notre-Dame de la Paix in Namur.

23. Blin, *Selected Letters,* to Sister Angela Witmeere, superior at Dinant, August 3, 1831.

24. Blin, *Lettres,* to Sister Angela Witmeere, superior at Dinant, August 10, 1831. Translation my own.

25. Quoted in Tomme, p. 338.

26. From *Souvenirs of Contemporaries,* quoted in Tomme, p. 338. Translation my own.

27. Blin, *Selected Letters,* to Sister Celine Monseu, superior at Thuin, October 20, 1831.

28. Blin, *Lettres,* to Sister St. John, superior at St. Hubert, October 24, 1831. Unpublished and untranslated; translation my own.

29. Tomme, pp. 331–32.

30. Quoted from *Souvenirs of Contemporaries* in Tomme, p. 332. Translation my own.

X. Threat from Within: 1832–1835

1. Letter written by Mother St. Joseph to the Viscount Blin de Bourdon, January 1832, and quoted in Tomme, pp. 341–42.

2. Quoted in Tomme, p. 343.

3. Father Méganck, S.J. was rector at the new Jesuit college in Namur, Notre-Dame de la Paix. In the French text of her letter, Mother St. Joseph referred to Father Méganck as *Monsieur* Méganck, the title used for secular clergy. This was due to the fact that, until 1833, the Jesuits had to live more or less clandestinely as diocesan priests because of the opposition on the part of the liberals to the erection of their college in Namur.

4. Mother St. Joseph is referring to Julie and to Father Varin as founder and foundress. In her typically self-effacing fashion, she has left mention of herself as cofoundress out of the equation.

5. Blin, *Selected Letters,* to Sister Ignace, superior at Jumet, August 10, 1832.

6. The new bishop of Namur, Jean-Arnold Barrett, was of Irish descent on his father's side. Exiled by Napoleon in 1811, he returned to Liège in 1813 and was named vicar general in 1814. Consecrated on June 16, 1833, he immediately expressed his desire to visit his entire diocese. During the visitation he confirmed more than fifty thousand and returned exhausted to Namur.

7. Blin, *Lettres,* to Sister Marie Lucie Lavoine, superior at Liège, June 17, 1833. Unpublished and untranslated; translation my own.

8. From the *Souvenirs of Contemporaries,* quoted in Tomme, p. 348.

9. Blin, *Selected Letters,* to Sister Caroline Dubois, superior at Dinant, August 1, 1832.

10. Ibid.

11. From the Annals of the Congregation, quoted in Tomme, pp. 346–47.

12. Quoted in Tomme, p. 345.

13. Blin, *Selected Letters,* to Sister Marie Lucie Lavoine, superior at Liège, April 17, 1833.

14. Ibid., to Sister Ignace Goethals, superior at Jumet, May 7, 1833.

15. It seems particularly ironic that the two sisters at the heart of the plot, which almost led to a schism in this congregation that owed so much to Saint Ignatius and the Company of Jesus by way of its origins and apostolic spirit, had as names in religion the names of two of Ignatius's own original companions, Francis Borgia and Francis Xavier.

16. Blin, *Lettres,* to Sister Marie Steenhaut, superior at Ghent, May 15, 1834. Unpublished and untranslated; translation my own.

17. Blin, *Selected Letters,* to Sister Marie Lucie Lavoine, superior at Liège, September 5, 1834.

18. Ibid., to Sister Ignace, superior at Jumet, February 27, 1835.

19. Ibid., to Sister St. John Cardon, superior at St. Hubert, April 6, 1835.

20. Ibid., to Sister Ignace, superior at Jumet, May 25, 1835.

21. From the *Testimony of Sister Marie Virginie,* quoted in Tomme, p. 362.

22. Blin, *Selected Letters,* to Sister Ignace, superior at Jumet, June 1, 1835.

23. Ibid., June 16, 1835.

24. Ibid., to the Sisters of Jumet, June 1835.

25. Quoted in Tomme, p. 362.

26. From letters to Sister Julienne on July 4 and 15, 1835, quoted in Tomme, pp. 366–67.

27. Blin, *Selected Letters,* to Sister Marie Lucie Lavoine, superior at Liège, June 30, 1835.

28. Ibid., to Sister St. John Cardon, superior at St. Hubert, August 17, 1835.

29. The confidential seal was lifted in 1938 by Mother Monica of the Passion, superior general.

30. From *Souvenirs of Contemporaries,* quoted in Tomme, pp. 367–68.

XI. Woman of Influence: 1836 and Beyond

1. Blin, *Selected Letters,* to Sister Aloyse Servais, superior at Verviers, March 2, 1836. The reference to the "storm" refers, of course, to the recent attempts to "reform" the congregation.

2. Ibid., to Sister Constantine Collin, superior at Jumet, March 26, 1836.

3. From *Témoignages des contemporaines,* quoted in Tomme, pp. 372–73.

4. Ibid., p. 373.

5. The Sisters of Notre Dame continued the direction of Harscamp until December 1869.

6. Blin, *Selected Letters,* to Sister Aloyse Servais and the sisters of Verviers, January 1837.

7. The first railroad on the European continent had been constructed in Belgium, and the line from Brussels to Malines had been in operation since May 5, 1835. However, a line through Namur was still to be completed.

8. Letters from Sister Ignace to Sister St. Jean, May 31, June 30, July 31, 1837, quoted in Tomme, p. 388.

9. Ibid., December 1, 1837.

10. Tomme, p. 389.

11. Ibid., p. 390.

12. Ibid., p. 391.

13. Ibid.

14. Blin, *Selected Letters,* to Sister Marie Lucie Lavoine, superior at Liège, January 15, 1838.

15. Tomme, p. 393.

16. Ibid., p. 394.

17. Ibid., pp. 394–95.

18. Ibid., p. 397.

19. Just a little over a year after Julie's death, July 27, 1817, Mother St. Joseph had quietly overseen the transfer of her friend's remains from the municipal cemetery to the newly completed garden chapel. See Roseanne Murphy, S.N.D. de N., *Julie Billiart: Woman of Courage* (Mahwah, N.J.: Paulist Press, 1995), p. 192.

20. From the *Témoignage de Soeur Marie-Laurentine,* quoted in Tomme, p. 401.

21. From the Annals of the Motherhouse and quoted in Tomme, p. 403. Translation my own.

22. Col 3:14, quoted in McGoldrick, p. 179.

BIBLIOGRAPHY

Aelred of Rievaulx. *Spiritual Friendship.* Ed. M. Basil Pennington, O.C.S.O. Trans. Mary Eugenia Laker, S.S.N.D. Cistercian Fathers Series 5/2. Washington, D.C.: Cistercian Publications Consortium Press, 1974.

Bankson, Marjory Zoet. *Seasons of Friendship: Naomi and Ruth as a Pattern.* San Diego: LuraMedia, 1987.

Bernard of Clairvaux. *On Loving God.* Ed. Emero Stiegman. Trans. Jean Leclercq, O.S.B., and Henri Rochais. Cistercian Fathers Series, 13 B. Kalamazoo, Mich.: Cistercian Publications, 1995.

Billiart, Marie-Rose-Julie. *Lettres de Sainte Julie Billiart Fondatrice des Soeurs de Notre-Dame de Namur.* Rome: Presses de l'Université Grégorienne, 1976.

Blin de Bourdon, Françoise. *Autres autographes.* General Archives, Sisters of Notre Dame. BC 280. Namur, Belgium.

———. *Ecrits spirituels.* General Archives, Sisters of Notre Dame. BC 272. Namur, Belgium.

———. *Lettres.* General Archives, Sisters of Notre Dame. BC 200. Namur, Belgium.

———. *The Memoirs of Mother Frances Blin de Bourdon.* Trans. Sister Thérèse of the Blessed Sacrament Sullivan, S.N.D. Westminster, Maryland: Christian Classics, 1989.

———. *Selected Letters of Mother Saint Joseph Blin de Bourdon, S.N.D.* Trans. Sister Mary Frances McCarthy, S.N.D. Westminster, Maryland: Christian Classics, 1990.

———. *Vie de Julie Billiart ou Les Mémoires de Mère Saint-Joseph.* Rome: Tipografia P.U.G., 1978.

Chappin, Marcel, S.J. *Pie VII et les Pays-Bas: Tensions Religieuses et Tolérance Civile 1814–1817.* Roma: Università Gregoriana Editrice, 1984.

Charry, Jeanne de, R.S.C.J. *Sainte Madeleine-Sophie Fondatrice de la Société du Sacré Coeur de Jésus.* Paris: Casterman, 1965.

———. *Joseph Varin, S.J.: Lettres à Sainte Madeleine-Sophie Barat (1801–1849).* Rome: n.p., 1982.

Clair, Charles, S.J. *La Bienheureuse Mère Julie Billiart, Fondatrice et Première Supérieure Générale de l'Institut des Soeurs de Notre-Dame de Namur.* Paris: Arthur Savaète, 1906.

Cobb, Richard C. *The Police and the People: French Popular Protest 1789–1820.* London: Oxford University Press, 1970.

Cristiani, L. *Madame de Franssu, Fondatrice de la Congrégation de la Nativité du Notre-Seigneur (1751–1824).* Avignon: Aubanel Frères, 1926.

Cunningham, Agnes, S.S.C.M. "Mission in the French School of Spirituality." Alive for God in Christ Jesus: Conference on the Contemporary Significance of the French School of Spirituality. Buffalo, N.Y.: St. John Eudes Center, August 18–24, 1995, 73–82.

D'Angelo, Mary Rose. "Woman Partners in the New Testament." *Journal of Feminist Studies in Religion* 6/1: 65–86.

d'Arenberg, Prince Jean. *La Couronne de Belgique et le Saint-Siège (1830–1831).* Enghien: Studium Arenbergense, 1991.

de Sales, Saint Francis. *Introduction to the Devout Life.* Trans. Allan Ross. London: Burns Oates and Washbourne Ltd., 1937.

Destremau, Noelle. *Une Soeur de Louis XVI: Madame Elisabeth.* Paris: Nouvelles Éditions Latines, 1983.

Deville, Raymond. *L'École Française de Spiritualité.* Bibliothèque d'histoire du christianisme. Bruxelles: Desclée, 1987.

Dorchy, Henry. *Histoire des Belges des Origines à 1991.* Septième édition. Bruxelles: De Boeck, 1991.

Dumont, Georges Henri. *Histoire de la Belgique.* Bruxelles: Éditions Le Cri, 1995.

Durant, Will and Ariel. *The Story of Civilization: The Age of Napoleon.* New York: MJF Books, 1975.

———. *The Story of Civilization: Rousseau and Revolution.* New York: MJF Books, 1967.

———. *The Story of Civilization: The Age of Voltaire.* New York: MJF Books, 1965.

Fairchilds, Cissie. "Women and Family." *French Women and the Age of Enlightenment.* Ed. Samia I. Spencer. Bloomington: Indiana University Press, 1984.

Flinders, Carol Lee. *Enduring Grace: Living Portraits of Seven Women Mystics.* San Francisco: HarperSanFrancisco, 1993.

Forrest, Alan. *The French Revolution and the Poor.* Oxford: Basil Blackwell, 1981.

Gaffney, Patrick, Rev., S.M.M. "Louis-Marie Grignion de Montfort." *Alive for God in Christ Jesus: A Conference Exploring Contemporary Influences from the French School of Spirituality.* Buffalo: St. John Eudes Center, 1995, 201–12.

Gibson, Ralph. *A Social History of French Catholicism: 1789–1914.* London: Routledge, 1989.

Gobert, Cornélie. Letter to canonical postulator in response to request for testimonials. 25 November 1880. Ohio Province Archives, Sisters of Notre Dame. Cincinnati, Ohio.

Goubert, Pierre. *The Ancien Régime: French Society 1600–1750.* Trans. Steve Cox. New York: Harper & Row Publishers, 1969.

Graham, Ruth. "Women versus Clergy, Women pro Clergy." *French Women in the Age of Enlightenment.* Ed. Samia I. Spencer. Bloomington: Indiana University Press, 1984.

Guidée, Achille, S.J. *Vie de R.P. Joseph Varin.* Paris: Charles Douniol, 1860.

Haseldine, Julian. "Friendship, Equality and Universal Harmony." *Friendship East and West: Philosophical Perspectives.* Ed. Oliver Leaman. Surrey: Curzon Press, 1996, 192–214.

Heilbrun, Carolyn G. *Writing a Woman's Life.* New York: Ballantine Books, 1988.

Hilden, Patricia Penn. *Women, Work, and Politics: Belgium 1830–1914.* Oxford: Clarendon Press, 1993.

Holtman, Robert B. *Napoleonic Propaganda.* New York: Greenwood Press, 1950.

Houssaye, Henry. *Waterloo 1815.* Évreux: Christian de Bartillat Éditeur, 1987.

Huertas, Monique de. *Madame Elisabeth: Soeur de Louis XVI.* Paris: Librairie Académique Perrin, 1985.

Hufton, Olwen. "Women in Revolution." *French Society and the Revolution.* Ed. Douglas Johnson. London: Cambridge University Press, 1976.

———. "The reconstruction of a church 1796–1801." *Beyond the Terror.* Ed. G. Lewis and C. Lucas. London: Cambridge University Press, 1981, 21–53.

———. *Women and the Limits of Citizenship in the French Revolution.* Toronto: University of Toronto Press, 1992.

———. *The Prospect Before Her: A History of Women in Western Europe 1500–1800.* New York: Vintage Books, 1998.

Jensen, Joseph, O.S.B. "Friendship: Old Testament and New Testament." *The Collegeville Pastoral Dictionary of Biblical Theology.* Ed. Carroll Stuhlmueller, C.P. et. al. Collegeville, Minn.: Liturgical Press, 1996, 348–49.

Johnson, Douglas, ed. *French Society and the Revolution.* Cambridge: Cambridge University Press, 1976.

Joset, Camille, S.J. "L'origine des Facultés de Namur: 1831–1845." *Études d'Histoire & d'Archéologie namuroises.* Publications Extraordinaire de la Société Archéologique de Namur, 1952, 969–84.

Lacouture, Jean. *Jésuites*. 2 vols. Paris: Éditions du Seuil, 1991–92.

Langlois, Claude. *Le Catholicisme au Féminin: Les congrégations françaises à supérieure générale au XIXe siècle*. Paris: Les Editions du Cerf, 1984.

La Vergne, Yvonne de. *Madame Elisabeth of France*. Trans. Cornelia C. Craigie. London: B. Herder, 1947.

Lefebvre, Georges. *The French Revolution from 1793–1799*. Trans. John Hall Stewart and James Friguglietti. New York: Columbia University Press, 1964.

———. *The Great Fear of 1789: Rural Panic in Revolutionary France*. New York: Pantheon Press, 1973.

———. "The Place of the Revolution in the Agrarian History of France." *Rural Society in France: Selections from the Annales Economies, Sociétés, Civilisations*. Ed. Robert Forster and Orest Ranum. Trans. Elborg Forster and Patricia M. Ranum. Baltimore: Johns Hopkins University Press, 1977, 31–49.

Linscott, Mary, S.N.D. *This Excellent Heritage: An Introduction to the Constitutions of the Sisters of Notre Dame*. N. p.: privately printed, 1995.

Littré, Émile. *Dictionnaire de la langue française: contenant la nomenclature, la grammaire, la signification* de *mots, la partie historique, l'étymologie*. 2 vols. of 4. Londres: Hachette, 1863 and 1872.

Lough, John. *An Introduction to Eighteenth-Century France*. London: Longmans, 1960.

Lough, John, and Muriel Lough. *An Introduction to Nineteenth-Century France*. London: Longman Group Ltd., 1978.

Mabille, Xavier. *Histoire politique de la Belgique*. Bruxelles: CRISP, 1986.

Martin, Marie de Saint Jean, O.S.U. *Ursuline Method of Education*. Rahway: Quinn & Boden Company, Inc., 1946.

Masteller, Jeanne. *Education of French Women in the Seventeenth and Eighteenth Centuries*. Unpublished master's thesis. Wright State University, 1986.

Mathon, G., G.-H. Baudry, and P. Guilluy, eds. *Catholicisme: Hier, Aujourd'hui, Demain*. Encyclopédie publiée sous la direction du Centre Interdisciplinaire des Facultés Catholiques de Lille. Paris: Letouzey et Ané, 1982.

Mauzi, Robert. *L'idée du bonheur dans la littérature et la pensée françaises au XVIIIe siécle.* Paris: Librairie Armand Colin, 1960.

McBrien, Richard P., ed. *The HarperCollins Encyclopedia of Catholicism.* San Francisco: HarperCollins, 1995.

McGoldrick, Terence A. *The Sweet and Gentle Struggle: Francis de Sales on the Necessity of Spiritual Friendship.* Lanham, Md.: University Press of America, 1996.

McManners, John. *French Ecclesiastical Society under the Ancien Régime.* Manchester: Manchester University Press, 1960.

———. *The French Revolution and the Church.* New York: Harper & Row, 1969.

McNamara, Jo Ann Kay. *Sisters in Arms: Catholic Nuns Through Two Millennia.* Cambridge: Harvard University Press, 1996.

Mitchell, Alan C. "The Social Function of Friendship." *Journal of Biblical Literature* 111.2: 255–72.

Molette, Charles. *Guide des sources de l'histoire des congrégations féminines françaises de vie active.* Paris: Editions de Paris, 1974.

Morel, Alain. "Power and Ideology in the Village Community of Picardy: Past and Present." *Rural Society in France. Selections from the Annales Economies, Sociétés, Civilisations.* Ed. Robert Forster and Orest Ranum. Trans. Elborg Forster and Patricia M. Ranum. Baltimore: Johns Hopkins University Press, 1977, 107–25.

Murk-Jansen, Saskia. *Brides in the Desert: The Spirituality of the Beguines.* Traditions of Christian Spirituality Series. Ed. Philip Sheldrake. New York: Orbis Books, 1998.

Murphy, Roseanne, S.N.D. de N. *Julie Billiart: Woman of Courage.* Mahwah, N.J.: Paulist Press, 1995.

Partridge, Mary Xavier, S.N.D. *The Life of Blessed Julie Billiart Foundress of the Institute of Sisters of Notre Dame.* Ed. James Clare, S.J. London: Sands and Co., 1909.

Petitfrère, Claude. "The origins of the civil war in the Vendée." *The French Revolution in Social & Political Perspective.* Ed. Peter Jones. London: Arnold, 1996.

Phillips, C. S. *The Church in France: 1789–1848.* New York: Russell & Russell, 1966.

Quinn, Patrick. "St. Thomas Aquinas and the Christian Understanding of Friendship." *Friendship East and West: Philosophical Perspectives.* Ed. Oliver Leaman. Surrey: Curzon Press, 1996, 270–79.

Rapley, Elizabeth. *The "Dévotes": Women and Church in Seventeenth-Century France.* Montreal: McGill-Queen's University Press, 1990.

Raymond, Janice G. *A Passion for Friends: Toward a Philosophy of Female Affection.* Boston: Beacon Press, 1986.

Roegiers, Jan. "Pretres Assermentés et Curés Réfractaires: L'Enjeu Politique Fondamental." *Deux Aspects Contestés de la Politique Révolutionnaire en Belgique: Langue et Culte Études sur le XVIIIe Siècle XVI.* Ed. Roland et Mortier, Hervé Hasquin. Groupe d'étude du XVIIIe siècle. Bruxelles: Éditions de l'Université de Bruxelles, 1989.

Rosner, Frances, S.N.D. and Tinsley, Sr. Lucy, S.N.D. *The Letters of St. Julie Billiart.* Rome: Gregorian Press, 1974.

Schmitz, Yves. *Guillaume Ier et la Belgique.* Bruxelles: Ad. Goemaere, 1945.

Simon, Alois. *La Politique religieuse de Léopold Ier.* Bruxelles: Ad. Goemaere, 1953.

———. *Le Cardinal Sterckx et son Temps (1792–1867).* Wetteren: Éditions Scaldis, 1950.

Sister of Notre Dame. "Origine de l'Institut des Soeurs de Notre-Dame de Namur." Unpublished article. General Archives, Sisters of Notre Dame. DA 120. Namur, Belgium.

———. "Souvenirs et Dépositions des Soeurs de Notre-Dame au sujet de Mère St. Joseph." General Archives, Sisters of Notre Dame. BF 515. Namur, Belgium.

Soille, J. "Le 'Schisme' des Ursulines." *Notes pour servir à l'histoire du Stévenisme.* 1ière Série. Gembloux: Éditions J. Duculot, S.A., 1958.

Spencer, Samia I. "Women and Education." *French Women and the Age of Enlightenment.* Ed. Samia I. Spencer. Bloomington: Indiana University Press, 1984.

Surin, John Joseph, S.J. *Spiritual Letters of Father Surin, S.J.* Trans. M. Christopher, O.S.F. London: Thomas Richardson and Son, 1875.

Tackett, Timothy. *Religion, Revolution, and Regional Culture in Eighteenth-Century France: The Ecclesiastical Oath of 1791.* Princeton, N.J.: Princeton University Press, 1986.

Tallett, Frank. "Dechristianizing France: The Year II and the Revolutionary Experience." *Religion, Society, and Politics in France Since 1789.* Eds. Frank Tallett and Nicholas Atkin. London: The Hambledon Press, 1991.

Terlinden, Charles. *Guillaume Ier et l'Eglise catholique.* 2 vols. Bruxelles: Librairie Albert Dewit, 1906.

Thompson, William M., Ph.D. "The Christocentric Trinitarianism of the French School of Spirituality." Alive for God in Christ Jesus: A Conference Exploring Contemporary Influences from the French School of Spirituality. Buffalo: St. John Eudes Center, 1995, 29–44.

Timmermans, Linda. *L'accès des femmes à la culture: (1598–1715).* Bibliothèque littéraire de la Renaissance, Series 3, vol. XXVI. Paris: Honoré Champion Éditeur, 1993.

Todd, Janet. *Women's Friendship in Literature.* New York: Columbia Press, 1980.

Tomme, Clara, S.N.D. *Histoire de la Vénérée Mère Saint-Joseph.* Marchienne-au-Pont: L. Téchy-Tomme, 1920.

Valschaerts, Colette, S.N.D. "Les Origines N.D. en France et en Belgique." General Archives, Sisters of Notre Dame. DA 156. Namur, Belgium.

Wadell, Paul J., C.P. "Friendship: Pastoral-Liturgical Tradition." *The Collegeville Pastoral Dictionary of Biblical Theology.* Ed. Carroll Stuhlmueller, C.P. and et al. Collegeville, Minn.: Liturgical Press, 1996, 349–53.

Woodrow, Alain. *The Jesuits: A Story of Power.* London: Geoffrey Chapman, 1995.

Wright, Wendy M. *Bond of Perfection: Jeanne de Chantal and François de Sales.* Mahwah, N.J.: Paulist Press, 1985.

———. "The Salesian and Bérullian Spiritual Traditions." Alive for God in Christ Jesus: Conference on the Contemporary Significance of the French School of Spirituality. Buffalo, N.Y.: St. John Eudes Center, August 18–24, 1995, 157–68.

INDEX